The Arab Conquest of Sp
710–797

A History of Spain

General Editor: John Lynch

María Cruz Fernández Castro	*Iberia in Prehistory*
J. S. Richardson	*Roman Spain*
Roger Collins	*Visigothic Spain, 409–711*
Roger Collins	*The Arab Conquest of Spain 710–797*
Roger Collins	*Caliphs and Kings: Spain 798–1033*
Bernard F. Reilly	*The Conquest of Christian and Muslim Spain, 1031–1157*
Peter Linehan	*Spain, 1157–1312*
Angus MacKay	*Spain: Centuries of Crisis, 1300–1474*
John Edwards	*The Spain of the Catholic Monarchs, 1474–1520*
John Lynch	*Spain 1516–1598: From Nation State to World Empire*
John Lynch	*The Hispanic World in Crisis and Change, 1598–1700*
John Lynch	*Bourbon Spain, 1700–1808*
Charles J. Esdaile	*The Emergence of Modern Spain, 1808–1939*

The Arab Conquest of Spain

710–797

Roger Collins

BLACKWELL
Oxford UK & Cambridge USA

First published 1989
First published in paperback 1994
Reprinted 1995, 1998

Blackwell Publishers Ltd
108 Cowley Road
Oxford OX4 1JF, UK

Blackwell Publishers Inc
350 Main Street
Malden, Massachusetts 02148, USA

British Library Cataloguing in Publication Data
A CIP catalogue record for this book is available from the British Library

Library of Congress Cataloging in Publication Data
Collins, Roger, 1949–
The Arab conquest of Spain
Includes index.
1. Spain—History—711–1516. I. Title.
DP99.C58 1989 946'.02 88–33356
ISBN: 0–631–15923–1 — ISBN: 0–631–19405–3 (pbk)

Typeset in 11 on 13pt Garamond
by Vera-Reyes, Inc.

This book is printed on acid-free paper

For the headmistress, staff and students
of the Royal School, Bath

Contents

Preface

Although major social and intellectual developments and transformations rarely allow themselves to fit exactly into the artificial chronological compartments into which history is normally divided, and which vary from culture to culture, there is something satisfying about taking a look at Spain in an exclusively eighth-century context. For one thing, it has never been done before. For another, it seems to make more sense than might be expected. There is a curious symmetry about the history of the peninsula in this span of time, moving from the sophisticated unitary state and ideology of the late Visigothic kingdom, through a period of disintegration and change, to the reconstituted unity so laboriously achieved by the first Umayyad rulers of Córdoba. By taking the century as a whole, it is easier to see that real discontinuity came in its middle decades and not from the supposedly decisive year of the Arab conquest, 711. The traditional divide between Visigoth and Arab, and between the types of scholar who study the one and the other, hides more than it reveals.

As this book is part of a series, of which the next two volumes are to come from the same word processor as this, I have felt justified on occasion in leaving the treatment of certain topics which apply to the eighth century but for which the evidence is fuller and clearer in the ninth and tenth for inclusion in subsequent books. Similarly, the proposed existence of a book on the Visigothic period has meant that I have been able to limit my discussion of the preceding century to one or two themes of direct relevance to the present volume. A fuller presentation of the Visigothic background would not have been possible or suitable here. Although purists might object, I have given all dates exclusively by the standard Christian calendar and have not included Year of the Hegira equivalents, not least as this can seem cumbersome and off-putting.

I am exceedingly grateful to the Leverhulme Trust for the generous grant of a Research Fellowship in the years 1984–6, which enabled most of the work for this book to be undertaken. The dedication to my wife, her staff and students is a token of thanks for support of all kinds in the writing of it. Not the least was that of some of the third element of this triumvirate, whose constant cries of 'Have you finished your chapter yet?' spurred me on when making heavy weather of one of the central parts of the book.

R.J.H.C.

List of Abbreviations

Latin Texts

CSM *Corpus Scriptorum Muzarabicorum*, ed. J. Gil (2 vols, Seville, 1973)

MGH *Monumenta Germaniae Historica*

AA	*Auctores Antiquissimi*
Leges	*Leges Nationum Germanicarum*
SRG	*Scriptores Rerum Germanicarum*
SS	*Scriptores* – series in folio

Chronicle of 754: all such references are to the edition of J.E. López Perreira, *Crónica muzárabe de 754* (Zaragoza, 1980)

Adefonsi Chronica, or *The Chronicle of Alfonso III*: see *Chronica Albeldensis*

Chronica Albeldensis or *The Chronicle of Albelda*: this text with the *Adefonsi Chronica* is cited in the edition by J. Gil, *Crónicas asturianas* (Oviedo, 1985), with introductory sections by J.L. Moralejo and J.I. Ruiz de la Peña

Arabic Texts Cited in Translation

Akhbar Machmua: ed. and tr. E. Lafuente y Alcántara, *Akhbar Machmua: colección de tradiciones* (Madrid, 1867)

Al-Maqqarī: tr. (and reorganized) P. de Gayangos, *The History of the Mohammedan Dynasties of Spain* (2 vols, London, 1840–43)

Ibn 'Abd al-Ḥakam: tr. J.H. Jones, *Ibn Abd el-Hakem, History of the Conquest of Spain* (Göttingen, 1858)

Ibn al-Athīr: tr. E. Fagnan, *Annales du Maghrib et de l'Espagne* (Algiers, 1901)

Ibn 'Idhārī: *Bayān al-Mugrib*, tr. E. Fagnan, *Histoire de l'Afrique et de l'Espagne* (2 vols, Algiers, 1901, 1904)

Ibn al-Qūṭiyya: tr. J. Ribera, *Historia de España de Abenalcotía el Cordobés* (Madrid, 1926)

Other Texts

DHEE *Diccionario de historia eclesiástica de España* (4 vols, supplement, Madrid, 1972–86)

see
Halsall
sources &
/ interpretation

Introduction

assumption of textual sources...

archaeology

— authorial intention of Arab authors & how they produced their histories versus. Common perception of role of historian

unreliable.

'fiction' of much of history

If ever there has been a 'Dark Age' in the history of the Iberian peninsula it could probably be said to be co-terminous with the eighth century. This is not to use the term in the sense of dark and sinister deeds, of general rapine, slaughter, disorder and barbarism, though these were to be found in abundance in this period, not just in Spain, but throughout the Mediterranean and the Near East. However chaotic these events may seem to be, it should be possible to make a pattern from them, and to suggest causes and consequences that put them into more comprehensible shape. Where the eighth century in the peninsula may be held to be 'dark' is in the original sense of evidential obscurity. Skilled, or otherwise, as the historian may be in suggesting explanations for random or complex sets of events, this does depend on some prior sense of reliance upon the reality of the individual components of the story that is to be told or the structures to be uncovered. Source criticism precedes analysis, let alone narrative. If it does not the result can be mere fiction.

Fiction, indeed, may be said to be the root of the problem in this particular case. Not in the sense that the modern novelist writes it, but in the sense that Arab authors in the Middle Ages may have had a taste for it too. In many respects the linguistic and educational divide between the trained medieval historian and the professional Arabist has made this a particularly dangerous area for representatives of either side to wander about in, at least without some form of safe conduct from the other. Those few scholars who have ever been interested in the problems of this period, either from the perspective of the history of Spain or as a discrete area of

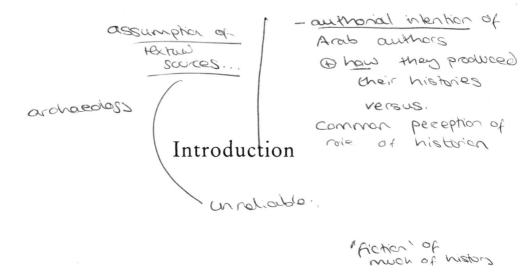

Islamic expansion, have tended to fall foul of the mines that the other side has either laid or could have detected for them. Thus the Arabists have consistently had difficulty understanding the preceding Visigothic period in the peninsula, and therefore have built their analyses of the society that followed on flawed foundations.[1] The fault here lies with the historians who should have taught them better. However, their neglect of, or lack of appreciation of, Latin sources is less easily forgiven.[2] On the other hand, certain overly dogmatic approaches to the Arab materials on the part of linguistically untrained historians has led to equally serious errors and disagreements.[3]

In these circumstances it might be better to steer clear of such shark-infested waters. However, without taking risks and making mistakes no progress at all will be achieved in advancing the understanding of an important and neglected period. Why its sources have been a cause of so many problems is neither a reflection of their scarcity, nor of any particular linguistic difficulties inherent in them. In comparative terms the eighth century in Spain is relatively well served in respect of the quantity of literary evidence available.[4] To a certain extent, also, linguistic competence particularly in the matter of the Arab texts becomes an issue of secondary importance in relation to the far greater problem of trying to answer the basic question of why they give us the kind of information they do and in the form that was chosen to convey it.

This is to return to the problem of fiction. Here, respectfully, it is necessary to point out that despite the many and considerable benefits their works have conferred, none of the scholars of the early Islamic period in Spain has ever fully faced up to the problem of trying to define the nature of the content of the Arab sources. This is not to say that source criticism has been totally absent, but it has been directed exclusively towards the establishing of an order of preference between competing and often contradictory works.

[1] See below pp. 7–8.

[2] For example the very limited use made by E. Lévi-Provençal in his discussion of the first half century of Arab rule in Spain of the only source, a Latin one, that was exactly contemporary with the period under consideration. See below pp. 52–65.

[3] As for example the controversies between C. Sánchez-Albornoz and a number of leading Arabists, including E. Lévi-Provençal and P. Chalmeta.

[4] For other regions of Western Europe see the accounts in W. Levison and H. Löwe, *Deutschland Geschictsquellen im Mittelalter*, vol. II (Weimar, 1953).

Thus, for one school of thought the testimony of the anonymous *Akhbar Machmua* is to be given precedence in virtually any circumstances because it was held to be in large part a genuine eighth-century composition. On the other hand, there are those who rightly consider the *Akhbar Machmua* to be wholly eleventh-century compilation, and give greatest credence to anything that seems to bear the hallmark of Ibn Hayyān.[5] So it goes on.

One of the most interesting developments in the modern historiography of early Arab society and the rise of Islam has been the recent trend towards a far more rigorous and critical scrutiny of the sources of the early Islamic tradition and the life of the Prophet Muḥammad.[6] Much of this remains highly controversial, but its roots lie in a tradition of sceptical scholarship that goes back to the critical study of *hadīth*, the traditions relating to the life and sayings of the Prophet, carried out by Ignaz Goldziher in the 1880s.[7] These re-evaluations have gone far beyond the attempt to re-shuffle the pack as far as the order of priority of the sources is concerned. Rather, the most valuable modern work has been based upon a fundamental re-appraisal of the ideological purposes of the medieval authors, and of the factors conditioning the way in which they received and transmitted the information they used for those purposes. Such an approach needs to be extended more widely, but it can run into serious opposition from the anti-intellectual tendencies of religious orthodoxy and the hostility of some modern Muslim scholars, who regard the application of Western intellec-

[5] This was essentially the point that divided C. Sánchez-Albornoz and E. Lévi-Provençal; see the former's 'La sana celosa de un arabista', *Cuadernos de Historia de España*, 27 (1958), pp. 5–42, reprinted in his *Estudios polémicos* (Madrid, 1979), pp. 111–52. However, both of them were arguing about essentially late sets of traditions, neither of whose claims to a real eighth-century origin can be maintained. For the very strong argument to the effect that the nearest the Arabs came to any form of record making or historical composition in the latter period was the compiling of bare lists of names and dates see J. Schacht, 'On Mūsā B. 'Uqba's *Kitāb al-Maghāzī*', *Acta Orientalia*, 21 (1953), pp. 288–300.

[6] R. Sellheim, 'Prophet, Chalif und Geschichte: die Muhammed-Biografie des Ibn Isḥāq', *Oriens*, 18/19 (1965/6), pp. 33–91; also J. Wansborough, *Quranic Studies* (Oxford, 1977), P. Crone and M. Cook, *Hagarism* (Cambridge, 1977), M. Cook, *Early Muslim Dogma* (Cambridge, 1981).

[7] For a short review of the historiographical argument over the reliability or otherwise of the early Arab sources see F.M. Donner's introduction to the English translation of A. A. Duri, *The Rise of Historical Writing among the Arabs* (Princeton, 1983), pp. vii–xvii. Duri's book provides a good example of what may be called the conservative approach to this problem.

tual traditions to the study of Islam and Arab history as manifestations of colonial imperialism.[8] Fortunately, neither of these factors apply directly to the study of the period of Islamic domination in Spain.

To refer to Arab authors whose works convey information relating to events in the Iberian peninsula in earlier periods than their own as being historians is to beg a vital question. Our own assumptions as to the nature of history and what the historian's task consists of are so deeply engrained in the traditions of our society that it is all too easy to transfer them to those whom we could thereby too casually classify as being Arab historians. It would, perhaps, be wiser to analyse the texts of such authors to see what their presuppositions and intentions were before their works are thus labelled as being self-consciously historical. Such an investigation is hardly the province of this book or of this author, but its very absence must justify the caution, indeed timidity, with which the Arab texts are here approached.

The flatly contradictory nature of many of the Arab traditions relating to events reported as having occurred in the early period of Islamic domination in Spain raises the suspicion that the deepest and most primitive level of Arab record making in this society consisted of originally little more than the compiling of sets of names of office holders, and subsequently of small amounts of bald annalistic reporting, rather similar to the kind of thin chronicle writing that was being practised by the Christians in the peninsula in the same period. Thus, the later generations of those who may for convenience be labelled literary historical writers had not much more than a few names and some very dry 'facts' to go on. They thus might have known in outline a little of what had happened, but nothing of the why or how . This, to put it crudely, they invented.

Consistency and coherence between the various sources can often be found, but it is clear enough, often from the explicit statements the authors make, that there was much mutual borrowing, or that earlier and now generally lost sources were common to the later extant accounts. To accuse the medieval Arab writers of downright invention is to make a charge that they would not

[8] See for example the introduction to M. Sadok Bel Ochi, *La Conversion des berbères à l'Islam* (Tunis, 1981), pp. 5–6, and N.A. Faruqi, *Early Muslim Historiography* (Delhi, 1979), pp. xvii–xx.

necessarily have found damning. We should only do so because of the nature of our presuppositions as to what the historian's duty is supposed to be. In fact a clear parallel can be made between the expanded and genuinely literary historical works of the medieval Arab authors and the kind of 'fictionalized' historical writing that became popular in Ireland in the twelfth century. The *Lebor na Cert* and the *Cogadh Gaedhel re Gallaibh* are probably generically closer to the nature and aspirations of the Arab authors than anything produced in the Latin historiographical tradition.[9]

These Irish works have themselves, once their character was detected, been taken to task by modern scholars for the deceptive nature of their contents. Once again, though, what counts is the authorial purpose. But just as no one would now turn to the *Cogadh* for a fully reliable account of the activities of the Vikings in Ireland, despite a leaven of earlier annalistic matter in the work, so too should it seem methodologically unwise to have recourse to such patently hybrid texts as the *Akhbar Machmua*, the *Fāth al-Andalus* or the supposed lecture notes of Ibn al-Qūṭiyya for sound information on the history of Islamic Spain (*Al-Andalus*) in the eighth or ninth centuries. Even more generically homogeneous books, such as those of Ibn al-Athīr and Ibn Khaldūn, can be equally tainted. This leaves the would-be historian of eighth-century Spain in no inconsiderable difficulty in terms of the trust, if any, to put in his sources. Particular problems will be discussed here as they arise, but it may well be that the process of source criticism is not taken far enough, and a naive reliance on worthless materials will manifest itself. On the other hand, hyper-criticism, as its opponents like to call it, is preferable to the writing of romance, and if this book is to err it would be better on the side of the former than of the latter. But before such problems with the Arabic sources take the centre of the stage, it is necessary to have a brief look at the last stages of a society in which that language was still unknown.

[9] *Lebor na Cert*, ed. M. Dillon (Dublin, 1962); *Cogadh Gaedhel re Gallaibh*, ed. and tr. J.H. Todd (London, 1867). On these texts see K. Hughes, *Early Christian Ireland: Introduction to the Sources* (London, 1972), pp. 285–98. To these texts could be added the *Fragmentary Annals of Ireland*, ed. J.N. Radner (Dublin, 1978).

1

A Developing Kingdom

The Visigothic Twilight?

Those societies in the past which have been unfortunate enough to have had their political order violently overthrown by military defeat at the hands of external enemies have often not only suffered the indignity of thus being made to disappear, but also have had to endure some form of posthumous historiographical *damnatio memoriae*. Where they have not been immediately consigned to the scholarly dustbin, it is only because various historians have wished to hold them up as moral bad examples. Thus a number of early medieval societies have earned opprobrium for their failure to withstand invasion. The straightforward military explanation, to the effect that in most battles someone has got to lose, is deemed too simplistic. It is felt necessary to find some set of underlying causes for why an army at a given place and time was not able to come up to scratch. There is an extraordinary unspoken assumption common to many of the interpretations of such events that there must have been something morally wrong about the losing side. The defeat of the Vandals at the hands of the Byzantines, the fall of the Visigothic kingdom before the Arab invasion, the Viking raids on England and the Carolingian Empire in the ninth century, and the Norman conquest of the Anglo-Saxon state have all been seen in such a light. To have proved so vulnerable to aggression such societies had to be decadent.

Such interpretations are far from being just the product of a particular moralizing perspective of late nineteenth- and early twentieth-century thinking. They can be found as far back as the immediate aftermath of the events themselves. The Byzantine historian Procopius blamed the Vandals for their own defeat on the grounds of their addiction to soft living and such unbarbaric indulgences as bathing. The Anglo-Saxon missionary and archbishop Boniface felt that the Arab conquests of Spain and parts of southern France could only be explained by the inhabitants having given themselves over to lust and fornication.[1]

Fortunately, more sophisticated and sympathetic studies of these particular societies have, in most cases, led to the making of fairer assessments of them, and their ultimate fates have ceased to weigh as indictments against them. The great exception, however, remains that of Visigothic Spain, for whose demise such archaic explanations are still all too frequently produced.[2] Some of the reasons behind this strange survival are themselves of interest, and stem from a particular set of preoccupations in the Spanish intellectual tradition. In part these have to do with such disparate influences as the impact on the intelligentsia of the humiliating elimination of the vestiges of Spanish Empire in 1898, and the longer term conflicts between national identity and the strength of regional cultures. Such considerations have led to the emergence of a distinctive set of questions that Spanish scholars in this century have wished the history of the peninsula to answer for them. Non-Spanish historians have no such justification for such an approach to their evidence, even though it was an English Presbyterian minister, the Reverend Dykes Shaw, who in 1910 was amongst the earliest of the proponents of the decadence explanation for the fall of Visigothic Spain.[3]

The effects of the dominance of this particular school of interpretation have been regrettable not only for the history of the peninsula in the period of the Visigothic kingdom, but also for their impact on the study of the subsequent early phases of Arab

[1] Procopius, *History of the Wars*, IV.vi.5–9, ed. H.B. Dewing (Cambridge, Mass., and London, 1916), vol. II, p. 256; Boniface, *Epistle* 73, to king Aethelbald of Mercia (746/7), ed. M. Tangl, *MGH Epistolae Selectae*, I (1955), p. 151; On various aspects of 'decadence' as interpreted in antiquity see S. Mazzarino, *The End of the Ancient World*, tr. G. Holmes (London, 1966), especially Part One.

[2] For a survey of interpretations see L.A. García Moreno, *El Fin del reino visigodo de Toledo: decadencia y catástrofe, una contribución a su crítica* (Madrid, 1975), ch. 1: 'Historia de una problema'.

[3] R. Dykes Shaw, 'The Fall of the Visigothic power in Spain', *English Historical Review*, 21 (1906), pp. 209–28.

rule. The nature of the linguistic divide between periods in which Latin and then Arabic constitute the dominant languages of the sources of historical evidence is so great that the Islamic conquest marks as much a caesura in modern scholarship as it did in the development of society in the peninsula in the eighth century. To put it simply, historians of Visigothic Spain do not study Arab Spain, and the orientalists who have worked on the history of *Al-Andalus* have not ventured into the previous period. The consequence has been that for the relatively few who have worked on Spain in the period of Islamic domination their views on the preceding Visigothic kingdom have come at second hand. They have relied on what the modern students of Visigothic Spain have told them, and if in consequence their views on that society have been scarcely more sophisticated than those of St Boniface, who is to blame them when this is the impression they have received from so much of what is available for them to read on the final stages of the kingdom?[4]

One major casualty of this misleading historiographical perspective has been any sense of continuity across the period of the Arab and Berber invasion. Only now is this being remedied, and some Spanish orientalists are looking for elements of the survival or the revival of indigenous pre-conquest social organization and administration in the society of Umayyad *Al-Andalus*.[5] This is valuable, and a vital corrective to the intellectual 'iron curtain' that once existed between the two periods and areas of study. Even so, such scholars have tended to be highly disapproving of many of the salient features of Visigothic society, again largely because of the way it has been presented in the existing historiography. But if valid continuities are to be detected, then these will have to depend upon well-founded assessments of the Visigothic kingdom, and especially of its final phases.

If presuppositions be avoided, then Spain in the later Visigothic period emerges as somewhat less like a realization of one of the paintings of Hieronymus Bosch than it is usually depicted. The most striking features of it in an early medieval context are the degree to which an area with poor communications and enormous

[4] Among the most recent victims may be included T.F. Glick, *Islamic and Christian Spain in the Early Middle Ages* (Princeton, 1979), pp. 27–33.

[5] Especially Joaquin Vallvé, by whom see most recently *La División territorial de la España musulmana* (Madrid, 1986).

geographical and cultural diversity was able to maintain not just the aspiration but also something of the reality of political unity. When the diversity of kingdoms that existed in Anglo-Saxon England at this time, or the divisions amongst the Merovingian Franks, or the problems of the Lombard rulers of Pavia with their overmighty dukes in Spoleto and Benevento be recalled, then the continued unity of the Iberian peninsula under a single source of secular authority becomes all the more surprising.

Similarly, in terms of ecclesiastical institutions, the metropolitan bishops of Toledo had achieved by the last quarter of the seventh century an authority and a primacy that was unique in Western Europe.[6] Not even the Pope could count on such support from neighbouring metropolitans, who in the Spanish case were technically equal to their *de facto* primate. The pressure for uniformity in ecclesiastical discipline and liturgy prefigured and in practice exceeded that which was aspired to in the 'Carolingian Renaissance' of the time of Charlemagne. In intellectual terms the leading Spanish churchmen of the seventh century had no equals before the appearance of Bede.

Although complaints are still levied against the politics of the kingdom by those who seem to want the Visigoths to have pulled a Frankish form of dynasticism out of thin air, or to have instituted clearly a form of elective monarchy that is held to have been traditional, but which almost certainly never existed, in practice royal succession amongst the Visigoths in the later seventh century was extraordinarily smooth, and certainly no whit more violent than that to be seen in the same decades in the various kingdoms of the Franks, Lombards, Anglo-Saxons and in the Byzantine Empire.[7] References to Gregory of Tours' joke about the *morbus gothicus*, in which he was writing about events occuring no later than the 550s, are anachronistic in the later seventh century. From 642 to 710 no succession to the kingship in Spain led to murder or

[6] On this see, *inter alia*, R. Collins, 'Julian of Toledo and the royal succession in late seventh century Spain' in *Early Medieval Kingship*, eds P. Sawyer and I. Wood, pp. 30–49; J. Orlandis, 'Las Relaciones intereclesiales en la Hispania visigótica', *Communio*, 12 (1972), pp. 403–44, republished in his *La Iglesia en la España visigótica y medieval* (Pamplona, 1976), pp. 61–93; *Historia de la iglesia en España*, vol. I, ed. R. García-Villoslada (Madrid, 1979), pp. 491–4.

[7] For the arguments on royal succession see J. Orlandis, *El Poder real y la sucesión al trono en la monarquía visigoda* (Rome-Madrid, 1962); also R. Collins, *Early Medieval Spain: Unity in Diversity, 400–1000* (London, 1983), pp. 113–15.

war in the centre of the realm. The only partial exception to this was the short-lived attempt in 673 of a rebel count to create an independent kingdom in the north-east. That such a thing happened is less surprising than that this was not a more frequent occurrence in view of the peninsula's considerable cultural diversity and its difficult geography.

In general the Visigothic kingdom has suffered most from its modern critics in the very areas in which it achieved most. Its large and relatively comprehensive law book, the *Forum Iudicum*, the last version of which appeared in the reign of Egica (687–702) has frequently been used as a stick with which to beat the society that produced it. Yet in terms of its aspirations and the nature of its content it has no parallel in the legislation of the Germanic successor states to the Late Roman Empire. The book itself and the legal procedures that it employed not only derived from Roman prototypes but also proved satisfactory in practical application for roughly 600 years after the disappearance of the kingdom.[8] There has also long existed a tendency to take the normative declarations of intent in the code as if they were expressions of reality. In this way the social conditions of such groups as the Jews and fugitive slaves have generally been presented in a lurid glow, and this in turn serves as the backdrop against which this decadent society is seen to meet its eternal judgement through the agency of Muslim invaders.[9]

Whilst all of these arguments could and should be debated in a more extended way, this would not be appropriate in the context of a book devoted to the history of the peninsula in the eighth century. Enough, though, has perhaps been said to indicate that the starting point of the present enquiry is a far more sympathetic and optimistic view of Spanish society on the eve of the Arab conquest than is normally allowed. However, one or two particu-

[8] On the continued use of the code see R. Collins, '*Sicut lex Gothorum continet*: law and charters in ninth- and tenth-century León and Catalonia', *English Historical Review*, 100 (1985), pp. 489–512; *id.*, 'Visigothic law and regional custom in disputes in early medieval Spain', in *The Settlement of Disputes in Early Medieval Europe*, eds W. Davies and P. Fouracre (Cambridge, 1986), pp. 85–104; M. Zimmermann, 'L'Usage du droit wisigothique en Catalogne du IXe au XIIe siècle: Approches d'une signification culturelle', *Mélanges de la Casa de Velazquez*, 9 (1973), pp. 233–81.

[9] E.A. Thompson, *The Goths in Spain* (Oxford, 1969), pp. 246–8, 271–4, 317–19.

lar areas of argument require slightly fuller treatment here because of their bearing on conditions that existed after the conquest.

Visigothic Hispania *and its Neighbours*

An assumption that has been common, and that has been all too rarely challenged, is that of the essential isolation of Spain for much of the Visigothic period. To some degree this has been conditioned by a framework of interpretation that sees the history of Spain as a whole being best represented by a pattern of long periods of isolationism and exclusivity on the part of the peninsula in relation to the outside world, punctuated by a succession of shorter, rather hectic, phases of catching up, in the course of which Spain becomes almost uncritically receptive of outside influences. In Early Medieval terms the late sixth century is taken as a clear example of one of the latter periods, whilst the ensuing seventh century can be seen as being typical of one of the epochs of isolation.[10]

Apart from the general attractiveness of such a pattern, and its relevance to modern political arguments, a number of different pieces of evidence have been advanced to support such a view of the prevailing character of the Visigothic kingdom, especially in its final phases. These include stringent regulations in the law code relating to dangers to be apprehended from the actions of enemies outside the kingdom and traitors within, controls on the movements of foreigners, notably merchants, and fears of the threat posed to the existing order by the activities of fugitives and exiles. To these general indications have been added such particular instances as the royal prohibition placed upon Bishop Fructuosus of Braga's proposed visit to the East, probably a pilgrimage to the Holy Places (*c.*650).[11]

The growing Arab menace and an apparently paranoid fear of Jewish conspiracies can be added to this mixture of factors seen as producing a citadel mentality amongst the rulers of the kingdom,

[10] L. Musset, *Les Invasions: les vagues germaniques* (Paris, 1969), pp. 295–6, is judicious on the matter of supposed 'isolation', but his arguments against it can be taken much further.

[11] E. A. Thompson, 'Two notes on Saint Fructuosus of Braga', *Hermathena*, 90 (1957), pp. 54–63.

above all in the second half of the seventh century, with obvious implications for the reduction of foreign contacts and the restrictive nature of the frontiers. Archaeological evidence has also been advanced that looks to support such a view, especially in relation to the frontiers in Septimania between the Visigothic kingdom and its Frankish neighbours.[12]

Even such an institution as the Papacy, which presented no threat to the security or integrity of the Visigothic realm, and might have been the ally and point of recourse for its Church, is represented in a modern historiographical perspective as having made no significant impact on Spain at this time. All papal interventions are seen as having been resisted; and the last of them, in 684, to such an extent that it has even been suggested that only the Arab conquest saved the Spanish Church from open schism from Rome; which is rather a high price to have to pay for the maintenance of oecumenism![13] Similarly, relations with the Byzantine Empire are presented solely within a context of conflict, marked by the successful Visigothic termination of the imperial enclave in the south-east of the peninsula in the first quarter of the seventh century, and finally the unprovoked Byzantine naval raid on the Spanish coast at the very end of it. In fact the only region outside the peninsula in this period with which it has been suggested that Spain enjoyed direct and peaceful relations, albeit of only a limited and cultural kind, is Ireland.[14] Unfortunately, the arguments in support of direct contact between the two fail to convince, largely because they ignore the navigational conditions of the Bay of Biscay and the limitations these imposed on medieval shipping.[15]

[12] E. James, 'Septimania and its frontier: an archaeological approach', in *Visigothic Spain: New Approaches*, ed. E. James (Oxford, 1980), pp. 223–41.

[13] For a more balanced view see F.X. Murphy, 'Julian of Toledo and the condemnation of Monothelitism in Spain', *Mélanges J. de Ghellinck*, vol. I (Gembloux, 1951), pp. 361–73.

[14] J.N. Hilgarth, 'Ireland and Spain in the seventh century', *Peritia*, 3 (1984), pp. 1–16, reinforces the same author's previous considerations of this relationship; all three of his articles on the subject may be found in his *Visigothic Spain, Byzantium and the Irish* (London, 1985), items VI, VII, and VIII.

[15] These factors would reinforce the arguments of E. James, 'Ireland and western Gaul in the Merovingian period', in *Ireland in Early Medieval Europe*, eds D. Whitelock, R. McKitterick and D. Dumville (Cambridge, 1982), pp. 362–86.

The details of such arguments and counter-arguments hardly matter here, but one thing they do seem to establish is that for the transmission of texts of Spanish origin to Ireland, as clearly did occur in the middle and later seventh century, intermediaries were required. Two regions in which such cultural interchange probably did occur, and which are of significance not just for the restricted debate on Spanish–Irish contacts but also for the wider problem of the peninsula's supposed isolation, are the lower Loire and northern Italy. The former raises the question of the extent of contacts between Visigothic Spain and its Frankish neighbours. Periods of open conflict between the two were distinctly rarer in the seventh century than in the preceeding one, and as far as the limited evidence available is concerned seem to have come to an end in the 630s, apart from some short-lived assistance from Aquitaine rendered to the rebel Paul in 672. Obviously a certain wariness and sensitivity to the Pyrenean frontiers did exist, as testified to by the law code, but various levels of commercial contact between the Visigothic and Frankish kingdoms look to have been maintained. Beyond that other reasons at least led Frankish travellers into Spain, as evidenced by a hitherto neglected text. This is a letter from the epistolary collection of Bishop Desiderius of Cahors (*c.* 630–55). This document, which can not be dated more closely than to the period of the episcopate as a whole, is in the form of a letter of introduction and recommendation in the name of Bishop Desiderius and is addressed to all 'Lord bishops, abbots, together with all *viri magnifici*, counts, tribunes, *defensores*, *centenarii* and indeed all men holding ecclesiastical and public office'. The recipients were requested to grant free and untroubled passage to a certain priest called Antedius. The nature of the document makes it the nearest the Early Middle Ages came to producing a passport, and it is brief and to the point:

> We request, lords, that you will deem us worthy of being prayed for, and that you will receive this commendation of the bearer of this letter, the priest Antedius, together with a boy, the companion of his journey, because he does not, like many *girovagi*, undertake wanderings for their own sake, but rather seeks the province of the Spains for purposes of reasonable pilgrimage. Act, therefore, that he may be troubled by

no-one nor receive any injury, but rather, with your aid, he should return safely, whence he came. May you always recall the benefits of the Lord with us.[16]

Perhaps the most surprising thing about this letter is that it has survived at all, being something that may be classed as an administrative document, although preserved in a collection of letters of literary character. It is reasonable to assume that many more such 'to whom it may concern' documents once existed, and that Frankish travellers in Visigothic Spain numbered more than just the priest Antedius and his boy. That pilgrimage should have been their purpose is far from surprising. There were a large number of major martyrs' shrines in Spain, not least in the Ebro valley, and the cults of several of them had spilled over into France, even as far north as Paris, where the Frankish king Childebert I (511–58) had endowed his monastery, the future Saint-Germain, with relics of St Vincent of Zaragoza. Trade and pilgrimage were not the only reasons for Franks to enter Spain, and probably Spaniards to travel to Francia. Diplomacy also led to periodic interchanges, though these might not always be so satisfactory in the outcome.[17] A passing reference in the *Life* of St Babolenus, a Merovingian abbot, provides a fortuitous sidelight on this aspect of Spanish-Frankish relations. When the Neustrian and Burgundian king Clovis II (638–57) sent abbot Sigefred of Saint-Germain on a diplomatic mission to Spain he was arrested by the Visigothic ruler at Zaragoza and detained in prison for so long a time that Babolenus was appointed to succeed him as abbot.[18] Such undiplomatic treatment of an envoy may have been politically inspired, but it is also conceivable that Sigefred was attempting to augment his monastery's collection of Vincentian relics by dubious means.

Chance and casual as such references and pieces of evidence are, they at least hint at a wider and more complex series of interrelationships and exchanges between Visigothic Spain and Francia than

[16] *Desiderii Episcopi Cadurcensis*, *Epistolae*, II.8, ed. W. Arndt, Corpus Christianorum, series Latina, vol. 117 (1957), p. 332.

[17] See in general J. Orlandis, 'Comunicaciones y comercio entre la España visigótica y la Francia merovingia', in his *Hispania y Zaragoza en la antigüedad tardia* (Zaragoza, 1984), pp. 171–80.

[18] *Vita Sancti Baboleni*, ed. D. Bouquet, *Recueil des historiens des Gaules et de la France* (2nd edn, Paris, 1869), vol. III, p. 569.

are generally allowed. Indeed there are grounds for suspecting that there was very probably a great deal more interchange at every level, commercial, cultural and personal, in the western Mediterranean in the seventh century than is traditionally assumed. One illustration of this reveals that Spanish ecclesiastics were far better informed about developments in the Church as a whole than the isolationist view of peninsula culture would give credit to. Taking an example that at first sight must seem unpromising, Bishop Eugenius II of Toledo (646–57) is attributed by his successor Ildefonsus in his *De Viris Illustribus* with the composition of a short work on the Trinity, which he was apparently 'desirous of sending to Libya and the *Partes Orientis*'. This *De Trinitate* is now lost, other than for a possible fragment preserved in the monastic library of Silos.[19] Although at the moment we have hardly any of the text, something can be made of the very existence of the work itself and its subject matter, as vouched for by Ildefonsus. A work on the Trinity, written in the years of Eugenius's episcopate and which its author, unusually, wanted to send to North Africa (*Libya*) and to Latin-reading churches in the eastern Mediterranean can only have been prompted by the Monothelete controversy, which reached its height in the later 640s.[20] It caused particularly strong feelings in Africa and amongst various monastic groups in the east. The publication of the imperial *Typos* by Constans II in 648, seen in Rome as supporting the Monothelete doctrine, was condemned by Pope Martin I in a synod at the Lateran in 649, and this in turn led to the latter's arrest and detention in Constantinople. Only in 681 was reconciliation finally effected between Constantinople, Rome and Carthage.

Another case in which an appreciation of the wider implications can make more sense of something normally only considered in a Spanish context comes in what may be called the matter of the missing *acta* of the Eighteenth Council of Toledo. This is also of significance in trying to make a fair estimate of the state of health of the Spanish Church on the eve of the Arab conquest. That such a council was held, the last of the great series of 'national' councils

[19] Library of Santo Domingo de Silos, Nájera fragments no. 18.

[20] Monotheletism still lacks a full modern study, but for an outline account see the chapters by L. Bréhier in *Histoire de l'Eglise*, vol. V, eds A. Fliche and V. Martin (Paris, 1947), pp. 103–76.

of the Visigothic period, in the reign of Wittiza, and probably in the year 702 is known from a later reference to it.[21] However, no trace of its canons can be found in any of the numerous manuscripts of the Spanish canonical collections. This has generally been taken to imply that the final version of the *Hispana*, the authoritative compilation of Spanish conciliar *acta* added to the Oecumenical, African and Gallic collections, was made soon after the holding of the Seventeenth Council of Toledo in 693, as this was the last assembly whose pronouncements were included.[22] The canons of the Eighteenth Council therefore came too late to be included, and the Arab conquest of 711 put an end to the making of such compilations.

On the other hand, although many of the manuscripts of the *Hispana* originate in Francia, and the collection was to exercise its greatest influence there, there are several lines of purely Spanish transmission. Moreover, the survival of the record of the deliberations of the council held in Córdoba in 839 shows that the preservation of canonical texts continued to have a high priority amongst the Christians under Muslim rule.[23] Thus, although the disappearance of the *acta* of the Eighteenth Council may be the result of no more than accident, some alternative explanation would seem preferable.

One that might be considered links this problem with another: the posthumous reputation of the Visigothic king Wittiza (694–710) in later Christian tradition in the peninsula. In a chronicle written probably in Toledo in the middle of the eighth century his reign is singled out as representing a period of particular splendour and revival, especially in relation to the preceding harsh regime of his father Egica (687–702). At a subsequent point in his work, though, the chronicler seems to temper his previously unstinted praise of the monarch when in writing of Bishop Sindered of Toledo he complains that the latter 'continually vexed the holy and illustrious men in the church', not 'through the zeal of

[21] One folio of a manuscript containing the index to the acts of this council survived until 1936; see G. Martínez Díez, *La Colección canónica hispana*, vol. I (Madrid, 1966), pp. 166–7. This came from the monastery of Celanova, and it is possible that it was of ultimately Andalucian origin.

[22] Ibid., p. 325.

[23] *Concilium Cordubense*, ed. J. Gil, *CSM*, vol. I, pp. 135–41.

holy wisdom' but at the instigation of the king.[24] By itself this makes but little sense. However, the late ninth-century chronicles written in the Asturian kingdom reveal quite unambiguous feelings about Wittiza. For the compiler of the *Ad Sebastianum* version of the *Chronicle of Alfonso III* he was 'infamous and profligate in his morals', and, quoting the Psalmist, 'like the horse and the mule that have no understanding'.[25] He is here accused of having several wives and numerous concubines, and to avoid ecclesiastical censure he is said to have 'dissolved the councils, covered over the canons, and depraved the whole order of religion'. Moreover, 'he ordered bishops, priests and deacons to have wives'.

In so far as any attention has been paid to these abusive accusations at all, they have generally been seen in the context of rival traditions allotting responsibility for the fall of the Visigothic kingdom to the Arabs to either Wittiza and his family or to Roderic, the last king (710/11–711/12).[26] In the Asturian legends the relatives of Wittiza play a dark part, as traitors and collaborators with the Arabs. The *Chronicle of Alfonso III* is clear that disaster befell Spain because of the evils of Wittiza's behaviour and what he had done to the Church. On the other hand the treatment of Roderic and his father, opponent and victim of Egica, is highly favourable in the Asturian tradition, whilst to the Toledan author of the *Chronicle of 754* the last Visigothic king had seized his kingdom by force.[27] Thus two traditions certainly existed, and historians have taken their messages seriously enough to see civil war and usurpation as having a vital role to play in the events of 710–12. In many cases, indeed, they have taken the stuff of the later legends rather more seriously than they deserve, but no attention has been given to the references to Wittiza's activities in respect of the Church, which not only feature in the more full-blooded but

[24] *Chronica Muzarabica* or *Chronicle of 754*, section 44, ed. J. Gil, *CSM*, vol. I, p. 32. The division into sections is the work of modern editors; the original form was by the regnal years of the emperors. This is preserved in the fragments of the earliest MS of the work: London B.L. Egerton 1934, and Madrid R.A.H. 81.

[25] *Adefonsi Tertii Chronica*, section 5, ed. J. Gil, in *Crónicas asturianas*, eds J. Gil, J.L. Moralejo and J.L. Ruiz de la Peña (Oviedo, 1985), pp. 119, 121.

[26] These traditions are surveyed in R. Menéndez Pidal, *Florestá de leyendas heróicas españolas: Rodrigo el último godo* (Madrid, 1925), pp. 14–54.

[27] *Chronica Muzarabica*, 43, ed. J. Gil, p. 31; *Adefonsi Chronica*, 5–7, ed. J. Gil, pp. 119–23.

later account in the Asturian source, but also seem to lie behind the elusive remark of the more reliable chronicler of 754.

To take the words of the *Chronicle of Alfonso III*, the accusations it contains of Wittiza's subverting the councils, upturning the canons and so forth are strong but unspecific, though it is noteworthy that they point to a conciliar and canonical context. What, though, of the only concrete claim, that the king made the clergy marry? Is this not mere vulgar abuse? However, in 692 the Council 'in Trullo', also known as the 'Quinisext Council', was held in Constantinople. The third, fourth, fifth and sixth canons of this assembly all dealt with the subject of clerical marriage. The outcome of the council's deliberations was that, although second marriages and marriages after ordination were forbidden, otherwise a married clergy was perfectly acceptable. These provisions were met with outright hostility in Rome and a refusal by successive popes to accept the acts of this council.[28] The kind of direct tactics that had been employed against Pope Martin I in the Monothelete controversy were now beyond the power of the emperors in the 690s and early eighth century, and so Roman acquiescence could not be enforced. On the other hand, as is well known, the Eastern Church preserved a married clergy thereafter.

The previous oecumenical council, the Third Council of Constantinople of 680/1, had had its acts distributed to all of the major component Churches of Christendom, and the acceptance of the principal theological definition promulgated by that council had been the cause of the holding of the Fourteenth Council of Toledo in 684.[29] The impetus for this search for unanimity, which was necessary to make such conciliar decisions truly oecumenical, came from the emperor Constantine IV (668–85).[30] His son Justinian II seems to have been equally determined to achieve such status for his own council, that of 692, and indeed Roman opposition would have made such canvassing of wider support even more imperative. Rome, equally, seems to have sought for and obtained broader backing for its stand amongst the Latin churches.

[28] E. Caspar, *Geschichte des Papsttums*, vol. II (Tübingen, 1933), pp. 632–40.

[29] Ibid., pp. 587–607; F.X. Murphy, 'Julian of Toledo'; *Concilios visigóticos e hispano-romanos*, ed. J. Vives (Barcelona-Madrid, 1963), pp. 441–8.

[30] See in general A.N. Stratos, *Byzantium in the Seventh Century*, vol. IV, 668–85 (Amsterdam, 1978), pp. 119–31.

In this context of controversy over the council of 692 and its canons, which centred on two different approaches to clerical marriage and celibacy, it is impossible to believe that Spain remained unaffected or in ignorance of what was going on. The implications of the later chronicle references might suggest that in the peninsula the imperial council and its policies received the backing of Wittiza, who, through his pliant metropolitan of Toledo, Sindered, had the decisions of the 'Quinisext Council' ratified by a Spanish assembly, that is to say the Eighteenth Council of Toledo. This would, for the opponents of such a reform, have seemed like a defiance and overturning of numerous earlier western conciliar pronouncements on clerical celibacy. The Eastern Church's decisions on the subject were successfully resisted by Rome and the West in general, but it looks as if briefly they were received in Spain under royal patronage in the early eighth century. The strength of opposition, and indeed the subsequent fate of both dynasty and kingdom, must have driven Spanish churchmen to take the earliest opportunity to repudiate XVIII Toledo, and if the events of 711 meant that they could hold no more such 'national' synods at which the acts could be formally condemned, at least the non-inclusion of its canons in the *Hispana* collections has served the same purpose. In the small Christian kingdom in the Asturias which came into being as the result of a successful revolt against the Arabs *c.*718/22, the formal abrogation of Wittiza's ruling on married clergy is recorded in one version of a late ninth-century chronicle as having been decreed by the king Fruela I the Cruel (757–68).[31]

Overall, the accumulation of small and disparate pieces of evidence that either relate directly to or only make sense in the context of the wider Mediterranean world in the seventh century leads to the clear impression that Spain in the late Visigothic period was far from isolated. Indeed the impression is strong that it remained very much involved in the broader political and cultural developments of the time, and maintained a wide and various range of contacts with its neighbours. One of these, however, is almost totally obscured from our view, and that is Byzantine North Africa. Communication had certainly existed between Spain and the African kingdom of the Vandals up to the fall of the latter in

[31] *Adefonsi Chronica* (Roda version), 16, ed. J. Gil, p. 134.

533.[32] Under the re-established imperial control fugitives from religious persecution in Africa had taken refuge in Spain. This was particularly a product of the period of the controversy over the 'Three Chapters' in the reign of Justinian I (527–65), and the resulting migration of monks and manuscripts had greatly enriched both the monastic life and the libraries of the south of Spain.[33] Indeed it was upon these African foundations that much of the 'Isidoran Renaissance' may have rested.

Africa, once the intellectual centre of western Christendom, becomes strangely silent by the later sixth century. Yet something of the level of cultural and educational life can still be learnt from the works of those such as Bishop Victor of Tunnunna or the poet Corippus who left the province compulsorily or voluntarily, and whose works have thereby survived.[34] Likewise, although he had passed some years in Italy prior to his despatch to Britain in 668, the culture of Abbot Hadrian of St Augustine's monastery in Canterbury must be taken as a testimony to the learning still flourishing in his native North Africa.[35] The strange silence of seventh-century Africa is at least in part the product of the region's subsequent history. The eventual disappearance of Christianity and the elimination of Latin as the speech of its inhabitants inevitably involved the loss in the passage of time of enormous numbers of manuscripts, and quite conceivably also of whole works whose transmission had been exclusively African.

The close links that have existed between southern Spain and much of North Africa, still visible even in the present, are far from being just a product of the common domination by an Arab and Muslim culture during the medieval centuries. The probable origin of the Iberians in northern Africa, the attempted domination of parts of the peninsula by Carthage, and the strong African influ-

[32] Procopius, *History of the Wars*, III.xxiv.7, ed. H.B. Dewing, vol. II, p. 196.

[33] J. Fontaine, *Isidore de Séville et la culture classique dans l'Espagne wisigothique* (Paris, 1959), pp. 854–9.

[34] *Flavio Cresconio CORIPO: El Panegirico de Justino II*, ed. A. Ramírez de Verger (Seville, 1985), pp. 11–13.

[35] Particularly interesting is the suggestion made by B. Bischoff in the discussion following the lecture of T.J. Brown, 'An Historical introduction to the use of Classical Latin authors in the British Isles from the fifth to the eleventh centuries' that the recipient of the lost epistle of Bishop Julian of Toledo to an Abbot Hadrian was indeed this Hadrian of Canterbury: *Settimane di studio del centro italiano di studi sull'alto medioevo*, vol. XXII (1975), p. 299.

ence on early Spanish Christianity all depended upon the ease of communication between the two regions. This, too, was why the Emperor Justinian was interested in establishing an imperial enclave on the south-eastern coast of the peninsula in 551 and in expelling the Visigoths from theirs around Ceuta.[36] The Visigoths had thought of a crossing from Spain into Africa in 418, and then the Vandals had achieved it in 429. The interrelationships and occasional interdependence between Spain and Africa under Arab rule are but part of a broader pattern that can be traced from Antiquity to the present.

In the late Visigothic period it is possible that their hold on Ceuta, terminated by Justinian in the 540s, was re-established.[37] This, however, is of little consequence in comparison with the wider range of contacts and exchanges that had long existed previously across the straits of Gibraltar. Obviously the principal point of contact was with Carthage and the easily accesible *Africa Proconsularis*, but an elusive reference in the *Vitas Patrum Emeretensium* to an attempted Arian evangelizing in Mauretania shows that the Visigoths were far from ignoring the western parts of North Africa, which lay close to hand.[38] As well as the occasional influx of refugees and their books Visigothic Spain was the beneficiary of trade with Byzantine Africa, and shipping from the eastern Mediterranean that made its way, as it occasionally did, through the Straits of Gibraltar and into northern waters obviously depended upon the hospitality of Spanish ports. Above all, though, what some have seen as the sub-Byzantine style of Visigothic southern Spain really owes its character to the strength of North African contacts.[39] For example the well-known carved pilasters of Mérida, which have survived divorced from any architectural context, have no equivalents in the existing churches of the Visigothic period in the centre and north of the peninsula, and indeed

[36] The failure to understand the limited and pragmatic nature of Justinian's intentions in the peninsula has helped perpetrate the mistaken belief in a Byzantine enclave encompassing Córdoba and most of the province of Baetica. For the most judicious treatment of this problem see E.A. Thompson, *The Goths in Spain*, pp. 320–3.

[37] R. Collins, *Early Medieval Spain*, p. 112.

[38] *Vitas Patrum Emeretensium*, V.xi.15, ed. J.N. Garvin (Washington, 1946), p. 242.

[39] H. Schlunk, 'Byzantinische Bauplastik aus Spanien', *Madrider Mitteilungen*, 5 (1964), pp. 234–54.

could not be accommodated within them either in terms of design or decoration, being too small to be nave arcading and too large to be part of a chancel screen. It is only by comparison with some of the Byzantine period churches of North Africa that their actual situation and function within a church building becomes clear, and also, whilst of distinct design, that their carved decoration finds counterparts. In these ways it is possible to get some sense of the Visigothic kingdom both as existing within a Byzantine influenced cultural milieu, mediated via North Africa, and at the same time being remarkably open to developments in the eastern Mediterranean.

Such an impression, however, requires also to be modified by a sense of the diversity of economic, social and cultural forms within the peninsula itself. A superficial but telling example of this comes from a comparison of the remaining buildings and architectural fragments from the later Visigothic period.[40] Virtually all of the peninsula had been given a political unity, that was largely the work of the Visigothic king Leovigild (569–86), and the metropolitans of Toledo had imposed a striking degree of uniformity on the Spanish Church by the late seventh century with royal backing. But for all that both the ideology and the practicalities of the unity of *Hispania* were the products of the Visigothic period, few of the elements of it were securely established. From the first stirring of revolt after the Arab conquest a peninsula-wide political unity was not to be re-established until 1580 (and that was to last only sixty years). What the future for the Visigothic kingdom might have been had the Arab invasion never taken place is impossible to say. Its achievements had been considerable. Some of these were to be lost almost immediately: one consequence of the conquest was to be that *Hispania* became no more than a geographical concept for the rest of the Middle Ages. But in other respects the legacies of this relatively short period that followed the end of Roman rule in the peninsula continued to make themselves felt for centuries to come, and even in certain respects upon the new masters of Spain.

[40] H. Schlunk and T. Hauschild, *Hispania Antiqua: die Denkmäler der frühchristlichen und westgotischen Zeit* (Mainz, 1978).

2

Adjusting to Conquest

Problems of Evidence and Interpretation

The nature of the conquest and the character of the ensuing settlement are clearly crucial to any understanding of questions of continuity with the Visigothic past and the social and economic position of Christians under the ensuing Islamic rule. Here the first priority lies with the assessment of the available evidence. Sources for the history of Spain in the late Visigothic period are generally scanty, and being composed largely of legal materials, both secular and ecclesiastical, tend to be normative rather than descriptive.[1] Strictly historical sources are rare and thus descriptions of events, politics and personalities are hard or impossible to make. However, partial and restricted as this evidence might be, the greater part of it has at least the virtue of being of contemporary date. For the conquest of 711 and the first two centuries of the Arab domination of the peninsula this is a quality all too rarely to be looked for in the available evidence.

The greatest part of the source material for the general history of this period comes from the writings of Arab historians and geographers, several of whom worked centuries after the events they describe and were not themselves natives of *Al-Andalus*. There exist serious problems of interpretation connected with works that in genre are very different to their approximate equivalents in the

[1] R. Collins, *Early Medieval Spain: Unity in Diversity, 400–1000* (London, 1983), pp. 123–8.

Latin literary tradition.[2] To some extent for present purposes these problems do not matter, in that alongside the more substantial literature of the conquerors there remains the vestiges of the Latin learning of the conquered.[3] These texts, as well as being generally earlier in date, are more significant in the reconstruction of many of the features of Christian society and culture under Muslim rule than most of the Arab writings, which make all too little direct mention of the subject population and its character. Even so, the Arab sources are the prime or only evidence for certain events or features of life in *Al-Andalus*.

Although major changes in the society and culture of *Al-Andalus* were to occur during the three centuries of the rule of the Umayyad dynasty (756–1031), in many ways the fundamental features of the Arab and Berber settlement were created in the preceding period of the rule of the governors. Unfortunately, these years, from the beginnings of the conquest in 711 up to the successful revolt that resulted in the formation of the Umayyad Amirate, are amongst the worst documented of any. These four decades are the furthest removed in time from the earliest Arab writers whose historical accounts are now available.[4] Nor have any administrative texts survived, with one partial but significant exception. Admittedly, this is also a problem to be encountered in the subsequent and generally better documented Umayyad period. But unlike the latter, the years of the rule of the governors are largely lacking in dated coinage, which if nothing else provides a strict chronological framework for the reigns of the Umayyad Amirs and Caliphs.[5] For the governors, however, there is the greatest difficulty to be encountered in even trying to pin down the approximate limits of their periods of office. Problems of dating are indeed so controversial, as a result of the limitations of the

[2] Ibid., pp. 146–9; on Arab historiography see D.M. Dunlop, *Arab Civilisation to AD 1500* (London and Beirut, 1971), pp. 70–149.

[3] The texts are all conveniently edited in *CSM*.

[4] The earliest Spanish Arab historian whose work is now extant is Aḥmad ar-Rāzī (*c.*950/70), but his text basically only survives via a lost Portuguese translation of *c.*1300: *Crónica del moro Rasis*, eds D. Catalán and M. Soledad de Andrés (Madrid, 1975); still valuable is P. de Gayangos, *Memoria sobre la autenticidad de la crónica denominada del moro Rasis* (Madrid, 1852).

[5] G.C. Miles, *The Coinage of the Umayyads of Spain* (2 vols, American Numismatic Society, 1950) is the fullest catalogue and study.

available evidence, that even for an event as supposedly crucial to the future development of Western Europe as the Battle of Poitiers there can be no unanimity about when it actually took place.[6]

This particular example is a good one in that it also highlights the problems of the availability of evidence for this period in general. Contemporary Frankish Latin sources are exceedingly meagre.[7] This is true to such an extent that historians have turned to Arabic accounts, all of which are several centuries later in date, to try to fix an exact chronology for the battle.[8] This they have done because those sources offer an apparently detailed dating, not just for this episode but for the period in general. Most of it relates exclusively to Spanish or North African developments, and has little bearing on what was happening north of the Pyrenees, but when it does seem pertinent historians faced with such a problem as finding a date for the Battle of Poitiers, and with it of course a significant part of the career of the Frankish Mayor of the Palace, Charles Martel, have been all too happy to take the seductively detailed information that the Arab sources offer. Unfortunately, a comparison of the principal accounts, notably those to be found in the anonymous eleventh-century *Akhbar Machmua*, the fourteenth-century Berber history of Ibn Khaldūn or the seventeenth-century compilation of al-Maqqarī, shows that no two authors will be found to be in agreement, despite the assuredness and minuteness of the chronological information that they offer.[9]

In fact such deceptive impressions of chronological and numerical accuracy may be seen as being a standard feature of Islamic historiography.[10] Admittedly, even apparently late sources, such as the work of al-Maqqarī, can be extremely valuable when they incorporate substantial portions of the work of earlier and otherwise lost historical writings.[11] But only the most optimistic com-

[6] The generally accepted date is October 732, but cases could be made for both 733 and 734; see ch. 3 below.

[7] They consist of one of the continuations of the so-called *Chronicle of Fredegar* and the first section of the *Chronicle of Moissac*; see *The Fourth Book of the Chronicle of Fredegar*, ed. J.M. Wallace-Hadrill (London, 1960), pp. 80–103.

[8] J. Deviosse, *Charles Martel* (Paris, 1978), appendix: pp. 315–22.

[9] See also the calculations of E. Lafuente y Alcántara in the appendix to his edition of the *Akhbar Machmua*, pp. 220–39.

[10] M. Cook, *Muhammed* (Oxford, 1983), pp. 63–4 is instructive on the way later Arab sources embroidered earlier accounts.

[11] Al-Maqqarī, tr. P. de Gayangos (see list of abbreviations).

mentators have ever suggested that there once existed Arab historical works written in the early eighth century in the western Mediterranean areas.[12] Indeed it is hard to feel confident that any of the known Arab historians of subsequent generations could have had access to precise information on such subjects as the chronology of the governors of *Al-Andalus*. Outside of Spain itself, such evidence could at best have been worked out only from the administrative documents of the Umayyad government in Damascus, and whether such texts, insofar as they ever existed, survived the overthrow of the dynasty in 750 is open to question. It is likely then that any such information was gathered on the basis of traditions to be found in *Al-Andalus* and possibly North Africa. The uncertainty of their transmission is clearly reflected in the significant variations in the dates proposed by the rival sources. Thus, alluring as the chronological guidance offered by the main Arab historical works may be, they should be treated with considerable scepticism, and only given weight in relation to the testimony of the one account that is effectively contemporary with the period under consideration.

This is the so-called *Chronicle of 754*, which has gone under a variety of alternative names, including *The Mozarabic Chronicle*, the *Chronicle of Isidore of Beja (or Pacensis)*, and *The Anonymous Rhyming Chronicle of Córdoba*.[13] The multiplicity of names reflects the variety of theories that have been advanced as to its character and the location of its author. Apart from two attempts

[12] C. Sánchez-Albornoz argued that certain sections of the *Akhbar Machmua* were of eighth-century date in his study, *El Ajbar Machmua. Cuestiones históricas que suscitá* (Buenos Aires, 1944). This was rightly criticized by Arabists, the chief of whom, P. Chalmeta, was later accused by Sánchez-Albornoz of 'orgullosa megalomanía'!, see his 'Réplica al arabista Chalmeta', *Cuadernos de Historia de España*, 59/60 (1976), p. 434. For the limited nature of contemporary Arab records in this period see J. Schacht, 'On Mūsā B. 'Uqba's Kitāb al-Maghāzī', *Acta Orientalia*, 21 (1953), pp. 288–300; similar conclusions were reached in R. Sellheim, 'Prophet, Chalif und Geschichte: die Muhammed-Biografie des Ibn Isḥāq', *Oriens*, 18/19 (1965/6), pp. 33–91. For briefer statements based on these conclusions see J. Schacht, 'The Kitāb al-Tārīh of Halīfa b. Hayyāt', *Arabica*, 16 (1969), pp. 70–81; P. Crone, *Slaves on Horses* (Cambridge, 1980), p. 14 and n. 87.

[13] *CSM*, I, pp. 16–54, and most recently J.E. López Perreira's edn: *Chronicle of 754* (see list of abbreviations); for earlier editions offering different titles for the work see J. Tailhan, *Anonyme de Cordue. Chronique rimée des rois de Tolède et de la conquête de l'Espagne par les arabes* (Paris, 1855), T. Mommsen, *Continuationes Bizantia-Arabica et Hispana*, in *MGH AA*, XI, pp. 334–68, and pp. 328–9 for the attribution of the work to 'Isidorus Pacensis' in the sixteenth century.

to place its writing in Syria, it has generally been accepted that the work is of Spanish origin, and that its composition took place very soon after the last dated occurrences recorded in it, which is to say in 754.[14] These considerations make of it the most substantial piece of chronicle writing carried out in the peninsula after the first quarter of the seventh century, and it was not to have a successor in Latin historical composition before the compilation of a series of short chronicles associated with the court of the Asturian king Alfonso III in the late ninth century.[15] It is thus the only detailed peninsula witness of Christian origin to the Arab conquest and its aftermath. Moreover, as has been suggested, it considerably predates not only the earliest surviving Arab accounts, but also many of the traditions upon which the latter were to be built up.

Indeed it probably would not now be necessarry to go into the question of the events of the conquest itself in any detail if there had not been an almost wilful refusal on the part of the majority of historians who have ever discussed it to apply any form of serious source criticism to it. In virtually every case what has happened has been that the accounts of the Arab sources have been taken as providing the primary level of information.[16] Certain of the more overtly fanciful elements in these have been rejected or rationalized, but otherwise the emphasis has been placed on making these disparate accounts cohere into a single narrative. When it is appreciated that not one of these versions on which such weight is being placed can be dated any closer to the events they purport to describe than 300 years the dangers of such a procedure become all too obvious. Moreover, instead of starting with the earliest datable sources, here represented by the *Chronicle of 754*, and looking with a critical eye at the gradual elaboration of the stories in progressively later works, the tendency in this case has been to start with the most recent and fullest versions of the story and to go backwards in time trying to make the earlier and more reliable

[14] Previous interpretations are usefully discussed in J.E. López Perreira, *Estudio crítico sobre la Crónica Mozárabe de 754* (Zaragoza, 1980), pp. 9–18.

[15] R. Menéndez-Pidal, 'Las primeras historias de la Reconquista', *Boletín de la Real Academia de la Historia*, 100 (1932), pp. 582–623 was the first modern edition and study, but see now *Crónicas asturianas*, eds J. Gil, J.L. Moralejo and J.L. Ruiz de la Peña (Oviedo, 1985).

[16] An honourable exception here is E.A. Thompson, *The Goths in Spain* (Oxford, 1969), pp. 249–51 whose brief treatment is based exclusively on the account of the *Chronicle of 754*.

texts cohere to them. This has even led to unjustifiable emendation of the text of the *Chronicle of 754* when it can thereby be made to fit in with the fantasies of the later Arab stories.[17]

What is required is for us to begin with the evidence that is nearest in time to the events themselves, and then to see how much of that survives into the later retellings of them. The 754 chronicler's account is, not surprisingly, brief and poignant, and also not always unambiguous. However, the narrative outline is more or less clear. In 711 (on the death of Wittiza?) Roderic was made king by a section of the Visigothic nobility; possibly the palatine aristocracy is being referred to here by the authors' use of the word *Senatus*. This, however, was not unopposed. Moreover, in the same year he was faced by the Arab invasion. Mūsā ibn Nuṣayr (the chronicler's 'Muza'), governor of Arab-ruled North Africa, sent an army into Spain under the command of 'Tariq Abu Zara'. This is said to have followed on from a prior series of raids and incursions in which some towns had been sacked. Roderic met the Arab forces in battle in the *Transductinis promonturiis*.

That he was there defeated is clear enough, but the chronicler's explanation is far from being so. He attributes it to the Visigothic army's flight and says this was due to its having accompanied the king 'in rivalry' and 'deceitfully', and 'out of ambition for rule'. Roderic himself is said in consequence to have 'lost his kingdom together with his fatherland with the killing of his rivals'.[18] It is possible that the text is corrupt, but as it stands it may imply that the army was divided by faction and this led to disaster, in course of which many of the king's potential rivals were killed. On the other hand it may even suggest that Roderic had indulged in a pre-emptive strike against his opponents, in consequence of which the army was weakened and thus unable to resist the Arab forces. In either case, such an impression would fit in with the general pattern of Visigothic regnal succession in which the opening years of any reign were crucial for the monarch's attempts to establish his military and political credibility. In this particular case the lack

[17] In the edition by J.E. López Perreira, p. 70, and note 13 on p. 71; the emendation was suggested by R. Dozy, *Recherches sur l'histoire et la littérature de l'Espagne pendant le Moyen Age* (2 vols, Paris, 1881), vol. I, p. 5. The emendation turns Oppa into the villain required by the legend; the text makes sense as it stands.

[18] *Chronicle of 754*, 52, p. 68.

of unanimity at his accession made Roderic's position particularly vulnerable.

The *Chronicle of 754* makes no further reference to Ṭāriq, but records the arrival in Spain at Cádiz in 711 of his superior, Mūsā. This latter is said to have proceeded to Toledo and pacified the adjacent regions. There he also carried out the execution of a number of members of the indigenous aristocracy who seem to have been involved in the escape from the city of Oppa, son of the former king Egica, and thus brother of Wittiza. It is not certain that this Oppa also perished in consequence. The chronicler makes it clear from his linking of the attacks of external enemies, in other words the Arabs and Berbers (*Mauri*), with internal 'frenzy' that localized warfare was endemic. He laments the disasters that had befallen Spain in language borrowed from Isaiah. The passage in which he records the burning of cities, the crucifying of men and the slaughter of children is a generalized impression of the violence of this tumultuous period, but he does make specific reference to the fall of Zaragoza. Mūsā himself was recalled by the Caliph Walīd, and left Spain before the end of 712, after a period of fifteen months in the peninsula, taking with him some of the captive Visigothic nobles and much loot. Once returned to Damascus, he fell foul of the Caliph, and was only saved from execution by a timely payment drawn from the substantial spoils of his African and Spanish activities.[19]

A certain amount of disentanglement is required as far as this account is concerned, as it is not strictly chronologically sequential. Firstly, though, it is important to note that the chronicler's dating systems, here using the regnal years of the Byzantine emperor and the Umayyad Caliph, the Arab years of the Hegira and the Spanish era, are generally mutually consistent. Although the work is structured chronologically around the regnal years of the Byzantine emperors, in fact the primary system of dating is, unsurprisingly, that of the Spanish era. More than that; it is also notable that the chronicler's dating for beginning of the reign of the Visigothic king Wittiza, which is not in accordance with that worked out on the basis of later king lists and generally accepted by historians, has been proved to be correct by the discovery of a

[19] *Chronicle of 754*, 54–5, pp. 70–4.

fragmentary but clearly dated charter belonging to the reign.[20] It has generally been held to have begun in 698, but it is now certain that this should be revised to 693/4.[21] It is necessary to stress here the indications of reliability for this author's dates as the chronology he provides for the conquest is at variance with that normally credited. He has Roderic's reign begin in 711 and end in 712, as opposed to 710 and 711.[22]

More important than the matter of dating are the implications of this account for the sequence of events themselves. Firstly, there were a series of initial destructive Arab raids on southern Spain. Secondly, in 711 there were two Arab forces operating in the peninsula: one, and this was probably the first to arrive, was the army of Arabs and Berbers led by Ṭāriq 'and others', and the other was the army under their superior, Mūsā, which landed at Cadiz and made its way to Toledo. Thirdly, continuing to follow the chronicler's chronology, in 712 the first of these armies defeated the main forces of the Visigothic king Roderic, who seems previously to have been engaged in a struggle for power with internal rivals. His own fate is not here recorded, but a later reference, *c.* 715, to his widow suggests a death in the battle or soon after.[23] Fourthly, Mūsā at Toledo executed an unspecified number of members of the indigenous aristocracy for their involvement with the brother of a former king. A reasonable guess may be that this latter had been chosen or even consecrated as king himself at this time. His fate is uncertain but may have been the same as theirs. Fifthly, in this period of 711/12 Mūsā and his deputies established control over not only the former Visigothic capital and parts of the centre and south of the peninsula, but also extended their authority as far as the Ebro valley and Zaragoza. These events, and the

[20] J. Canellas López, *Diplomática hispano-visigoda* (Zaragoza, 1979), doc. no. 192, p. 255.

[21] The previous and hitherto standard dating was worked out by K. Zeumer in his 'Die Chronologie der Westgotenkönige des Reiches von Toledo', *Neues Archiv*, 27 (1902), pp. 409ff.

[22] *Chronicle of 754*, 52, p. 68. The chronicler makes no reference to the death or the fate of Wittiza, though (44, p. 62) he seems to suggest that his reign lasted for 15 years. It would thus look to have ended *c.*710. It is possible that his premature death – he was probably less than 30 at the time – opened the way for the disputed succession the chronicler alludes to. On the other hand he may have been overthrown by Roderic.

[23] Ibid., 59, p. 78.

accompanying local struggles and civil war produced considerable destruction and loss of life.

In certain respects this outline conforms with that to be drawn from the principal Arab accounts of the conquest of the peninsula. These are generally in agreement that Mūsā ibn Nuṣayr, when governor of *Ifrīqīya* sent his freedman Ṭāriq into Spain and that a victory won by the latter over the army of the Visigothic king Roderic laid the whole kingdom open to conquest by the Arab and Berber forces. Mūsā, aware of the scale of his lieutenant's success hastened to cross the straits, and, in some of the accounts, to stress his own superiority over his deputy publicly humiliated the latter. Subsequently both he and Ṭāriq undertook a campaign that brought much of the peninsula into submission. He was at this point recalled by the Caliph, and taking Ṭāriq with him, returned to Damascus. There he fell into disfavour with the new Caliph, Sulaymān (715–17), and died in poverty.[24]

There is, however, a significant degree of difference between certain elements in the Arab sources and the *Chronicle of 754*. In the former the conquest, as well as being effected by a numerically tiny force, was essentially the product of a single battle. Some of the Arab accounts record a previous raid by a certain Ṭārif, but their basic presentation is of a clear-cut and decisive Muslim intervention in the affairs of the peninsula, in which a small army of 'true believers' invaded a kingdom and conquered it virtually at a stroke. On the other hand the *Chronicle of 754* gives the impression of both considerable prior raiding by Arab forces from Africa and also the presence of probably two Arab and Berber armies in the peninsula for anything up to a year before the crucial battle with Roderic. This too, in the light of subsequent campaigning by some of the governors who were to follow Mūsā, was not as immediately decisive as the Arab accounts suggest. Moreover, the Arabs themselves were intervening in the peninsula in a time in which there were already serious internal divisions and possibly civil wars taking place. The impression of events given by the *Chronicle of 754* must surely have a greater ring of authenticity to it than the overly clean-cut and ideologically influenced presentation of the Arab accounts. There also remains the problem of those features in the Arabic sources that might be considered as legendary: such

[24] Ibn 'Abd al-Ḥakam, pp. 18–28; *Akhbar Machmua*, pp. 17–23.

things as the role of 'Count Julian', the rape of his daughter, Mūsā's flogging of Ṭāriq, and the story of the locked chamber in Toledo.[25] Is it possible to sieve these accounts and just accept certain parts of them as being fundamentally historical and others as deriving from essentially literary traditions? The same problem is to be encountered in Christian sources relating to these events dating from after the eighth century.

Before considering further such later Christian and Muslim accounts of these episodes, it should also be asked if there is any other contemporary evidence that can be placed alongside the testimony of the author of the *Chronicle of 754*? The immediate answer must be that, regrettably there is very little. Certainly some archaeological evidence is indicative of the abandonment or destruction of settlements at this time, and the volume of this may be increased in the course of future excavation.[26] More specific, though, may be the indications of coinage. For the reign of Roderic coins are only known from two mints, those of Toledo and of *Egitania* (Idanha la Velha in central Portugal). Admittedly, the numbers involved, amounting to only a dozen examples, are small, and further coins may be found with other mint names. However, it is significant that there also exist coins of the same style in the name of a king Achila, who also features in two regnal lists. These were struck exclusively in the mints of Narbonne, Gerona and Tarragona.[27] Thus, although the sample is small, it has been suggested that Roderic and Achila were ruling simultaneously, with the latter controlling the provinces of Narbonensis and Tarraconensis, whilst his rival held the centre and south of the peninsula.[28] Significantly, the two regnal lists that include the name of

[25] Ibn 'Abd al-Ḥakam, pp. 19–20 (Julian and his daughter), pp. 21, 26 (table); *Akhbar Machmua*, pp. 19–20 (Julian and his daughter), p. 27 (table); see also the works of R. Menéndez-Pidal in n. 38 below, and R. Basset, *La Maison fermée de Tolède* (Oran, 1898). H.T. Norris, *The Berbers in Arabic Literature* (London and Beirut, 1982), pp. 69–70 is brief but very pertinent here.

[26] P. de Palol, 'Las Excavaciones del conjunto de "El Bovalar"', in *Los Visigodos: Historia y civilización* (Murcia, 1986), pp. 513–25, describes one such site, whose destruction *c.*713 is dated by finds of coins of Achila II, including the first one known of this reign from the mint of Zaragoza.

[27] G.C. Miles, *The Coinage of the Visigoths of Spain: Leovigild to Achila II* (American Numismatic Society, 1952), pp. 442–3 (Roderic), pp. 444–6 (Achila).

[28] E. Lévi-Provençal , *Histoire de l'Espagne musulmane* (3 vols, Paris/Leiden, 1950–1), vol. I, pp. 6–7; R. Collins, *Early Medieval Spain*, pp. 151, 253–4.

Achila lack that of Roderic.[29] This explanation would certainly fit in with the indications of civil war given by the chronicler. There are no grounds whatsoever for trying to equate Achila with Oppa.

Despite a general resemblance in outline, there are remarkably few points of similarity in detail between the testimony of this, the only eighth-century account of these events, and their subsequent treatment in later Spanish sources, both Latin and Arabic. The Christian ones, in the form of the two versions of the *Chronicle of Alfonso III*, are nearest in time, being compositions of the late ninth century, albeit both now in early tenth-century recensions.[30] For these texts, which here diverge one from another fairly substantially, the conquest could be attributed to a single simple explanation: the treacherous behaviour of the sons of the Visigothic king Wittiza. The succession of Roderic, who in the fuller, Roda version of the chronicle was presented as the grandson of the former king Chindasuinth, led the disappointed heirs of the previous ruler Wittiza to collude with the Arabs, bring them into the kingdom, and desert the monarch in the crucial battle.[31]

This is linked with the next episode in the chronicle, the Asturian revolt and the victory of its first king Pelagius over the Arabs at Covadonga. In this one of the sons of Wittiza in particular has a role to play as collaborator with the Arabs. This is Oppa, variously presented in the two versions as bishop of Seville or bishop of Toledo. In fact here the chronicle betrays its source, as in both versions, and particularly the longer Roda one, Oppa and Pelagius are given an extensive passage of heroic dialogue in the build up to the account of the battle. This is quite at variance with the highly laconic style of the rest of this work, and the implication must be that the source is fundamentally not a historical one. The Oppa character is obviously some form of reminiscence of the Oppa, brother of Wittiza, of the *Chronicle of 754*, here transformed into his son. The authors of the two versions could not even agree on the see to which to assign him, though a tenth-century set of episcopal lists seems to indicate the existence of a bishop Oppa of Seville at some point in the early eighth century.[32] There is nothing

[29] *Cronica Regum Visegothorum*, ed. K. Zeumer, *MGH Leges*, I, p. 461 – *Continuationes*: B.

[30] J. Gil et al., *Crónicas asturianas*, pp. 45–76.

[31] *Adefonsi Chronica – Rotensis*, 6, ed. J. Gil, p. 120.

[32] Ibid. – *Rotensis*, 8, *Ad Sebastianum*, 8, ed. J. Gil, pp. 123, 124.

here that challenges the version of events given in the 754 chronicle, and the nature of its account is such that it would be highly unwise to try to supplement the earlier text with elements taken from this source. The 'sons of Wittiza' look tempting, but should be resisted.[33]

With the Arab records of the conquest, fantasy, already present in the *Chronicle of Alfonso III*, becomes the dominant feature. As literature this material is interesting, but not as anything else. Even what may be regarded as the strictly historical elements in such records may be seen to have been affected by the need to present the conquest as further proof of the validity of the message of Islam as evidenced in martial triumph. More than that, though, there exist serious problems to be faced in taking such accounts as having direct points of historical contact with the realities of events in the early eighth century. Firstly, there are no certain lines of oral tradition (*hadīth*) that link the principal extant Arab accounts with the period in which these events occurred. Secondly, the relative wealth of detail provided on the conquest is in stark contrast with the poverty of the same sources' treatment of the subsequent history of *Al-Andalus* prior to the tenth century. In other words the conquest was an episode that attracted legendary embroidering, as the fundamental features of its treatment in these texts indicate. Not all elements of the stories are present in full in all of the sources, and there are interesting variants. But the striking consistencies that can be found are not indicative of the greater veracity that should be attributed to these tales; rather they are symptomatic of the highly-developed nature of the legendary core by the time these materials came to be included in the extant texts. There is no point turning to the *Chanson de Roland* for a historical account of the battle fought in 778 between the Basques and the rearguard of Charlemagne's army.[34] Yet in terms of genre and distance in time between event and literary treatment of it this is just what those who wish to believe in the Arab accounts of the conquest of Spain in 711 might be willing to do.

A number of objections might be offered to such a sweeping dismissal of the whole of the Arab tradition on the conquest.

[33] The 'sons of Wittiza' and other elements in these tales continue to beguile historians of this period: M. Coll i Alentórn, *Els Successors de Vitiza en la zona nord-est del domini visigòtic* (Barcelona, 1971).

[34] R. Collins, *The Basques* (Oxford, 1986), pp. 118–23.

Certain authors in particular who included accounts of it in their works may seem deserving of more respect. For example there is the supposedly early work that includes a section on the Arab conquests of North Africa and Spain by Ibn 'Abd al-Ḥakam, dated to the mid-ninth century, and there is also the late tenth-century version given by Ibn al-Qūṭiyya ('Son of the Goth'), a self-proclaimed descendant of the Visigothic king Wittiza. But in neither case does the text of their works survive in original form.[35] Nor, in the case of Ibn al-Qūṭiyya, even assuming this is not just another of a fairly numerous series of examples of spurious genealogizing, does a distant familial connection guarantee the authenticity of stories of this kind.[36]

Without wishing to go further into the problems connected with these materials here, it is sufficient to suggest that there is nothing in them that requires us to reject the account of the conquest given by someone writing just forty years after it, nor should anything in them command such respect that it is necessary to use it to complement the work of the author of the *Chronicle of 754*. Even in matters of chronology the earlier Arab sources are convincingly vague whilst the later ones are suspiciously precise. There is only one element in the Arab versions that requires fuller consideration in this context, in that it has been held to have received corroboration from the *Chronicle of 754*, and that is the role of 'Count Julian'.[37]

This individual is found in a number of the Arabic sources, and is portrayed as holding office in Ceuta, generally under the aegis of the Visigothic king Roderic, though this is left rather vague. In the most developed form of the story the rape of Julian's daughter by Roderic whilst she was entrusted to the court school in Toledo leads the former to plan revenge. This he encompassed by submitting to Mūsā ibn Nuṣayr, the governor of *Ifrīqīya*, and assisting the Arabs under Ṭāriq to cross the straits and carry out the invasion of

[35] C. Sánchez-Albornoz, *En torno a los orígenes del feudalismo*, vol. II, *Fuentes de la historia musulmana* (2nd edn, Buenos Aires, 1974), pp. 64–8, 166–72, who is probably harder on the former and more trusting of the latter than either deserve.

[36] R. Collins, *Early Medieval Spain*, pp. 190–1.

[37] See most recently A.M. Howell, 'Some notes on early treaties between Muslims and the Visigothic Rulers of Al-Andalus', in *Actas del I congresso de historia de Andalucía*, vol. I (Córdoba, 1978), pp. 3–14.

Spain.[38] Even the most romantic of historians have tended to pass by the rape story, but the existence of Julian himself and his role in abetting the Arab conquest have received an extraordinarily high level of credence. This has been assisted by an argument that sees Julian as identifiable as a certain Urbanus, who features once in the *Chronicle of 754*. It is suggested that the difference of name could be explained by palaeographic confusion, though it would require a fairly drunken scribe to have perpetrated such an error.[39]

It is only because historians are so reluctant to part with any form of evidence, however far-fetched, that not only are such stories taken seriously but are also made to condition the interpretation of materials that are intrinsically far more reliable. Urban thus has to fit Julian, rather than Julian be seen as at best a distant literary echo of Urban. Of this Urban the *Chronicle of 754* reports that he was an African, brought up as a Catholic Christian, and a confident of Mūsā, whom he accompanied on his expedition to Spain.[40] As previously mentioned, it is methodologically dubious to approach the available Arab sources on the basis of feeling that it is possible merely to discard certain elements that are too preposterous for credence and take the rest as if it were a core of reliable historical evidence that traversed the centuries between the events and their recording essentially unsullied and unaltered. There is no point in pretending that bad evidence is good because it is virtually all that there is. In this case there is not even that excuse because, by Early Medieval standards, the *Chronicle of 754* offers really very good evidence in that it is both close in time to the events that it describes, and presents an account that is intrinsically credible both in terms of historical methodology and common sense.

Military Occupation and the Restoration of Order

The chronology of the chronicler of 754 is credible in respect of the period of the Arab governors who ruled *Al-Andalus* from 711 to 756, in that the degree of its exactitude varies. That is to say it

[38] R. Menéndez-Pidal, *Floresta de leyendas*, pp. 39–54; for the texts see his *Reliquias de la poesía épica española* (2nd edn, Madrid, 1980), pp. 8–20.

[39] E. Lévi-Provençal, *Histoire de l'Espagne musulmane* (Paris/Leiden, 1950), vol. I, p. 13, see the discussion and bibliography in n. 1.

[40] *Chronicle of 754*, 57, p. 76.

becomes increasingly precise as it approaches the decades in which the author himself lived and worked, and is least confident about the earliest part of this period. Such frailty is more credible than the contradictory certainties of some of the later Arab writers.[41] Intrinsically more important, though, than problems of dating are the all too brief pieces of information that the chronicler provides in respect of the activities and achievements of the individual governors. In a number of cases his account corroborates details to be found in the later Arab traditions, which might otherwise be treated with less respect than they deserve.

A case in point is the story of the killing of the second of the governors, 'Abd al-Azīz ibn Mūsā, probably late in 715. He had been entrusted with authority over the conquered territories by his father when the latter was recalled to Damascus to report to the Caliph Walīd I. In the Arab tradition, 'Abd al-Azīz married the widow of Roderic, the last Visigothic king, and under her influence was tempted both to make use of a crown, and to scheme how to get his Arab companions to perform acts of obeisance before him in Seville.[42] These unegalitarian tendencies led the latter to assassinate him. The 754 chronicler has a fundamentally similar tale to tell in that he records that at the instigation of his wife Egilona, widow of Roderic, 'Abd al-Azīz was planning to 'throw off the Arab yoke from his neck and retain the conquered kingdom of Iberia for his own'.[43]

This is a peculiarly interesting and quite credible tale. The Arabs and their Berber mercenaries represented a very small percentage of the population of Spain in 715. Although the royal *comitatus* had been dispersed in the defeat of Roderic, and most regions of the peninsula subjected to a superficial pacification in the subsequent years, the Arab hold was clearly precarious, and indeed in *c.* 718 the Caliph 'Umar II was said to have considered seriously the idea of abandoning the conquest. Visigothic royal traditions had hardly been touched by the events of the conquest, and the expectations of the bulk of the population were directed at a

[41] For an attempt to reconcile the latter see appendix III of the edition of the *Ajbar Machmua* by Lafuente.

[42] *Akhbar Machmua*, pp. 31–2; C. Sánchez-Albornoz, *La España musulmana* (6th edn, Madrid, 1982), vol. I, pp. 66–9 for the Pseudo-Ibn Qūṭayba; Ibn 'Abd al-Ḥakam, pp. 26–7.

[43] *Chronicle of 754*, 59, p. 78.

strong, centralized, and purely peninsular monarchy. The potential for a re-assertion of independence was considerable, and it is indeed peculiar that only 'Abd al-Azīz ibn Mūsā was prepared to contemplate the possibility of using the conquest to create a personal monarchy. On the other hand his failure is easily explicable. Such a step clearly depended upon the articulation of indigenous traditions of government and royal authority, represented by such elements as the employment of regalia and ceremonial. Although similar developments were taking place within the Caliphal court at Damascus, these were at variance with the traditions of authority in pre-Islamic Arab society and with the fundamental egalitarianism of the prophetic message of Islam, and in due course helped contribute to the collapse of the Umayyad regime in Syria.[44]

It is notable that in the whole extent of the Arab conquests in the seventh and eighth centuries which stretched almost from the Punjab to the Pyrenees, that it was only in Spain that such a scheme of revolt by an Arab governor is to be encountered. This is probably due to the fact that virtually all of the conquered territories constituted parts of two great empires, and thus the individual regions had no traditions of autonomous self-government on which an indigenous movement of revolt could be focused. The only exception was the monarchy of the Visigoths confined to the Iberian peninsula. It is thus also perhaps not fortuitous that in 756 Spain was to be the first region of the hitherto politically united 'Arab Empire' to break decisively free of the secular authority of the Caliphs.

'Abd al-Azīz's three-year governorship (712–15) is notable not only for its dramatic end but also for laying the groundwork for the continuing Arab and Berber occupation of the peninsula. The eighteen-month period in which his father Mūsā had been present in Spain seems to have been too short to have contained more than military activity, but of 'Abd al-Azīz the 754 chronicler records that he was 'throughout three years peacefully subjecting all Spain to the yoke of taxation'.[45] This statement, typical of the stylistic

[44] For various interpretations of the collapse of the Umayyad Caliphate see M. A. Shaban, *The 'Abbāsid Revolution* (Cambridge, 1970), and P. Crone, *Slaves on Horses: the Evolution of the Islamic Polity* (Cambridge, 1980), pp. 37–57.

[45] *Chronicle of 754*, 59, p. 76.

brevitas advocated by Isidore and much followed by this author, essentially contains two elements.[46] Firstly that this governorship saw the effective pacification of the peninsula, and secondly that this was allied to the creation or adaptation of a system of taxation. This indeed was the normal pattern of the imposition of Arab rule in the period of the conquests, as testified to in such relatively early sources as the *Futūḥ al-Buldān* of al-Balādhuri (d. 892).[47] In general the main towns of regions occupied by Arab armies were offered simple terms: either they might surrender at once and be guaranteed a large measure of local self-government and religious toleration or, if they offered resistance, the population would be liable to enslavement. A number of local treaties were made on the basis of such offers in Syria, Palestine and Egypt.[48]

The same process, which allowed for the maximizing of the military potential of the Arab armies and the greatest rapidity of expansion, was also applied in Spain. In this case, indeed, historians are particularly fortunate in that the actual text of one of these treaties has survived, and this corroborates not only the general picture given by al-Balādhuri but also the statement of the chronicler of 754 in respect of the activities of 'Abd al-Azīz. The document contains the text of the treaty made by 'Abd al-Azīz ibn Mūsā with a certain Theodemir, lord of seven towns and their associated lands in the south-east of the peninsula. It has been preserved in three separate later works, including a fourteenth-century biographical dictionary, and is dated to the fourth day of the month of Recheb in the ninety-fourth year of the Hegira (5 April AD 713).[49] This in itself helps to confirm the chronology presented by the 754 chronicler. On the basis of his information it is possible to deduce that Mūsā ibn Nuṣayr left Spain towards the end of 712, whereas the Arab accounts would keep him there until the last months of 713.

The treaty itself stipulates that those who surrender and 'submit themselves to the patronage of God' and become clients of his

[46] On *brevitas*, see J. Fontaine, *Isidore de Séville*, p. 768.

[47] Al-Balādhuri, *Futūḥ*, tr. P. Hitti, *The Origins of the Islamic State* (New York, 1916), pp. 187, 223, 246–7, 249, 271–5, 338–40.

[48] Ibid.; see also A.J. Butler, *The Arab Conquest of Egypt* (2nd edn, Oxford, 1978), pp. 249–74, 310–27.

[49] F.J. Simonet, *Historia de los Mozárabes de España* (Madrid, 1867), pp. 797–800 for texts; also, the useful discussion of Theodemir and the treaty in J.B. Vilar, *Orihuela musulmana* (Murcia, 1976), pp. 18–44.

Prophet will not be killed, enslaved or separated one from another or from their wives and children. They will retain their own lords and will not be molested in the performance of their religion, nor would their churches be destroyed. These terms of capitulation are here extended to the towns of Orihuela, 'Valentila' (which some have argued to be Valencia), Alicante, Mula, 'Bigastro', 'Eyya' and Lorca. The inhabitants were in return required not to give refuge to deserters from or enemies of the conquerors, not to conceal the existence of such enemies nor threaten those who lived under the protection of the Arabs. In addition they were to pay a set annual tribute *per capita*. This consisted of one dinar (the Arab gold coin, though probably here indicating a weight of precious metal), four measures of wheat, four of barley, four jugsful of grapejuice, four of vinegar, two of honey and two of oil per head. For every slave a half payment would be expected.[50]

The implications of this treaty for the history of the earliest period of the Arab occupation of the peninsula are considerable. As the pattern to be found elsewhere in the lands conquered in the seventh and early eighth centuries makes clear the making of this agreement would not have been a unique occurrence in the peninsula.[51] Indeed there are very good grounds for believing that such a treaty was made with the inhabitants of Pamplona.[52] Thus the conquest effected by the chance outcome of a single battle was followed by the making of a series of such treaties with many of the cities and even smaller settlements, probably through the persons of those holding authority in them, that is to say the Visigothic counts. Such agreements indicate that, at least initially, land tenure remained unaffected by the events of 711, as did the functioning of local authority. In this case this was represented in the person of Theodemir, in whose name the treaty was drawn up. By good fortune something more is known of him from a previous stage of his career. In the *Chronicle of 754* he appears in an unusual

[50] J. Vallvé, *La División territorial de la España musulmana* (Madrid, 1986), pp. 189–91, assumes that the amounts stipulated in the treaty were not those to be paid by each inhabitant, but rather were those to be received by each member of the Arab army. He can thus argue that this proves the existence of slave soldiers. There is no justification for such a belief, and at the very least the matter would require fuller argument.

[51] See above n. 47 and n. 48.

[52] R. Collins, *The Basques*, p. 116.

parenthetical entry, which, in reporting his death, provides a synopsis of his achievements. He is recorded as having, under the joint rule of Egica and Wittiza (694–702), defeated a Byzantine naval raid on the kingdom.[53] This otherwise unrecorded episode should probably be linked to the despatch of a fleet to Africa by the short-lived emperor Leontius, which was driven from Carthage by the Arabs in 698/9.

Taxes, in the form of the annual tribute specified in the treaty with Theodemir, were certainly imposed as the price for continuing local autonomy and religious freedom, but there are no grounds for assuming these were necessarily heavier than those that existed in the time of the Visigothic monarchy. Precision on this point is not possible as the evidence for Visigothic taxation, other than for the fact that it existed, is very slight.[54] However, it has been shown that in other Mediterranean regions conquered by the Arabs the existing Byzantine forms of taxation became the basis of the subsequent exactions.[55] Certainly the items specified in the treaty made with Theodemir do not correspond exactly with those known to have been levied as tax from the non-Islamic populations of Egypt and Syria, so they may have been closer to the norms of the Visigothic monarchy.[56] It may also reasonably be assumed that the precise character of the tribute varied from location to location, as some of the items expected of the inhabitants of these seven towns could not have been produced in some of the other regions of the peninsula.

The making of such a series of local arrangements, which barely troubled the existing local order of the peninsula, was obviously a highly satisfactory expedient for the opening phase of the conquest, leaving the Arab and Berber armies unencumbered by the demands of garrisoning a large number of hostile settlements and free to proceed rapidly with the pacification of other areas. It must be remembered how limited were the forces available to the first

[53] *Chronicle of 754*, 87, p. 112–114. The placing here is due to editorial emendation; in the manuscript and in previous editions this section comes earlier in the work. See the edition by J. Gil: *CSM*, I, p. 34 = section 47. For the relocation of this section see J.E. López Perreira, *Estudio crítico sobre la crónica mozárabe de 754* (Zaragoza, 1980), pp. 40–3.

[54] E.A. Thompson, *The Goths in Spain*, pp. 126–31.

[55] M.A. Shaban, *Islamic History A.D. 600–750* (Cambridge, 1971), pp. 37–9, 43.

[56] Compare the details given by Balādhuri, see n. 47 above, and in general D.C. Dennet, *Conversion and the Poll-tax in Early Islam* (Cambridge, Mass., 1950).

governors of *Al-Andalus* and how substantial the area over which they had to seek to impose their authority. However, some cities did resist. Mérida held out against a prolonged siege until the mid-summer of 712.[57] It is likely that according to precedent terms would have been offered, but having been rejected it is regretable that no information survives as to the fate of the inhabitants on their eventual surrender. However, it is clear that in such circumstances the male population of the city might be put to death and the women and children enslaved.[58] This seems to have occurred in Zaragoza in 712. Similarly, accordingly to Arab traditions, the Visigothic count of Córdoba and his troops put up a short-lived resistance from an improvised fortress after the Arab seizure of the city. They were all put to death on capitulation.[59]

Thus a number of places did resist the blandishments of the conquerors' proffered terms, and may well have suffered in consequence. There were probably also cities that the Arabs were not prepared to allow the same degree of freedom as was offered to others. Toledo, the former Visigothic capital, must surely have been a case in point as it was the obvious focus for a major revival of indigenous resistance. The last Visigothic kings received a large measure of their legitimation, at least in the eyes of the Church, from their ritual anointing in the *urbs regia* at the hands of the metropolitan bishop of Toledo.[60] The speed with which Ṭāriq or Mūsā may have been able to seize the capital probably had a vital part to play in paralysing the kingdom and preventing the resurgence of centralized opposition to the continuing conquest. One indication that Toledo did not enjoy the kind of freedoms conceded to Theodemir's towns is the rapid departure from Spain of the metropolitan bishop Sindered, deserting, as the chronicler of 754 saw it 'the sheep of Christ not like the shepherd but like the

[57] The traditions that require the siege to have lasted for several months can be reconciled with a departure of Mūsā for Damascus late in 712 if it be allowed that fighting between the Arabs and the forces of Roderic continued throughout the years 711–12, and that the siege began well before the decisive battle *in transductinis promonturiis*. See Sánchez-Albornoz, *España musulmana*, vol. I, pp. 52–4.

[58] *Chronicle of 754*, 54, pp. 70–2.

[59] *Akhbar Machmua*, pp. 9–11 of text, pp. 23–7 of translation.

[60] R. Collins, 'Julian of Toledo and the royal succession in late seventh century Spain', in P. Sawyer and I. Wood, *Early Medieval Kingship* (Leeds, 1977), pp. 30–49.

hireling'.[61] He appears as a signatory to the council held in Rome in 721.[62]

Another city that was probably singled out for different treatment was Córdoba, which, according to the later accounts, fell into the hands of the Arabs in a surprise attack in the aftermath of the defeat of Roderic. It, like Toledo, was thus a legitimate prize in that it had been taken in war and not by an agreed capitulation. It became the centre of the new governors' administration when this was transferred from Seville (*c*.716), which had also been retained for direct rule.[63] In all previous territories that had been conquered by the Arabs the standard practice had been for the existing centre of government to be downgraded and a totally new settlement to be created, which was initially an Arab preserve and military centre for the army (*jund*). Thus in Iran the Sassanian capital at Ctesiphon was abandoned and the new garrison cities of Kūfa and Baṣra founded. To these were later to be added Wāsiṭ, and Merv for Khorasan. In Egypt the Byzantine administrative and religious centre of Alexandria was replaced by Fusṭāṭ, that later grew into Cairo, and in Byzantine North Africa the new foundation of Kairouan fulfilled the role previously played by Carthage.[64]

It is thus interesting to note that Spain does not seem to adhere fully to this pattern. Certainly Toledo, which had been matched by no other city in western Europe outside Italy as the governmental and symbolic centre of a powerful monarchy, was permitted to play no such role under the new regime. Indeed it has been suggested that the city was deliberately severely damaged by the conquerors.[65] If so such actions, involving the destruction of public buildings and churches, were clearly intended to break the continuity with the traditions of the departed Visigothic monarchy and to symbolize the new and more lowly place assigned to Toledo under Arab rule. Both Ctesiphon and Carthage are thought to have

[61] *Chronicle of 754*, 53, p. 70.

[62] *Sacrorum Conciliorum Nova et Amplissima Collectio*, ed. J.D. Mansi, vol. XII, p. 265.

[63] A. Artajona Castro, *Anales de Córdoba musulmana (711–1008)* (Córdoba, 1982), doc. 4a, pp. 15–16.

[64] On Fusṭāṭ see A.J. Butler, *Arab Conquest*, pp. 339–45.

[65] I. Zamorano Herrera, 'Caracteres del arte visigodo en Toledo', *Anales Toledanos*, 10 (1974), pp. 7–149 provides a study of the fragmentary remains of the Visigothic art of the capital.

been abandoned in the wake of the conquests, though in the latter case at least there is evidence to suggest this was a more gradual process than has been often assumed, and a similar slighting of Toledo made a forceful point.[66] However, it is worth noting that the physical geography of the city's location imposes severe constraints. Being constructed within an incised meander of the river Tagus, which surrounds it on three out of four sides, the dimensions of the site were firmly fixed. Therefore, in a history of continuous human occupation over nearly two millennia new buildings have always had to be erected at the expense of the old, and few traces of the buildings of earlier periods of occupation can now be seen above ground level.

But whether it be the product of neglect or deliberate destruction Toledo suffered a period of profound decline throughout much of the earlier centuries of Arab dominance in the peninsula. On the other hand, the chosen centres of government both for the *Walis* or governors and the subsequent Umayyad Amirs were existing cities of considerable antiquity. No Spanish equivalents to Kairouan were built. This is particularly notable when it be considered that the conquest had been organized from Africa, in which the latter city had served as the exclusive religious, administrative and military capital for the Arabs ever since its foundation in 672. It is possible that such a new city was not created because initially the governors of *Al-Andalus* were regarded as subordinates of those of *Ifrīqīya*. On the other hand certain distinctive features of the conquest and settlement of Spain, which will be examined subsequently, may provide another explanation for this apparent anomaly.

It seems clear that in the immediate aftermath of the invasion the peninsula was effectively divided into different regions under two different types of authority: the quasi-autonomous areas ruled by local potentates such as Theodemir, and those which were directly under Arab control, and whose main towns provided the locations for garrisons. It looks as if even this latter element was not institutionalized before the govenorship of Al-Ḥurr (715–18), in whose time the *Chronicle of 754* records the setting up of garrisons

[66] See J. Lassner, *The Shaping of 'Abbāsid Rule* (Princeton, 1980), pp. 164, 177 on Arab traditions relating to the ruins of Ctesiphon, and the religious-political message they implied.

in Córdoba.[67] His successor As-Sāmh is credited with the same activity in Narbonne (c.721).[68]

'Abd al-Azīz's murder had been instigated by his brother-in-law Ayyūb, who in the Arab accounts served as an interim governor while his associates took the head of his assassinated predecessor and an account of his imputed crime to the Caliph. As the latter seems to have been looking for a way to disgrace and impoverish Mūsā ibn Nuṣayr he had little cause to blame the murderers of the latter's younger son. However, the appointment of a new governor of Spain remained in the hands of the *Wali* in Kairouan, who was 'Abdallāh, the unfortunate 'Abd al-Azīz's elder brother, and he sent Al-Ḥurr, apparently with orders to avenge him.[69] Leaving aside the Arab traditions, which concentrate almost exclusively on such feuds and personal conflicts, the *Chronicle of 754* continues to provide brief, almost elliptical, information on the social and administrative changes taking place in the peninsula at this time. As well as three years of fighting in 'Gallia Narbonensis', the former Septimania, where a last Visigothic king Ardo (713–20) was putting up some resistance, and the aforementioned garrisoning of Córdoba, Al-Ḥurr is credited with four other initiatives. Firstly, he is said by the chronicler to have 'sent the strong arms of the judges throughout Spain'. The precise meaning of this is not clear, in that it might imply the establishment of Islamic judges, *qāḍīs*. However, in the administrative terminology of the Visigothic period, the *iudices* were the chief civil officers of the towns, whose authority paralleled that of the counts. Certainly some form of new legislative and administrative order was imposed at this time, as one of this governor's other concerns was punishing those Berbers who had hidden loot.[70] In principle all of the spoils of the conquest should have been pooled and fixed percentages sent to Damascus and distributed amongst the conquerors.

The chronicler's other two references to Al-Ḥurr relate to matters with a direct bearing on the Christian subject population. He is said to have gradually imposed *vectigalia* on 'Hispania Ulterior'. This may be no more than to imply that the process begun in the time of

[67] *Chronicle of 754*, 64, p. 80.
[68] Ibid., 69, p. 84.
[69] *Akhbar Machmua*, p. 33
[70] *Chronicle of 754*, 62, pp. 78–80.

'Abd al-Azīz of the making of tribute-producing treaties was continued or brought to completion. On the other hand it may refer to the imposition of a new tax burden based upon land rather than capitation. The term *vectigalia* is archaic, as indeed is the use of 'Hispania Ulterior' for the southern parts of Spain, but it features in Isidore to whom the chronicler is indebted for many of his antiquarian usages. In the *Etymologiae* Isidore writes of *vectigalia* as a synonym for *tributa*, the origins of which he sees as the tax paid by a Roman 'tribe', but he admits that in his day it was paid by a region.[71]

An interpretation that would see this as representing a land tax might be reinforced by the chronicler's final comment on the governorship of Al-Ḥurr: ... *atque resculas pacificas Xpianis ob vectigalia thesauris publicis inferenda instaurat.* This is not easy to comprehend, and the work's most recent editor has rendered it in his accompanying Spanish translation as meaning that he 'imposed small fines on the Christians in return for peace in order to augment the revenues of the treasury'.[72] A better version might be that '... he restored the pacified estates to the Christians on account of the tax that would be brought to the public treasuries'. Apart from the fact that the attested usages of the rare word *rescula* imply a meaning of 'small estates' rather than 'fines', this alternative rendering makes perfect sense in the light of the standard forms of Islamic taxation.[73] All Muslims were exempt on Koranic authority from the payment of any form of taxation, being merely obliged to engage in almsgiving, one of the five 'Pillars of Islam'. On the other hand the much needed revenues of the emergent Arab state had to be drawn exclusively from the poll and land taxes imposed on the non-Muslim subject population.[74] Thus, in the case of Spain, a restoration of estates to their former Christian owners meant a valuable augmentation of the revenues available to the governors, who were obliged to send some of their resources to the Caliphs and to provide adequate rewards for the Arab and Berber warriors under their command.

In other words, what the chronicler is so briefly describing is the

[71] Isidore, *Etymologiae*, XVI.xviii.8, ed. W. Lindsay (Oxford, 1911).
[72] *Chronicle of 754*, 64, p. 81 for the translation.
[73] J. Niermeyer, *Mediae Latinitatis Lexicon Minus* (Leiden, 1976), s.v. 'Recula', p. 894.
[74] D.C. Dennet, *Conversion and the Poll-tax*.

real beginnings of the establishment of Arab administration. Although fighting was still continuing along the borders of the former Visigothic kingdom the initial phase of conquest was over as far as the peninsula is concerned. Law had been imposed on the conquerors as well as tax on the conquered. Moreover the pre-conquest pattern of landownership was re-established, and some of the conquerors were forced to disgorge loot they had concealed and which belonged to the treasury. These significant fiscal measures clearly imply the existence of a proper financial administration. This same period also saw the introduction of a new Arab coinage in Spain, which, as under the preceding Visigothic monarchy, was exclusively gold, and was also bilingual in Arabic and Latin. This replaced a previous short-lived initial coinage of North African type or origin.[75]

Obviously, however extensive the restoration of the previous pattern of estate-ownership, quite a lot of land will have remained in the hands of the conquerors. In particular this will have included the former possessions of the Visigothic monarchy. The extent of its holdings have never been worked out; basically because the necessary evidence does not exist.[76] They may, though, be assumed to have been extensive. For one thing the Visigothic rulers had acquired the lands of the imperial fisc in Spain, which in turn may have included the possessions of emperors of Spanish origin such as the members of the Theodosian dynasty. Visigothic legislators in the seventh century had been concerned to maintain a fixed division between lands held by the individual kings by virtue of their office and those which constituted their own familial inheritance.[77] Lacking fixed principles of dynastic succession in the kingship, such a distinction was important. One consequence of this was that a body of estates marked as being exclusively royal will have been available to the conquerors, as also will have been the personal lands of the defeated king Roderic. Other properties possessed by the aristocracy who had resisted the Arabs may also have been acquired in the process of conquest, but these are the

[75] Catalogued and studied in M. A. Balaguer Prunés, *Las Emisiones transicionales arabe-musulmanas de Hispania* (Barcelona, 1976).

[76] E. A. Thompson, *The Goths in Spain*, pp. 127–8, R. Collins, 'Julian of Toledo', pp. 30–1.

[77] *Leges Visigothorum*, II.i.6, ed. K. Zeumer, *MGH Leges*, pp. 48–52; P.D. King, *Law and Society in the Visigothic Kingdom* (Cambridge, 1972), pp. 62–3, also ch. 2 for the relationship between 'the king and the law'.

estates most likely to have been restored by Al-Ḥurr. At the time, though, all of the lands still retained, together with more mobile loot, such as that the Berbers had recently been forced to disgorge, seems to have been held collectively under the authority of the governor in the name of the Caliph and the Community of Islam.

This changed in the time of the next governor, As-Sāmh (718–21). Under his rule the first attacks on Frankish, or more accurately Aquitanian, lands were begun. But as far as the peninsula is concerned he is attributed with two significant developments. Firstly the chronicler records that he instituted a *Descriptio* or tax assessment of his own devising of the whole of Spain, both 'Ulterior' and 'Citerior'. Secondly, he carried out a division by lot of the spoils, which had previously been kept in Spain undivided, and assigned a proportion of both the real and the moveable property to the fisc.[78] Thus, further steps were being taken both to establish an administration on a regular basis by the recording, and it may be assumed rationalizing, of the tax assessments owed by non-Muslims, and to underpin the conquest by the distribution of land to the conquerors. This is particularly notable when it be considered that at this time the Caliph 'Umar II (717–20) is reported to have contemplated ordering the abandonment of the Spanish conquest.[79]

The nature and details of the process of the distribution – *sorte* – by lot, of the lands held by the conquerors are hard to work out, as although something is known of the general distribution of Arab and Berber settlements this largely relates to conditions pertaining in the tenth and eleventh centuries.[80] Several movements of population in the interim make it hard to estimate to what extent this represents continuity with conditions in this opening phase of the occupation. Thus by the end of the governorship of As-Shām, just ten years after the invasion, order had in large measure been returned to the peninsula. What fighting was now going on was taking place in France, the pre-existing system of land tenure had been largely restored, though this may not have been completed until the governorship of Yaḥyā (725–28), and a system of taxation had

[78] *Chronicle of 754*, 69, p. 84.

[79] E. Lévi-Provençal, *Histoire de l'Espagne musulmane*, vol. I, p. 39.

[80] See P. Guichard, *Al-Andalus* (Barcelona, 1976), pp. 285–458 for a major attempt at reconstruction.

been established.[81] Many regions of the peninsula clearly enjoyed a large measure of local autonomy and the Christianity of the majority population was hardly under threat. Similarly the position of the Arabs and Berbers had been regularized and a land distribution had taken place, almost certainly on a tribal basis. Although these conditions may not have been uniform, in that the Arab and Berber presence was unequally distributed and certain major centres of population were under direct rule of the conquerors, the position of the subject population in many parts and in many respects can hardly have changed from the time of the rule of the Visigothic kings.

One development at this time, which may be thought to have had very significant long-term consequences for the future of Islam in the peninsula, was the successful revolt in the Asturias, which led to the formation of the tiny Christian monarchy there. This has traditionally been dated to the year 718, but the Spanish historian Claudio Sánchez-Albornoz made out a case for believing that 722 should be the preferred date.[82] This could have the virtue of relating this revolt and the defeat of an Arab and Berber punitive expedition to the death of As-Sāmh in battle with Duke Eudo of Aquitaine whilst besieging Toulouse.[83] This was the first major set-back to the Islamic forces since the conquest of Spain, and although the practical consequences were slight, it may have provided the necessary spur.

Equally significant, though, may have been the failure of the attempt to impose Berber settlement along the fringes of the mountainous northern regions of the peninsula and in Galicia. It is notable that major mountain chains marked the limits of Arab expansion in virtually all of the areas of their conquest.[84] Neither their tactics nor their forms of social organization equipped them to be mountain dwelling or occupying. The North African Berbers, whose native regions shared many points of geographical and climatic similarity with much of the Iberian peninsula, differed from their Arab overlords in these respects. Thus it is not surpris-

[81] *Chronicle of 754*, 69, 75, pp. 84, 90.

[82] C. Sánchez-Albornoz, *Los Orígenes de la nación española: el Reino de Asturias*, vol. II (Oviedo, 1974), pp. 97–135.

[83] *Chronicle of 754*, 69, p. 84.

[84] P. Hitti, *A History of the Arabs* (8th edn, London, 1964), pp. 206–23.

ing that they were positioned not only in the more mountainous regions of the south, as around Granada, but also in the Pyrenees and the Cantabrian and Galician mountains. However, at the very least the climate of the mountainous southern fringes of the Bay of Biscay was for them less than hospitable, as too may have been the local population. The revolt in the Asturias may itself have been a response to the settlement plans of As-Sāmh, and it seems that by the middle of the century Berbers located in Galicia preferred to take their movable loot and leave their lands in favour of a return to Africa.

In a traditionalist historiography the Asturian revolt and the elevation of Pelagius as the first ruler of this Christian realm has taken on a particular significance as the first step in a process that would culminate in the final elimination of any form of Islamic rule in the peninsula by the capture of Granada in 1492 by the 'Catholic monarchs' Ferdinand and Isabella. At the same time it marked the commencement of a linear process that was to see the Asturian monarchy transform itself into the Leonese and that in turn into the Castillian and then into the Spanish kingdom of the Habsburgs. In other words this is seen as the beginning of the institutional history of the modern Spanish state and also of the Spanish national identity.[85] The latter is taken in this conservative centralizing tradition to be effectively identical with that of Castille.

One consequence of such a historiographical perception is that not only have the Arabs and Berbers been regarded as aliens whom it took seven centuries to get rid of, but also that the non-Muslim populations of southern Spain under their rule are treated as failed stock, and their culture has been seen as essentially non-contributory to the growth of Spanish nationhood. Fortunately, this way of thinking has come under increasing criticism amongst Spanish historians in recent decades, and it is not necessary to consider it here.[86] However, what is important to note now is that Pelagius's success in creating an independent Asturian kingdom, largely because the Arabs were too preoccupied to make any sustained efforts to

[85] See the arguments of C. Sánchez-Albornoz, *España un enigma histórica* (2 vols, Buenos Aires, 1956).

[86] The Asturian revolt and the kingdom that it gave rise to will be discussed in ch. 6.

eliminate it, not only represents the first breach in the political unity of the peninsula, imposed so laboriously by Leovigild in the late sixth century, but it also paved the way for the disintegration of the ideological unity within the Spanish Church that had been one of the great achievements of the Visigothic period. Initially, however, that sense of a 'national' Church continued to survive the elimination of the unitary monarchy that had largely brought it into being, and Toledo, whatever may have happened to the city physically, continued to enjoy an intellectual pre-eminence.

3

The Tenacity of a Tradition

Christian Chroniclers and Arab Rulers

It is possible that the *Chronicle of 754*, whose value as a historical source for the early Muslim period in Spain cannot be sufficiently stressed, is the best testimony in itself to the continuing intellectual vitality of Toledo even after the Arab conquest. However, as will become clear, it is not possible to locate its author in the former Visigothic capital with absolute certainty, although this is a view with much to recommend it. The overthrow of the Visigothic kingdom and its replacement by Arab rule, which once again integrated Spain, or most of it, as a component part of a Mediterranean-wide state, served, almost as the converse of the political and religious unification of the peninsula under Leovigild and Reccared, as the spur to historical composition. In the way that Isidore of Seville had answered a need to place the emergent Romano-Gothic monarchy in the broader perspective of the history of Rome's dealings with the Visigoths and also the Christian and Biblical chronology of the world, so in the aftermath of 711 the changed fortunes of the peninsula that resulted, and the sudden rise of new racial elements to political and cultural pre-eminence in it, required contemporaries to look at these events in a wider time scale.[1] For the first time for over a century chronicle writing came back into fashion. The

[1] J.M. Wallace-Hadrill, *The Barbarian West* (3rd edn, London, 1967), pp. 123–6; M. Reydellet, 'Les Intentions idéologiques et politiques dans la Chronique d'Isidore de Séville', *Mélanges de l'Ecole française de Rome*, 82 (1970), pp. 363–400.

master of this form at this time was to be the anonymous author of the *Chronicle of 754*, but he may have had at least two predecessors in the years after 711.

There is another Latin chronicle of this period that enjoys an exclusively Spanish manuscript transmission. This is the text entitled rather cumbersomely the *Continuatio Byzantia Arabica*, or, more conveniently, the *Chronicle of 741.*[2] This has been presented as a continuation of the *Historia Gothorum* of Isidore of Seville, but unlike that work it structures itself in the form of a series of brief accounts of the reigns of successive Byzantine emperors, from Phocas (602–10) to Leo III, ending in 741, rather than those of the Visigothic kings. An alternative, and perhaps more acceptable interpretation sees the work as a continuation of the *Chronicle* of John of Biclar (completed 602), with which it shares structural similarities.[3] What is extraordinary about this text is that with the exception of its final entry and a brief reference to the conquest of 711, it contains no material relating to Spain whatsoever. On the other hand, the dating system it seems to employ is that of the Spanish era. Its attachment to the tradition of John of Biclar's chronicle and the use of a distinctively peninsular form of dating would seem to make its Spanish origin incontrovertible, yet at the same time it is both well and exclusively informed about eastern Mediterranean events relating to the Byzantine Empire and the emergent Arab state.

Unfortunately, the manuscript tradition fails to help elucidate the problems of the text, in that the work now only survives in one thirteenth- and three sixteenth-century codices, the latter written for the noted antiquarian and canon of Toledo, and later Bishop of Segorbe, D. Juan Bautista Pérez (1537–97), whose collections have preserved a number of Spanish medieval historical works which would otherwise have been lost or poorly attested to.[4] Pérez found the text in a now lost manuscript from Soria. Apart from the view that it was 'antiquissimus' Pérez could give no further indication of the date of this manuscript. However, the fact that it probably also contained a copy of the *Chronicle of Alfonso III*, means that this

[2] *CSM*, I, pp. 7–14.
[3] T. Mommsen in *MGH AA*, XI, pp. 323–30.
[4] On whom see *DHEE*, III, p. 1971, and Supplement, p. 608.

'codex Soriensis deperditus' can not have been older the late ninth century.[5]

The *Chronicle of 741*, as it may be called for convenience, is of interest not only because it is a work that may have been composed in Spain in the earliest period of Arab rule, but also because of its standing in respect of the more informative *Chronicle of 754*. It has generally been claimed that the latter was largely dependent upon it for both chronology and information relating to eastern Mediterranean events. However, the latest editor of the *Chronicle of 754* has shown convincingly that such dependence is illusory, and that the compiler of that work probably did not have a copy of the *Chronicle of 741* available to him.[6] There is, however, one point of identity between the two texts, and that comes in the description of the expedition against Toulouse led by the Arab governor of *Al-Andalus* As-Sāmh and its disastrous outcome.[7] This, though, is the final item in the *Chronicle of 741* and is not only chronologically out of place but also quite at variance with the character of the rest of the work's contents. It would seem that, although the two authors wrote in ignorance of each other, their works were subsequently united in at least one strand of their manuscript transmission. In these circumstances it is quite conceivable that a subsequent reviser added the passage relating to the expedition of As-Sāmh from the *Chronicle of 754* to that of 741.

The *Chronicle of 741* in its present state is worthy of closer attention than it has generally been given. The existence of the *Chronicle of 754* has led to the general acceptance of the assumption that the two works are fundamentally similar in character. However, dissection of the actual contents might lead to doubt on this score. When reduced to its component parts the *Chronicle of 741* may be found to consist of entries of basically three kinds. Firstly there are a small number of dated references to the succession of some of the Visigothic kings with their lengths of reign, though only so far as Suinthila (621–31), the duration of whose

[5] For a description of the contents see T. Mommsen, *MGH AA*, XI, pp. 165–6.

[6] J.E. López Perreira, *Estudio crítico sobre la crónica mozárabe de 754* (Zaragoza, 1980), pp. 96–9.

[7] 741: *CSM* ed. = section 42, p. 14; 754: *CSM* ed. = section 57, pp. 37–8, López Perreira ed. = section 69, p. 84. The two texts, although not identical, are too close for coincidence.

rule is not noted. Then there are more substantial entries relating to changes of ruler in Constantinople. Here an era date is not always given, though the last year date of any sort in the work is the one relating to the succession of Constantine the son of Heraclius in 640 (*recte* 641).[8] As in the *Chronicle of John of Biclar*, the ruler's number in a notional list of emperors stretching back to Augustus is given, together with the length of his reign. This latter information is not always correct, especially in the case of the Heraclian dynasty. A brief account of each reign is given at the same point, though the treatment of Heraclius is far more substantial than that afforded any of his successors.[9] The last emperor to be mentioned in the work is Leo III (717–41), and his date of death has been associated with the date of the composition of the chronicle itself. His twenty-four-year reign is mentioned correctly, but there is no reference made to his successor.

The third and most significant component of the *Chronicle of 741* is a set of longer entries that detail the names, reign lengths and deeds of the Arab rulers from Muḥammad himself onwards. The last of these to be mentioned is Walīd II (743–44).[10] This alone would suggest that the chronicle as we now have it post-dates 741, and that it would at least be more exact to call it 'The Chronicle of 744'! However, the reference to Walīd II is linked with that concerning his predecessor, Hishām, whose long reign and achievements are not separately mentioned.[11] The impression must be that this final entry, different in scale and character to the other notices on the Arab rulers, was not an integral part of the source from which the rest of such material was taken.

Thus presented, it looks as if there were at least three separate sources for the *Chronicle of 741*. These are firstly the *Historia Gothorum* of Isidore, which ends with Suinthila, and from which the very small amount of information on the Visigothic kings was

[8] *CSM*, section 6, p. 8.

[9] Ibid., sections 6–18, pp. 8–9.

[10] Ibid., section 43, p. 14.

[11] Ibid. For a study of the sources of this chronicle see C.E. Dubler, 'Sobre la crónica arábigo-bizantina de 741', *Al-Andalus*, 11 (1946), pp. 298–332, but great caution is needed in considering some of the specific claims Dubler makes as to Byzantine and other Eastern Mediterranean texts being currently available in Spain.

culled.[12] Secondly, there was some form of Byzantine chronicle source. There are certain elements in the materials relating to the emperors that are common to both the *Chronicle of 741* and the *Chronicle of 754* and to the work of the ninth-century Byzantine chronicler Theophanes. There is no exact identification possible, but it would seem that a common source must underlie the similarities, particularly in some of the clearly legendary stories relating to the emperor Heraclius.[13] Finally, and perhaps most interestingly, there would seem to have been a work on the rulers of the Arabs, that in structure modelled itself closely on Isidore's *Historia Gothorum*. Common to both is a structuring on the basis of the individual rulers, who are named, their length of reign given, and whose deeds are described in a synoptic form. It would not be going too far to say that it looks as if this source may have been a *Historia Arabum*. This was written by a Christian, as its treatment of Islam indicates, but also someone whose sources of information or personal sympathies were Syrian and Umayyad in character. This is made clear by the deliberate omission of the Caliphate of 'Alī (656–61), cousin and son-in-law of the Prophet, whose reign was dominated by conflict with his eventual successor Mu'āwiya, the first of the Umayyad dynasty.[14] The text gives the regnal span of Yazīd II (720–24) and the succession of Hishām. As has been mentioned, the latter receives no further treatment, and the reference to his successor looks like a subsequent addition. This might indicate that the original version of the work was composed in the period of the reign of Hishām (724–43), quite possibly at an early state of it.

The *Chronicle of 741*, as now constituted, thus presents a series of problems. Its lack of information concerning Spain after 621 is surprising, and seems to indicate that the compiler had no more than Isidore's *Historia Gothorum* and perhaps his *Chronicle* to go on. The termination of era dating after the reference to the succession of Heraclius Constantine in 640/1 is also striking. Similarities between the Byzantine and Arab materials in the *Chronicle of 741* and the *Chronicle of 754* are numerous, but equally important are

[12] *Historia Gothorum*, sections 57–62, ed. C. Rodríguez Alonso, *Las Historias de los Godos, Vándalos y Suevos de Isidoro de Sevilla* (León, 1975), pp. 268–75.

[13] A.N. Stratos, *Byzantium in the Seventh Century*, vol. I (602–34) (Amsterdam, 1968), pp. 80–91.

[14] J. Welhausen, *Das arabische Reich und sein Sturz* (Berlin, 1902), ch. 2.

the differences. The *Chronicle of 754*, for example, can on occasion augment the information on the Arab rulers to be found in that of 741.[15] In other words, as with the Byzantine history, it looks as if the compilers of the two works had sources in common. In particular these would have included a Latin *Historia Arabum*, almost certainly written in the reign of Hishām (724–43), if not in Spain then in North Africa. It is quite possible that the compiler of the *Chronicle of 741* worked in the reign of the latter's short-lived successor Walīd II (743–44). As a whole the *Chronicle of 741* is a confused and confusing work that fails to integrate the elements of which it is composed in a workmanlike and satisfying way. This could not be said of its successor.

The author, regrettably anonymous, of the *Chronicle of 754* presents the first clear literary personality to be found in Spain across the divide of the Arab conquest. Some estimation of him needs to be formed before the information of his chronicle may be evaluated. It is thus particularly regrettable that no consensus of opinion exists as to the place in which he was working, and indeed it probably never will. Arguments have generally centred around the claims of Córdoba and Toledo, but the most recent editor has made a strong case for an unspecifiable centre in the Levante, the south-eastern coastal region of the peninsula, with Guadix as a possible contender.[16] Basically such arguments revolve around indications suggesting that the author displays special knowledge of one or other of these locations. Those relating to Córdoba are almost certainly the weakest, and there is nothing in his references to the city that inspires belief that the author was resident there. The Toledan information is both quantitatively greater and more localized. López Perreira, in the study accompanying his edition of the chronicle, discounts this on the grounds that the importance of Toledo was such that an author resident elsewhere in the peninsula might well be expected to be reasonably informed on subjects relating to its Church and leading personalities.[17] Faced, though, with such specifically localized information as the chronicler's quotation of the inscriptions set up on the city's restored walls by the Visigothic king Wamba (672–80), he has to claim that the

[15] For example, the tribal origin of the Caliph Abu Bakr: *Chronicle of 741*, 17, *CSM*, I, p. 9, compared to *Chronicle of 754*, 11, ed. J.E. López Perreira, p. 30.
[16] J.E. López Perreira, *Estudio crítico*, pp. 13–16, 64.
[17] Ibid., pp. 14–15.

author may have used an otherwise unknown Toledan chronicle of possibly early eighth-century date.[18] This, it must be admitted, is rather hard to credit, particularly in the light of the otherwise limited knowledge of late seventh-century events on the part of the 754 chronicler and the diminutive nature of the historiographical output of the late Visigothic period.[19]

López Perreira's own arguments in favour of a place of work in the Levante are certainly interesting. They consist of two features: the provision in the chronicle of some unusually detailed mention of political arrangements in the region, and the reference to a local bishop, Fredoarius of Guadix (*Acci*). The first of these, a parenthetical entry on two successive local potentates in the area of Orihuela, is strangely placed and out of keeping with the construction of the rest of the work.[20] The reference to the bishop of Guadix is equally inconclusive, in that his commemoration in the chronicle is linked to those of two Toledan clerics, and it is quite conceivable that he was resident in that city at the time of his death. Nor are there any good reasons for believing that a Toledan author would necessarily be ignorant of important figures elsewhere in the Spanish Church of his day. Thus, although the arguments in favour of the Levante have some weight, they are far from conclusive; any more, it must be admitted, than those relating to Toledo. The issue thus remains an open one, though priority might still be given to the claims of Toledo, not least in that the literary culture displayed by this author is quite consistent with the learning known to have been available in the former Visigothic capital in the late eighth century.[21] The Levante, however, offers no evidence of itself as an intellectual centre at that time at all.

What is clear enough is that the author of the *Chronicle of 754* was able to draw on both a historiographical tradition in chronicle writing that stretched back through Isidore to Eusebius, in the Latin version of Rufinus, and on the learning of the Visigothic church. As well as the *Historia Gothorum* and the *Chronicle* of

[18] Ibid., p. 104.

[19] Despite various hypotheses, no convincing case has been made out for any kind of historiographical composition between the time of Julian of Toledo's *Historia Wambae* and the 720s at the earliest.

[20] J.E. López Perreira, *Estudio crítico*, pp. 40–3.

[21] See *Ars Iuliani Toletani Episcopi*, ed. M.A.H. Maestre Yenes (Toledo, 1973), pp. xxix–lx.

Isidore, he seems to have known the latter's *Etymologiae*, a Christological treatise of Braulio of Zaragoza, Ildefonsus's *De Perpetua Virginitate*, Julian of Toledo's *De Comprobatione Sextae Aetatis*, as well as the collected *acta* of the Councils of Toledo.[22] There were doubtless more debts besides, but these works are what may be regarded as the classics of the literary production of the Spanish Church of the Visigothic period. Nor is it surprising that he had also read some of the works of non-Spanish origin that had been especially valued at that time, notably some of the writings of Gregory the Great. Thus in himself this author is proof of the continuity, at least qualitatively, of the learning of the Spanish Church across the divide of the Arab conquest. However, it is impossible from one example to quantify such survival, or to estimate local variation, but, as has been suggested above, such a continuity makes more sense in a Toledan context than in any other.

As a writer the author of the *Chronicle of 754* presents himself as someone primarily interested in history. Nor was this his only historiographical composition. He himself twice alludes to another work, which he calls an *epitoma*, devoted to the history of the civil wars fought between rival Arab factions in Spain around the years 742–46.[23] This work, unfortunately, is entirely lost. Its relative brevity may be assumed from the title he twice assigns to it, but on the other hand its structure must have been different to that of the chronicle he subsequently composed. Its subject matter seems to have been exclusively the civil wars, as he never alludes to it in any other context. A reference at the very end of his chronicle to a 'book of the words of the days of the *Saeculum*' has been taken as indicating the existence of a third work by this author or as giving the exact title of the lost *epitoma*, but is in its particular context purely metaphorical.[24]

What is particularly striking about his *oeuvre* is that these two works, the one extant and the other not, represent the only certain pieces of original historical composition undertaken in the peninsula since the writing of Julian of Toledo's *Historia Wambae* (*c.* 675)

[22] J.E. López Perreira, *Estudio crítico*, pp. 83–92.
[23] *Chronicle of 754*, 86, 88, pp. 112, 118.
[24] *Chronicle of 754*, 94, p. 126.

and before the late ninth century. Indeed they are, with the exceptions of the hypothetical *Historia Arabum* and the related *Chronicle of 741*, the only Latin historical works composed in southern Spain under Muslim rule. In themselves they represent an overt continuity with the Visigothic past in that the *Chronicle* starts its account with the period in which Isidore's historical works stop, and the character of the lost *Epitoma* may be suspected of owing much to the *Historia Wambae* of Julian, which dealt with a single episode, a military undertaking, in a short chronological context. On the other hand, the 754 chronicler was to have no known successor or continuator. Moreover, apart from one or two disparate pieces of information, such as the details of Wamba's inscriptions on the walls of Toledo, he tells us virtually nothing about the late Visigothic period that cannot be found in other sources. In other words he may have been little better informed about his own immediate past than we are today. The continuity, then, resided more in the sustained availability of a corpus of books than in much of a living tradition.

It is perhaps easy to overlook the chronicler's greatest achievement, which is his attempt to unify a wide diversity of chronological systems. Although capable of making mistakes in his calculations, his chronological concerns are also revealing of something of the wider context into which the peninsula fitted in the first half of the eighth century. For the essential framework of the *Chronicle* is provided by the reigns of the Byzantine emperors, but this the author also attempts to synchronize with the Spanish era, with the regnal dates of the Arab Caliphs, with the 'years of the Arabs', in other words dating by years of the Hegira, and with a universal dating based upon a supposed point of creation of the world in what we would call 5204 BC.[25] Imperial reign dating he would have found in the work of his Visigothic predecessor John of Biclar, but its use in his work is not antiquarian, but rather represents the continuing strength of Roman imperial traditions amongst the non-Muslim populations of the Arab world. The presentation in the contents of the chronicle of much material relating to the eastern Mediterranean is again not surprising once notions of the essential insularity of Spain in the Visigothic period are abandoned. At the same time the integration of the chronologi-

[25] J.E. López Perreira, *Estudio crítico*, pp. 28–35.

cal systems of the Arabs, both in the form of Hegira dating, the 'years of the Arabs', and the regnal lengths of the Caliphs, with the systems of calculation used in pre-Islamic Spain and in Byzantium put the new order in the peninsula into a wider historical context, and in this way made a bridge across the divide marked by the events of 711.

Obviously the Arab conquest put much of the peninsula into a position of closer contact with parts of the east, with which relations may have been less consistent under the Visigothic kingdom. This is particularly true of Syria and Egypt. But it would be unwise to see this as marking a fundamental change. John of Biclar's chronicle that covers the years 567–90 is the principal source of evidence for many of the events of those years not only in Spain but also in North Africa and the heartlands of the Byzantine Empire.[26] Although his access to such information was unusually good, as the result of his own prolonged sojourn in Constantinople, what is important to note is that John, writing for a readership in the peninsula, felt it worth including so much material relating to the world beyond Spain. So too the 754 chronicler deliberately sought to put events taking place within the peninsula into the context of a Mediterranean-wide account. In that sense what is striking is his apparent lack of information relating to Francia and Italy. The history of the Arabs over the course of the previous century and a quarter he knew about in some considerable detail, whilst the rise of the Carolingians impinged upon his perspective not a whit.

One thing the author of the *Chronicle of 754* might be expected to tell us, if only by implication, is what his reactions were to the recent conquerors of the peninsula, who differed from him in both race and religion. However, his reticence in these respects may seem perplexing. He writes about three distinct groups: the *Mauri*, the *Arabes*, and the *Sarraceni*. Of these the first can be easily identified as the Berbers. The latter two are used by the author quite interchangeably and synonymously. Both mean Arabs. This is perhaps surprising, in that for Isidore the two names had distinct applications: the *Sarraceni* were the Arabs of Syria and the north of the Arabian peninsula, whilst the *Arabes* were the inhabitants of

[26] J. Campos, *Juan de Biclaro, Obispo de Gerona. Su vida y su obra* (Madrid, 1960), pp. 56–67.

the Yemen.[27] The peculiarity of the chronicler's usage lies in the fact that such a distinction, of little concern to Isidore, should have been of considerable significance in the first half of the eighth century, when a supposedly traditional feud between northern and southern Arabs is normally held to have been the motivating force behind a major political division between two sections of the conquerors, and the cause of several civil wars, affecting Spain not least of all.[28] One of those conflicts was indeed the subject of this author's other and lost work; so it is reasonable to assume he was both aware of and particularly interested in such divisions amongst the Arabs, and yet he apparently fails to take advantage of the existence of alternatives amongst ethnographic labels available to him to distinguish between the two great groupings. This too, when he had the authority of Isidore to justify such a procedure. Perhaps, as will be seen, this usage implies that the roots of the feuds amongst the Arabs at this time did not lie in a notional traditional hostility between the northern and southern Arabian tribal confederacies.

The other perplexing absence of comment relates to the religion of the conquerors. At no stage in his account does he make any reference to Islam. Nor does he regard the Arab Muslims as heretical Christians, let alone pagans. That he was not himself a Muslim is clear enough from various features of his narrative, such as his treatment of Muḥammad, who is presented as the first military leader of the Arabs.[29] His prophetic role is confined to his own people.[30] The chronicler was, on the other hand, well aware that the Arabs were not Christians, in that he uses that designation as his standard epithet for the indigenous inhabitants of the Iberian peninsula.[31] A number of explanations can be advanced for this reticence. For one thing his readership would have been well enough aware of the religious divide between the conquered population and the bulk of the conquerors. In addition publicly to revile the Prophet was a capital offence, certainly by the mid-ninth century and most probably from the start of the Muslim domi-

[27] Isidore, *Etymologiae*, IX.ii.49 (*Arabes*), IX.ii.57 (*Saraceni*), ed. M. Reydellet (Paris, 1984), pp. 64, 68.

[28] W.M. Watt, *A History of Islamic Spain* (Edinburgh, 1965), pp. 28–9, 31.

[29] *Chronicle of 754*, 8, p. 28.

[30] Ibid., 11, p. 30.

[31] Ibid., 74, 75, 79, 91, pp. 88, 90, 96, 102.

nation.[32] Thus a considerable difficulty existed in respect of how Muḥammad could be described once the religious dimension of his activity was invoked. The secular and neutral depiction of him and of his followers in the chronicle was thus a sensible expedient, especially if, as is likely, the author was working in Toledo under direct Arab rule. A similar lack of sectarian zeal led the compiler of the *Chronicle of 741* to be thought of as a Spanish or eastern Mediterranean convert to Islam, but neither of these writers needs to be seen as anything other than Christian. In this way it is possible to see that the conquest of 711 did not necessarily result in overt religious antagonism.

On the other hand it is important to note that the conquest was not regarded as just another occurence in the tangled skein of history. For the author of the *Chronicle of 754* in a note of unusual feeling the fall of the Visigothic kingdom was likened to Adam's fall, to the fall of Troy, to the Babylonian capture of Jerusalem and to the sack of Rome.[33] Although it may seem parochial to equate events in just one region of the Mediterranean with a scheme of world history, this is what by implication the chronicler was doing. A sixfold succession of Ages leading to the Messianic coming, or in the Christian tradition to the appearance of Antichrist and the Second Coming, was a long-established feature of Jewish and Christian eschatological thinking, and in the Visigothic period had been represented not least by Julian of Toledo's polemical *De Comprobatione Sextae Aetatis*.[34] Julian's turning points were different to those listed by the 754 chronicler, but it looks as if the latter were manipulating this tradition in deliberately choosing four such examples to equate with the disaster that befell Spain. Thus, he saw himself and his contemporaries living in the last age of the world.

In addition to new historical compositions, a concern for the past also manifested itself in this same mid-eighth-century period in the making of new copies of the principal chronicles of the Visigothic kingdom. In 733 or 743 an anonymous scribe copied

[32] K.B. Wolf, *Christian Martyrs in Muslim Spain* (Cambridge, 1988), pp. 23–35.

[33] *Chronicle of 754*, 55, p. 72.

[34] Ed. J.N. Hillgarth, *Sancti Iuliani Toletanae Sedis Episcopi Opera*, Corpus Christianorum, series Latina, CXV (1976), pp. 143–212.

Isidore's *Chronicle*, and extended its chronology though not its historical contents up to the time of his own writing.[35] The manuscript itself has not survived, but it became the basis for another copy of the work made in the tenth century which was included in a manuscript of Isidore's *Etymologiae*, currently preserved in the library of the monastery of the Escorial. It has been suggested that this tenth-century manuscript was written in Mérida or Seville, but that the lost exemplar came from Toledo.[36]

Likewise in 742 another scribe made a copy of the *Chronicle of John of Biclar*, together with those of Eusebius, Prosper and Victor, in which he too brought the calculations of date up to his own day without adding to the substance of the text.[37] As in the previous case the original manuscript is no longer extant, but the eighth-century recension survived to be copied into a later manuscript which preserved the brief additional comments of the scribe. It is possible that the copy made in 742 was written in the fledgling Asturian kingdom, as in its present setting, a thirteenth-century manuscript now in Madrid, it accompanies a brief list of the kings of the Asturias that was clearly compiled in the reign of Alfonso II (791–842).[38] This immediately precedes the Eusebius-Prosper-Victor-John Chronicle with its eighth-century note. Although much of the rest of the contents of this manuscript is not integral to the core collection, the corpus of chronicles and the regnal list are. However, the chronicle group can be dated to 742 while the list can not be earlier than 791, or to be precise 14 September 790. Thus it is conceivable and indeed probable that the copy of the chronicle collection was written further south, possibly in Toledo, and only brought to the Asturias by the end of the century.

Such a conclusion may be reinforced by the answers to the vexed question of whether or not there existed an original eighth-century Asturian chronicle, which although no longer extant in its own right formed the basis for the earlier sections of the late ninth-

[35] MS Escurialensis T.II.24 (formerly Q.II.24); for text see T. Mommsen, *MGH AA*, XI, p. 506.

[36] M.C. Díaz y Díaz, *Códices visigóticos en la monarquía leonesa* (León, 1983), p. 306.

[37] Preserved as a copy in the MS Matritensis, bibl. universit. 134, fol. 25v; see T. Mommsen, *MGH AA*, XI, p. 169.

[38] Ibid., p. 168 for text.

century Asturian historical compilations.[39] Obviously this has a direct bearing on the utility or otherwise of the information contained in the latter as far as this period is concerned. Without wishing to obfuscate the issue much further it should also be mentioned that for some historians the question is even more complex, and that as well as a later eighth-century annalistic compilation an otherwise unknown late Visigothic historical text has been seen as underlying the opening sections of the Asturian chronicles.[40] This may be taken to explain the information relating to the period 670–710 therein contained but which may be found in no other sources. In fact, when this is dissected what can be found is the skeleton of a highly personalized narrative involving the individual monarchs of the late Visigothic period in complicated but interrelated network of feud, conspiracy and vengeance. To put it crudely it is a story, but one that, had it any underlying historical basis to it, might have been expected to have made its mark on the *Chronicle of 754*.

Apart from the traces of an epic tale of Pelagius, to which indeed the 'saga' of the last Visigothic kings may have been a prologue, there is nothing in the very brief accounts of the eighth-century Asturian kings that would require us to believe that this represents re-use of a virtually contemporary source. Argument has revolved around points of detail such as the list of towns captured and then depopulated by Alfonso I (739–57), but the structure of the relevant passage makes this the least chronicle-like element in the whole of these sections.[41] Although this requires arguing in greater detail, there are ultimately no strong grounds for belief in an eighth-century Asturian historical composition.

Toledo and the Spanish Church

History was not the only subject of interest to the Christian learned classes in the peninsula in the mid-eighth century. Nor are

[39] C. Sánchez-Albornoz, 'Un misterioso chrónicon del siglo VIII', in his *Investigaciones sobre historiografía hispana medieval* (Buenos Aires, 1967), pp. 109–214.

[40] M. Stero, 'El Latín de la crónica de Alfonso III', *Cuadernos de la Historia de España*, 4 (1946), pp. 125–35, A. Ubieto Arteta, *Crónica de Alfonso III* (Valencia, 1971), pp. 12–15.

[41] C. Sánchez-Albornoz, 'Un misterioso chrónicon', pp. 203–14.

all of the authors of this period anonymous. The *Chronicle of 754* gives some brief and tantalizing glimpses of the intellectual activity still taking place in the Church of its day, particularly in Toledo. In its discussion of events around the year 720 it makes a reference to three outstanding figures of the time: bishop Fredoarius of *Acci*, of whom nothing else is known, and two Toledan ecclesiastics, Urban and Evantius.[42] Of these the former is described as the veteran *Melodicus* of the cathedral of Toledo. This would seem to indicate an office like that of 'arch-chanter' or, in later medieval canonical parlance, cantor, which is to say the official responsible for the music and above all the singing in the cathedral. His colleague Evantius is described as archdeacon. All three men are praised for their wisdom and learning, and at a subsequent point in the chronicle the deaths of both Urban and Evantius are recorded as occurring around or in the year 737.[43]

It has been suggested that Urban served as a surrogate bishop of Toledo.[44] The metropolitan at the time of the conquest, Sindered, is recorded as having fled soon afterwards, and was certainly in Rome in 721. The date of his death is unknown and no further record of him exists. However, in strict observance of the canons, he could not be replaced as bishop during his lifetime, other than by his being deposed by a full council. This had happened to one of his predecessors, Sisbert, in 693.[45] Thus there certainly must have existed a hiatus in the episcopal succession in Toledo between the period of the conquest and the death of Sindered. However, there is no evidence that this was filled by the cantor Urban carrying out the episcopal functions. This is merely wishful thinking on the part of those faced by too little evidence to be used to answer too many problems. In fact there is some information that can be used to shed a little light on the question of episcopal continuity in the metropolitan see in the eighth century. This comes from the survival of three lists of bishops for the sees of Seville, Toledo and Granada (Elvira) preserved in a tenth-century manuscript prob-

[42] *Chronicle of 754*, 70, pp. 84–6.

[43] Ibid., 83, p. 106.

[44] H. Flórez, *España sagrada*, vol. V, pp. 322, 336; F.J. Simonet, *Historia de los Mozárabes* (Madrid, 1867), pp. 166–7.

[45] Acts of XVI council of Toledo (693): ed. J. Vives, *Concilios visigóticos e hispano-romanos* (Madrid/Barcelona, 1963), pp. 507–09.

ably dating from 992.[46] The lists themselves are nearly contemporary with the codex, as the only dated entry relates to the death of a bishop John of Toledo in the year 956 (era 994). Where they can be checked against other information, which is the case with much of the Visigothic period, these episcopal lists are accurate, and thus give reasonable grounds for confidence in respect of names for whom they provide the only evidence. Thus in the case of Toledo, fixed points exist with Sindered (*c.*704–21) and Cixila, both of whom feature in the *Chronicle of 754*, with the latter holding the see by 744.[47] In the tenth-century list of bishops two names may be found placed between theirs: Suniered and Concordius. It is thus a reasonable assumption that the approximately twenty-year gap was filled by the pontificates of these two men, and that it was they who were the bishops of the see in the time of Urban the cantor and Evantius the archdeacon.

Of the musician no work is now known, and it is not clear in his case whether the *doctrina et sapientia* praised by the chronicler translated itself into specific writings and compositions, though there exists the possibility that he was co-author of a hagiographical text. But from Evantius something more concrete has survived, in the form of a letter.[48] The immediate addressee of the work is unknown, but its subject is the existence of judaizing practices amongst the Christian population of Zaragoza. In such cases the recipient might have been expected to have been the bishop, but nothing is known of episcopal continuity or the lack of it in this see in the eighth century. The principal problem that Evantius sets out to deal with in the letter is the belief apparently prevalent in the city that certain forms of meat were unclean. For the archdeacon these Christians have been interpreting the Biblical passages 'in the Jewish manner' and 'according to the dead letter rather than the life-giving spirit'. He attempts to counteract the literal observance of Deuteronomic precepts, which is what he found the Zaragozans doing, by the application of a number of New Testament texts, particularly drawn from the Epistles, and by a reference to the *Pastoral Rule* of Gregory the Great.

[46] Ed. J. Gil, *CSM*, I, pp. xvii–xviii, n. 10, from MS Escurialensis d.I.1, fol. 360v.

[47] *Chronicle of 754*, 53, 88, pp. 68f, 116f.

[48] *CSM*, I, pp. 2–5. For Urban as hagiographer see below p. 75f.

The question that Evantius was attempting to answer was a serious one, and it should not be seen as the strange local by-product of the collapse of the pre-eminence of Christianity in the aftermath of the Arab invasion. Similar problems had confronted the leaders of the Church in the Visigothic period.[49] The real issue here was essentially an exegetical one, in that it revolved around the status of the Old Testament in the Christian revelation. The mutual coherence of the whole of the Bible was a long-established expectation in Christian thinking. This could be achieved by the application of allegorical exegesis, which by this period had been applied with considerable success to most of the prophetic and historical books of the Old Testament, and had provided ways of showing how their contents prefigured or directly related to the Christian message of the New Testament. However, the legal books of the Old Testament, Leviticus and Deuteronomy, fundamental parts of the Jewish *Torah*, presented real problems here. They could be explained as allegories much less effectively, in that the literal level of meaning was all too clear and potentially applicable, and the problem of the extent to which Jewish ritual observances should remain a fundamental part of the new faith had been a major and contentious issue in the earliest days of Christianity. Although the matter had been fought out and basically resolved at that time, it was far from definitively solved. It always remained possible for Christian communities to feel that the authority of the Biblical texts required them to obey the legal and ritual precepts of the Pentateuch literally.

Thus at the theoretical level the query to which Evantius was doubtless responding and the problem that his unnamed correspondant had put before him were neither unpredictable nor unprecedented. Some of the polemical writings of the Visigothic Church and also some of the ferocious legislation of the kingdom relating to its Jewish population had been concerned not with the Jews themselves so much as with the existence of what were seen as judaizing tendancies amongst some Christian communities.[50] What is interesting is why such problems continued to reappear, especially when a general resolution to them would seem to have been

[49] B. Saitta, 'I Guidei nella Spagna visigota', in his *Studi Visigotici* (Catania, 1983), pp. 59–170.
[50] R. Collins, *Early Medieval Spain*, pp. 129–42.

so long established. There are two possible, and not mutually exclusive, answers. Firstly, there is the fact that, logically speaking, literal observance was the most straightforward reaction to the twin postulates of the authority of the Bible and the contents of the legal books of the Pentateuch. Secondly, there exists the possibility of direct influence in a local context from Judaism.

It must be borne in mind that what is at issue here is not a matter of simple religion or popular piety. Bibles were expensive to produce and usually came in the form of multiple codices. A priest might by no means be expected to have owned one or might have only had some of the books.[51] Thus both the making known of the Bible text and its exposition were the products of readings in the liturgy and of preaching. If a local Christian community, such as that of Zaragoza, was tending to interpret the Bible in a particular way this was not the fruit of ordinary townsfolk's misunderstandings but of what was being taught to them in their churches. A second item of imaginative reconstruction that has to be understood is that much greater openness and mutual interpenetration existed between local Christian and Jewish communities in the Iberian peninsula and the Mediterranean in general at this time than the later and Eastern European images of the ghetto might lead the unwary into expecting. Thus it was possible for Jewish ideas and practices to make a direct impact on the leaders of local Christianity.

This could be particularly true of the question of the dating of Easter. The New Testament Passion narratives make the identification of Easter with the celebration of the Passover quite specific. What then was more natural than that the observance of the liturgical feasts of Easter should be pegged to the contemporary Jewish dating of the Passover? However, the systems of calculating the dates had diverged markedly in the course of the fifth and sixth centuries, as new and highly complex procedures were adopted gradually throughout the Church.[52] These took some while to establish themselves, and, for example were only fully accepted

[51] Compare, for example, the small number of Bibles in comparison to various liturgical books in the listings in C. Sánchez-Albornoz, 'Notas sobre los libros leidos en el Reino de León hace mil años', in his *Miscelanea de estudios históricos* (León, 1970), 273–91.

[52] Described in detail in *Bedae Opera de Temporibus*, ed. C.W. Jones (Cambridge, Mass., 1943), pp. 3–104.

into the calendar of the Celtic Church in the northern parts of Ireland and western Scotland in the early eighth century. Spain had not been as slow as this, and had accepted the new methods of calculating the date of Easter in line with Rome and other western Mediterranean Churches. However, the procedures were complicated, and the alternative form which linked Easter and Passover had the virtues of both antiquity and simplicity. Moreover, at a local level, they presented no questioning when it was seen that the celebrations of the Jewish and the Christian feast had diverged in date, although the Biblical texts equated them.

Thus it comes as little of a surprise to find that another letter or treatise of the first half of the eighth century was sent from Toledo, this time to Seville, to explain to the Christian community there that they were observing Easter incorrectly. The text of this has not survived, but its composition is recorded in the *Chronicle of 754*.[53] The author of the work, composed around the year 750, was a deacon called Peter. He was also the *Melodicus*, and therefore probably Urban's successor, and the chronicler records him as being 'very wise in all the Scriptures'. Although this letter is lost, there survives another which may be by the same Peter.[54] It is extant in only one manuscript, dating from the tenth century, in which it accompanies the fragment of another letter which contains a reference to the date of its writing being the era 802, which is AD 764. The letter of Peter has lost its conclusion and it is not possible to know the author's rank, but that he is an ecclesiastic is highly probable. The recipient was a bishop Felix of Córdoba, who, it has been suggested, was the author of the fragmentary epistle that accompanies this text in the manuscript.[55]

Coincidence of name, especially such a common one for a churchman, is not the only reason for associating the author of the letter with the deacon Peter of the *Chronicle of 754*. The nature of the contents would also seem to justify such a view. Peter was writing to the bishop about the dating of a liturgical fast on the tenth day of September. What had disturbed him was the question of a possible mutual observance of this by the Jewish and Christian communities. He became quite sarcastic with his correspondent on

[53] *Chronicle of 754*, 93, p. 124.
[54] *CSM*, I, pp. 55–7.
[55] Ibid., p. 58.

the matter and told him that if he was going to allow this to happen he may as well go the full length and introduce the complete Old Testament prescribed ritual for the feast of Tabernacles (Succoth). Once again what is illustrated here is the mutual closeness of Jewish and Christian communities at the local level. This is not just a question of good neighbourliness, rather it may suggest that positive difficulties could be caused by the two groups celebrating either festivals of opposed character at the same time or ones of similar type at slightly different times. In other words if the Christians could arrange to be celebrating or in mourning at the same time as the Jews normal social and possibly family interchange would not be disrupted. Despite the normative and minatory pronouncements of the Visigothic law code and some of the decrees of the Church councils, works like these letters can give us a more vivid impression of the realities of urban life in Spain by suggesting what it was that upset the ecclesiastical establishment. Unlike the Later Middle Ages, no pogroms are recorded in the annals of Jewish–Christian relations in these centuries, and in the individual localities mutual convenience may have been of greater weight than the rules of clerical, and in the Visigothic period secular, government.

For Evantius and Peter conditions were, of course, very different from those that had existed in the time of their predecessors in the struggle against judiazing or 'sabbathizing' (*sabbatizare*) practices.[56] The full weight of the law-making capacity of the state lay behind Isidore and Julian of Toledo in the seventh century, even if this may not have been translatable into fully effective action at a practical level. However, in the mid-eighth century there no longer existed a Christian king and ruling elite for whom the maintenance of uniformity of belief and practice was tantamount to the ensuring of the political and economic stability and well-being of the realm. The Arab governors could be at best neutral in disputes between sections of their Christian subjects, and had no interest in promoting their interests at the expense of the Jews.

In these circumstances it is significant to see the continued interest of the Church of Toledo in promoting or maintaining the uniformity in matters of doctrine and procedure of the whole Christian community in the peninsula. More than that, it looks as

[56] Letter of Peter, 2, line 7, ibid., p. 55.

if bishops from as far apart as Zaragoza and Córdoba still looked to Toledo to give the lead in matters affecting their own local Christian communities. Although the kingship, which had been so intimately tied to the capital, the *urbs regia* of the Visigothic monarchy, had disappeared, the unchallenged pre-eminence achieved by the Church of Toledo in the later seventh century clearly continued or was revived. Not only were its clerics still well enough equipped in intellectual terms to provide authoritative guidance on a wide range of issues of ecclesiastical discipline and doctrine, but this was also actively sought.

In this context it is perhaps surprising that the individuals of whom we are informed are almost all in lesser orders. It is deacons not bishops who are recorded in the chronicles and who wrote the scant remains of the literature now available to us. This is in contrast to the norms of the Visigothic period, in which the luminaries of the Church of Toledo, and therefore generally of the Church in Spain as a whole, were the bishops. This may be a matter of accident, but it is possible because of the traditions and past of the city that the Arab governors maintained a tight hold on it, and it is conceivable that its bishops were more titular than effective. Certainly in the first half of the century they made no mark.

Whatever the reasons for that strange silence, with the appearance of a certain Cixila, Toledo had its first bishop of whom we may have any writings since the time of Felix (693–*c*.700). His pontificate is recorded in the *Chronicle of 754* in an entry placed in conjunction with events dated to the year 744.[57] As has been mentioned, his existence is also confirmed by the episcopal list of 956. Certain caution has to be used in going much further than this in any statement about Cixila. The section relating to him in the *Chronicle of 754* has been regarded as an interpolation, and is certainly out of character with the rest of the work, in that as well as making some general remarks about the bishop it retells a miracle that occurred when he was confronting a Sabellian heretic.[58] The man had attempted to receive communion but was questioned by the bishop as to how he could hope to do so when tainted by such a sin. When the heretic denied that his beliefs were offensive

[57] *Chronicle of 754*, 88, p. 116f.
[58] Ibid., 88, pp. 116–18.

he was taken in a fit of demonic possession, much to the amazement of the rest of the congregation. Cixila was able, however, through prayer to restore him to both health and true belief. The section ends by recording the nine-year tenure of office and the death of Cixila.

Chronologically, a nine-year episcopate commencing in 744 would end in 753, and thus just prior to the probable date of composition of the Chronicle. The opening sentences of the section on Cixila, which record of him that he was 'learned in holy things, a restorer of churches, and, following the scriptures, most firm in faith, hope and charity', are in themselves quite in keeping with other biographical notes in the *Chronicle of 754* in respect of contents and vocabulary. The only stumbling block to the acceptance of this passage is the miraculous episode. In that Cixila was dead by the time of writing such a record is not incredible, and studies of the role of the supernatural in the early medieval consciousness are now so numerous and so sophisticated that we should not find it incredible for a Toledan cleric to believe the truth of such a story relating to one of his contemporaries.[59] Indeed, it would not be hard to rationalize the tale itself in that it reflects a basically psychological reaction to a situation of intense internal conflict. The Sabellian heretic was clearly attempting to take part within his own community in an act of worship in which the rest of the congregation differed from him in fundamentals of Trinitarian theological belief. Finally, it is worth noticing that another, and far more extended miraculous story is included in the earliest section of the Chronicle, which relates to the Visigothic period. This is the account of the visit in the 640s to Rome in search of some of the works of Gregory the Great of the Zaragozan deacon Taio.[60] Their whereabouts are revealed to Taio through a miraculous appearance by Gregory himself. This too has been taken for a subsequent interpolation in the text of the Chronicle, but its latest editor has made a strong case for accepting it as an integral part of the work on grounds of style and vocabulary.[61] Thus there exist good grounds for regarding the Cixila passage as equally authentic, and effectively none for doubting it.

[59] For the chronology see F.J. Simonet, *Historia de los Mozárabes*, p. 207, n. 1.
[60] *Chronicle of 754*, 23, pp. 38–44.
[61] J.E. López Perreira, *Estudio crítico*, pp. 65–74.

This is important for a number of reasons. Not the least of these is the existence of the so-called Sabellian heretic. His significance does not lie in the label assigned to him. Sabellius and the Sabellians were essentially a fourth-century group, whose reaction to the Trinitarian arguments of the period of the Arian controversy had been to affirm the absolute oneness of God.[62] For them Christ was God who had appeared physically on earth in the person of Jesus. This doctrine had been soundly condemned, and various credal formulations existed specifically to denounce it. It is not necessary to believe in the survival of secret cells of Sabellians from that time on into the middle of the eighth century. Any subsequent enunciation of ideas of a similar stamp would be sufficient for the holders to be dubbed 'Sabellians'. The Church had a repertoire of such labels ready to apply to almost any theological idea that diverted from the main stream of orthodox thought. Thus the Toledan Sabellian could have been no more than an isolated 'free-thinker'. What is significant, though, is the presumed nature of his thinking. To have earned the title of 'Sabellian' implies that his beliefs were more rigidly monotheistic, or to use an anachronistic term 'Unitarian', than was acceptable. In the context of Spain in the mid-eighth century it is probably not stretching conjecture too far to suspect that this may mark an Islamic impact on certain areas of Christian thinking.

Whether that be the case or not, Cixila is worthy of attention for a number of other reasons. The chronicler's delineation of him as 'restorer of churches' is tantalizing. Does it imply that the Christians were re-occupying churches abandoned or destroyed in the time of the conquest, and did such a programme extend beyond the confines of the city? Toledo had also been besieged for four weeks in the course of the civil wars between rival Arab factions in 742, and damage could have been inflicted then too.[63] Cixila's other main area of activity may have been literary. Here too, though, doubt and controversy await. There exists a text known as the *Vita Ildefonsi* (*Life of Ildefonsus*), though the alternative title of *Gesta Ildefonsi* (*Deeds of Ildefonsus*) would be preferable, the authorship of which in at least one manuscript is attributed to bishop

[62] J.N.D. Kelly, *Early Christian Creeds* (3rd edn, London, 1972), pp. 246–8.

[63] *Chronicle of 754*, 85, p. 110; J. Porres Martín-Cleto, *Historia de Ṭulayṭula (711–1085)* (Toledo, 1985), p. 17.

Cixila of Toledo.[64] The alternative attribution is to bishop Helladius of Toledo (615–33), which is extraordinary in that Ildefonsus (657–67) was one of his successors!

The work as now extant is in no sense a life of the bishop, in that it provides hardly any details of his career and writings, and in one of the manuscripts that transmit it this has been rectified by the biographical and bibliographical information on Ildefonsus added to his own *De Viris Illustribus* by his successor bishop Julian. The *Life* attributed to Cixila basically contains three things. Firstly an account of how Ildefonsus was sent by his master, bishop Eugenius II of Toledo, to study under Isidore of Seville, immediately prior to his being made abbot of the monastery of SS. Cosmas and Damian in the suburbs of Toledo. Secondly there is an account of Ildefonsus' devotion to St Leocadia, the patroness of the city, and the miracle that resulted from that, which took place in the presence of king Reccesuinth (649–72), and finally there is the story of the apparition of the Virgin Mary to Ildefonsus in which she invested him with a 'small present taken from the treasury of my Son'. It is implied that this is a garment, which in later tradition became fixed as a chasuble, and the whole scene was to be a very popular one in the art of sixteenth- and seventeenth-century Spain.

The ambiguity in the manuscript attribution of authorship inevitably arouses suspicions that if Helladius is clearly impossible there can be no certainty that Cixila is any more reliable. On the other hand there is a reference in the body of the work that at least seems to locate its composition in the right period. Between the two stories relating to St Leocadia and to the Virgin Mary the author passes over the opportunity of recording other miraculous occurrences brought about by Ildefonsus because it would be too laborious to provide a re-telling of the accounts to be found in the book by Urban and Evantius. The implication of the way these two are mentioned is that they were still alive, and probably superior in status to the author. In other words the work was composed before *c.*737, and this too is several years before Cixila's elevation to the episcopate. It is of course possible that this text was written at some later time and given a spurious sense of date and authenticity by a reference to two such men whom the real

[64] *CSM*, I, pp. 60–6. *Gesta* is used in the two oldest mss: Escurialensis d.I.1, and Madrid R.A.H. Aemil. 47.

author would only have known of from the *Chronicle of 754*. If so, the work would have to have been composed no later than the end of the tenth century, when it is first attested in the manuscript transmission.[65] More significantly, there is hardly any point to be seen in such a fraud. Had a later compiler wished to give spurious authority to his work it would have made sense to have contrived to make it seem to have been composed in or just after Ildefonsus' lifetime, but to locate it some 70 or 80 years later makes little sense, as this would not have provided a sense of absolute credibility. Furthermore, although the book by Urban and Evantius is alluded to, it is not given a title and the implication is that the readers of this work would know it well. In fact the case for doubting the period of composition of this work are not strong, even if ultimately Cixila's authorship of it can remain no more than a definite possibility.

The work itself presents a number of interesting features that have a bearing on the milieu in which it was produced. After the brief biographical introduction there follow the two miracle stories, which took place on the feast days of St Leocadia and the Virgin Mary, divided by the passage in which the author declines to offer a version of the events of an Advent Sunday, because of the existence of the book by Urban and Evantius. The work thus alludes to three liturgical feasts, in the course of which supernatural occurrences took place. These are the days of St Leocadia, the fourth Sunday in Advent, and of the Virgin Mary respectively. In the Calendar of the Visigothic Church the first and third of these fell on 9 and 18 December, with the movable Sunday feast falling in between them.[66] In this particular case even more exact dating is provided by the information given that the feast of the Virgin came on the seventh day after the Advent Sunday, which therefore must have fallen on the 11th of the month.[67] In the ten years of the pontificate of Ildefonsus this coincidence of day and date only occurred in the year 662.

The precise liturgical setting of these episodes is made clear by some of the points of detail presented within them. Thus, after the

[65] MS Escurialensis d.I.1, dated 992: see G. Antolín, *Catálogo de los códices latinos de la Real biblioteca del Escorial*, vol. I (Madrid, 1910), pp. 320–68.
[66] *Liber Mozarabicus Sacramentorum*, ed. M. Férotin (Paris, 1912), p. liii.
[67] *Vita Ildefonsi*, 6: *CSM*, I, p. 63.

miraculous levitation of the covering of St Leocadia's tomb, Ildefonsus exclaims one of the antiphons set for the Matins of the feast day, and which would have been found in the late seventh-century original of the León antiphonal.[68] Similarly, the miraculous appearance of the Virgin Mary occurred in the context of the Mass for the feast. Mention is also made of the three days of penitential litanies to be celebrated from 13 December, which had first been instituted by the decision of the Visigothic king Chintila and the bishops present at the Fifth Council of Toledo in 636. This practice thus clearly survived the Arab conquest.

The significance of all of this is hard to gauge. The miracles themselves could be classified as being of a very superior type. Not only does the patron saint of the city speak from her tomb, but an appearance of the Virgin Mary is quite unprecedented in Spanish hagiographical texts. Moreover the chronological context is both specific and sequential. These supernatural happenings follow one another in the course of a short period of time in a year that can be identified. In addition, in both instances they take place in the presence of the Visigothic king Reccesuinth. Interestingly, the author has pronounced views on this monarch, whom he sees as being troubled by the uneasy consciousness of his sins.[69] This, like the generally approving treatment afforded Wittiza in the *Chronicle of 754*, runs counter to the perspectives on Visigothic history later to be found in the Asturian kingdom, whose founder Pelagius was there portrayed as a descendant of the family of Chindasuinth.

A further distinctive element in this work is the presentation of Ildefonsus as the pupil of Isidore.[70] There is no contemporary evidence that would support such a view. Ildefonsus does not speak of it himself, and in Julian's *Elogium Ildefonsi* bishop Eugenius II of Toledo (646–57) is said to have been his master.[71] If the latter is the bishop Eugenius referred to in the eighth-century work, then the chronological impossibility of a relationship with Isidore, who died in 636, becomes all the greater, and if it is bishop Eugenius I (636–46) who is being referred to by Cixila then it

[68] Ibid., 3, p. 62; *Antifonario visigótico mozárabe de la catedral de León*, eds L. Brou and J. Vives (Barcelona/Madrid, 1959), fol. 48v, p. 52.

[69] *Vita Ildefonsi*, 4, p. 63.

[70] Ibid., 1, p. 61.

[71] Julian of Toledo, *Beati Ildefonsi Elogium*, ed. F. de Lorenzana, *SS.PP. Toletanorum quotquot extant Opera*, vol. I (Madrid, 1782), p. 94.

should be noticed that Ildefonsus makes no personal reminiscences of him, unlike of Eugenius II, in his *De Viris Illustribus*.[72] In fact, there are no grounds for placing any reliance on this tradition, but it should rather be seen as an early stage in the process that led to all of the great luminaries of the Visigothic Church being linked one to another either by family relationship or by ties of discipleship.[73] As far as the reality of seventh-century conditions can be gauged there did exist a number of bonds of master and pupil between some of the principal bishops of Toledo in the latter part of the century, and these were much valued, but these only connected with Isidore through bishop Eugenius II and only in so far as his own master, Braulio of Zaragoza, had been the friend and disciple of the great bishop of Seville. With the invention of the story of Ildefonsus' studying with Isidore the distant reality is subverted in the interest of promoting belief in the direct connection between the two men.

What this text, which may well be incomplete as we now have it, seems to indicate is a renewed sense of confidence and identity on the part of the Church of Toledo. At the end of the sixth century the city had emerged from relative obscurity to become the permanent governmental centre of the Visigothic monarchy; a true capital, whose only equivalent in western Europe was to be Lombard Pavia.[74] The cult of its obscure patron saint benefited enormously from the royal support it received from monarchs as different as Leovigild and Sisebut, and its bishops rapidly built on the privileged access the special status the city had acquired to seek to match it in terms of the hierarchical structuring of the Church in the kingdom.[75] In 610 they had made their see into the metropolitan bishopric of the province of Carthaginiensis, and by the 670s Toledo had become the dominant metropolitanate of the realm, able to impose its practices and authority over all of the ecclesiastical provinces of the realm. This was matched by the acquisition of

[72] *El 'De Viris Illustribus' de Ildefonso de Toledo*, ed. C. Codoñer Merino (Salamanca, 1972), sections XII and XIII of the text, pp. 132–4.

[73] R. Collins, *Early Medieval Spain*, pp. 71–80.

[74] E. Ewig, 'Résidence et capital pendant le haut Moyen Age', *Revue historique*, 230 (1963), pp. 25–72.

[75] For the earlier stages of this development see R. Collins, 'Mérida and Toledo, 550–589', in *Visigothic Spain: New Approaches*, ed. E. James (Oxford, 1980), pp. 189–219.

exclusive rights in respect of the liturgical processes of king-making.[76] From such a position Toledo had stood to lose most in the aftermath of the Arab conquest, but by the middle of the eighth century at the latest it appears to have re-established itself as at least the mentor of many or most of the other churches of the peninsula.

It was also, as the work attributable to Cixila shows, undertaking a re-evaluation of its past. A new historical perspective on the Visigothic monarchy had been created in which judgements on the merits of the individual kings loomed large. Where it can be compared this can be seen to be at variance with the realities of the individuals and periods concerned. At the same time, and probably more significantly, the Toledan clerics of these middle years of the eighth century seem to have reassessed the episcopal succession in the see, following a tradition already strong in the later seventh century, and in particular they seem to have given a special prominence to Ildefonsus. From the point of view of modern scholarship his writings may look less sophisticated and less well-informed than those of Julian, but throughout the medieval centuries it was to be Ildefonsus who, together with Isidore, was to be the most respected of the fathers of the Visigothic Church.[77] In a way this was less for what he wrote than for the effect of those writings, and the latter really means the miraculous signs of approval afforded to him by the patron saint of the city and by 'the Queen of Heaven'.

The root of Ildefonsus's appeal to his eighth-century successors lay in his writings: his liturgical compositions, some of which were almost certainly intended for use in the feast of Leocadia, and in his virulent and polemical defence of the Virgin in *De Virginitate Perpetua Sanctae Mariae*.[78] In these works he both honoured and placed under obligation the city's patroness and the *Theotokos*. Their gratitude and special relationship towards him are the themes of the miraculous occurrences recorded by Cixila. In part this validated and sanctified particular focuses of power. Thus Cixila records that after the appearance of the Virgin and the miraculous

[76] R. Collins, 'Julian of Toledo', pp. 30–49.

[77] Sr. A. Braegelmann, *The Life and Writings of Saint Ildefonsus of Toledo* (Washington, 1942); J.F. Rivera Recio, *San Ildefonso de Toledo* (Madrid, 1985).

[78] Ed. V. Blanco García, *Santos padres españoles*, vol. I, *San Ildefonso de Toledo* (Madrid, 1971), pp. 44–154. See also J.M. Cascante, *Doctrina mariana de S. Ildefonso de Toledo* (Barcelona, 1958).

vesting of Ildefonsus no bishop of Toledo ever used the throne upon which Ildefonsus had been seated at the time. The only one to break with this tradition was Sisbert, and he, as the author points out, had been rapidly deposed (by the Seventeenth Council of Toledo in 693 for his involvement in a conspiracy against King Egica).[79] More than just in such localized settings, the miraculous actions effected through the virtues of Ildefonsus transformed both the Church and the city of Toledo. Whatever befell it, and much had done so in the early part of the eighth century, the city and its clergy were special. The *urbs regia* of the Visigothic period had become *urbs sancta*. The development of the set of ideas that allowed the Church and city to retain their old authority in a new way looks to have been the work of a group of the clergy, including Urban, Evantius, Peter, Cixila, and quite probably the author of the *Chronicle of 754*, working in the 730s to 750s, who drew on, and in the case of the relationship of Ildefonsus to Isidore, distorted the traditions of the Visigothic past to create a response to new conditions that ensured fundamental continuity with those elements in that past which they valued. This they achieved in a period of great instability and change.

[79] *Vita Ildefonsi*, 7, *CSM*, I, p. 64.

4

The Conquerors Divided

A Peaceful Decade in the Peninsula

The first decade following the Arab invasion saw a wave of violence and military activity pass through the Iberian peninsula from south to north and then on across the Pyrenees into the former Visigothic region of Septimania. Certain areas were probably hardly touched; others, such as the Ebro valley and the region around Narbonne may have seen a disproportionate amount of fighting and destruction. In most cases, though, a period of initial disorder seems to have been followed by a restoration of stability and, as has been seen, either the revival of local forms of government or in some cases the imposition of direct rule by the Arab governors or their representatives. The making of local and regional treaties and the imposition of tax payable to the central authority marked this period of the restoring of order. Within the Iberian peninsula itself much of this had been achieved by 721, although fierce fighting was to continue in Septimania and parts of southern Aquitaine, and much of the following two decades seems to have been passed by most of the inhabitants in relative tranquility.

Once again it is the *Chronicle of 754* that provides both quantitatively and qualitatively the best information on this sparsely recorded period. Of the governor 'Anbasa ibn Suḥaym al-Kalbī ('Ambisa' to the chronicler), who was installed in 721, the chronicler reports that he 'doubled the taxes on the Christians'.[1] This in itself is rather ambiguous in that it is not clear if this should be

[1] *Chronicle of 754*, 74, p. 88.

taken as meaning that he thereby broke the existing treaties made with the various Christian towns and lords in which, as in the case of that made with Theodemir, precise rates of tribute had been specified. In general the chronicler appears to have approved of this governor, and records his capture of a number of unnamed towns and fortresses by surprise attack in the context of continuing and overall not very successful conflict with the Franks.[2] It is possible that the mention of a doubled rate of tax refers to the terms imposed on these newly-acquired towns and their inhabitants rather than the abrogation of existing treaties that the broader interpretation would imply, or it may also have just been applied to those Christians living in towns under what may be called direct Arab rule. However, it is significant to note that at this same period, in 725, a revolt broke out amongst the indigenous inhabitants of Egypt provoked by an attempt to introduce a five per cent increase in their taxation.[3]

It is important to appreciate that there is nothing necessarily arbitrary and localized about such developments, although our sources inevitably present them in an exclusively Spanish context. The reign of the Umayyad Caliph Hishām (724–43) was marked by attempts to increase tax yields from the non-Muslim subject population across the whole breadth of the Arab-ruled lands.[4] Indeed Muslims themselves became increasingly liable for such things as taxes due on lands which they acquired which had formerly been in non-Muslim ownership, and progressively more rigorous methods seem to have been resorted to in augmenting revenue and in chastising defaulters. 'Anbasa, like other governors was thus imposing on *Al-Andalus* the policy objectives of his caliphal master in Syria.

Arab traditions are few and slight as far as this governor is concerned, other than in reporting that he had been appointed to his office by the governor of *Ifrīqīya*. A fragment of the work of the eleventh-century historian Ibn Ḥayyān records that the revolt of the Asturias that was led by Pelagius took place during the

[2] Ibid.

[3] M.A. Shaban, *Islamic History A.D. 600–750* (Cambridge, 1971), p. 149 and n. 2. An attempt to tax Muslim Berbers is said to have led directly to the Berber revolt in the region of Tangier in 740: Ibn al-Athīr, p. 63.

[4] Shaban, pp. 138–52; P. Hitti, *A History of the Arabs* (8th edn, London, 1964), p. 223.

governorship of 'Anbasa.[5] As the latter has been generally accepted as falling within the years 721–25, this could be used to justify redating the revolt to 722 rather than to 718, which can be calculated from the information provided in the late ninth-century Asturian chronicles.[6] This, however, merely leaves the historian with the difficult task of weighing up the relative merits of an eleventh-century Arab account and a ninth-century Latin one. The roots of the latter seem to lie in a probably late eighth-century regnal list, whilst those of the former cannot be traced back anything like so far. At best the uncertainty has to remain, but the new dating is by no means as secure as it is now often assumed to be.

Both Arab and Christian sources agree in reporting 'Anbasa's death from natural causes soon after he had gone to take personal command of the forces being used against the Franks, which had previously failed to make much headway under a succession of deputies.[7] He appointed his own temporary successor in the person of 'Udra ibn 'Abdallāh al-Fihrī ('Hodera'), but the latter's responsibility seems to have been confined to withdrawing the army that 'Anbasa had commanded at the time of his death, and he was replaced within no more than six months by a properly constituted governor sent by the Caliph Hishām. This was Yaḥyā ibn Salāma al-Kalbī ('Iaie').

His tenure of office, which lasted for nearly three years, is particularly marked by his restitution of property to the Christians. As usual the chronicler's references are brief and elliptical. He qualifies Yaḥyā as 'terribilis potestator', which has been taken to have a prejudicial significance. On the other hand he records that the governor prosecuted the Arabs and Berbers in Spain on account of loot they had acquired illicitly, and returned much of the latter to the Christians.[8] It has been suggested, in the interests of resolving the apparent contradiction inherent in a Christian author

[5] Contained in Al-Maqqarī, II, pp. 34–5.

[6] This comes from the calculation of regnal lengths, starting from the well-established dates of the late ninth-century kings. Arab accounts have 'Anbasa dying in December 725: Ibn al-Athīr, p. 57.

[7] *Chronicle of 754*, 74, p. 88; Al-Maqqarī, II, p. 35; *Akhbar Machmua*, p. 35 records his appointment, but not his demise. See M. Rouche, *L'Aquitaine des Wisigoths aux Arabes, 418–781* (Paris, 1979), p. 112.

[8] *Chronicle of 754*, 75, p. 90.

criticizing a governor who went out of his way to benefit the Christian community, that the chronicler was here relying on an Arab account of these events, which was inevitably hostile to Yaḥyā.[9] One thing, though, that should be clear by now about the author of the *Chronicle of 754* is that he was not a fool. The idea that he should just have parroted a Muslim opinion without recognizing the implications of what he was writing is not worthy of consideration. The point is rather that to call him 'terribilis potestator', which is to say a terrifying wielder of authority is by no means uncomplimentary, and that the furious rage he is said to have directed against Arab and Berber miscreants is in no degree earning him the chronicler's censure.[10]

The important issue here is that this looks like a case of centrally imposed authority being used to bring about a restoration of social justice. The conquerors were forced by their own government to give up spoils which they were not entitled to, and the subject population benefited from a restitution of what had been taken from them improperly. In terms of movable property it is perhaps hard to imagine how this was carried out, but if what is at issue here is title to land then some form of inquisition could have been used to test the rights of ownership and to enable the dispossessed to make a legal challenge to those who had acquired their former holdings.[11] As in the case of 'Anbasa's increase of the tax burden on the Christians, the governor was doing no more than carrying out with some degree of relish and efficiency the bidding of his master the Caliph Hishām, whose regime was turning to increasingly severe methods to augment its revenue. The subsequent overthrow of the Umayyads in 750 has meant that in the Arab historiographical tradition they were rarely given credit for their achievements, whilst their shortcomings were magnified.[12] Thus the rule of Hishām was seen in Arab tradition as a time of peculiar fiscal extortion. However, this contemporary Christian evidence

[9] J.E. López Perreira, *Estudio crítico sobre la crónica mozárabe de 754* (Zaragoza, 1980), p. 107.

[10] For the meanings of *potestator* see J.F. Niermeyer, *Mediae Latinitatis Lexicon Minus* (Leiden, 1976), s.v. *Potestas*, pp. 819–20.

[11] For a hint of the form this type of proceeding might have taken see the story related of the *quāḍī* 'Abd ar-Raḥmān ibn Ṭārif al-Yaṣobī: *Historia de los jueces de Córdoba de Aljoxami*, ed. and tr. J. Ribera (Madrid, 1914, reprint 1985), pp. 82–3.

[12] P. Crone and M. Cook, *Hagarism: the Making of the Islamic World* (Cambridge, 1977), p. 33 and n. 43.

from Spain suggests that it may have been accompanied by more equitable treatment of the subject population, at least in terms of rights to property and security of title.

Sometime in the middle of the year 728 Yaḥyā either died or was replaced. A reasonable supposition would be that this was related to the appointment of a new governor of *Ifrīqīya*, still the immediate superior of the one in *Al-Andalus*.[13] Both Yaḥyā and his predecessor 'Anbasa belonged to the tribal confederacy of the Kalb, as had the governor of *Ifrīqīya*, Bashīr. On the latter's death in 727 he had designated another member of the same tribe to succeed him, but early in 728 his nominee was replaced by a governor chosen by the caliph, this time a member of another and rival confederacy, the Qays. Yaḥyā's immediate successor in *Al-Andalus* belonged to the same group.[14] Such dramatic changes of personnel and of factional ascendancy were used by the caliphs at this time for short-term political and financial advantages. Whatever the cause, there ensued a brief period of some instability in Spain. The new governor, Ḥujefa ('Odifa'), only held office for six months, and is severely if unspecifically criticized by the author of the *Chronicle of 754* for his 'levity'.[15] What this means in practice cannot be known, but the concept of *levitas* was one used by Latin writers of the Early Middle Ages to imply frivolity and the lack of appropriately dignified behaviour on the part of someone entrusted with high office.[16] The Asturian king Fafila (737–9) was killed by a bear when indulging in unsuitable 'levitas'.

Ḥujefa's successor 'Uthmān ibn Abi Naṣr was only in office for four months before being replaced in turn by Al-Ḥaytān ibn 'Ubayd al-Kalabī ('Aleittan'). The causes of what then occurred are by no means clear, but a group of leading Arabs in *Al-Andalus* united in a conspiracy to depose the new governor within ten months of his taking up office. His rule had been characterized by the Christian chronicler as confused and disorderly.[17] Al-Ḥaytān was able to forestall the conspirators, and seizing them, he had

[13] Ibn 'Abd al-Ḥakam, p. 32.
[14] Ibid., pp. 32–3. Cf. Ibn al-Athīr, p. 58.
[15] *Chronicle of 754*, 11, p. 92.
[16] See the account of the murder of the Frankish king Childeric II in *The Fourth Book of the Chronicle of Fredegar*, ed. J.M. Wallace-Hadrill (London, 1960), *continuationes*, 2, p. 81.
[17] *Chronicle of 754*, 78, p. 92.

them tortured and executed. Some of those involved had been men of considerable local influence and their relatives were able to persuade the governor of *Ifrīqīya* to act against his own nominee. Early in 731 the governor sent one of his officers from Kairouan with a secret commission to arrest Al-Ḥaytān and to install 'Abd ar-Raḥmān al-Ghafiqī in his place.[18] The latter had previously held office temporarily after the death of As-Sāmh and was the first local appointee for a decade. His selection may reflect some discontent amongst the leading Arabs settled in *Al-Andalus*, many of whom may have been there for up to twenty years by this time, with the continuing African suzerainty and the appointment of outsiders as governors.

Thus it may have been in part as a response to the internal difficulties of the previous few years that 'Abd ar-Raḥmān resumed the more aggressive attitude towards the Aquitanians that had characterized some of the earlier governors, such as his own mentor As-Shām. No mention had been made of such campaigning on the part of the governors themselves by the author of the *Chronicle of 754* since the death of 'Anbasa in 726.

Wars with the Franks

The dynamics of the Arab expansion from the time of the immediate successors of Muḥammad onwards are by no means easy to understand, not least due to the inadequacy of the available evidence. To take a view of it from the Spanish perspective, it seems extraordinary that within less than a decade of the invasion of the peninsula, the Arabs and their Berber mercenaries were campaigning across the Pyrenees, and that for the next fifteen years or more their principal military energies should have been concentrated in southern Aquitaine and Provence.[19] In the same way the conquest of Spain had been undertaken no more than twelve years after the completion of the subjugation of North Africa. What is striking is the lack of subsequent internal resistance in both Africa and Spain

[18] Ibid., 78, p. 94. Ibn al-Athīr, p. 58, merely reports that Al-Ḥaytān died in Feb/March 730, and was replaced by al-Gafiqī. Priority must be given here to the contemporary Latin source.

[19] See in general M. Rouche, *Aquitaine*, pp. 111–20.

and the apparent speed with which such conquests could be consolidated and new ventures undertaken.

The Arab incursions into Francia, and in particular into Aquitaine, had begun immediately after the elimination of the last pocket of Visigothic resistance with the capture of Narbonne in 720. As-Sāmh had no sooner taken and garrisoned the latter city than he launched an attack into Aquitanian territory, besieging Toulouse. Here, however, in a battle with the relieving army of the Aquitanian duke Eudo he was defeated and killed. As with the invasion of Spain, which followed so closely after the pacification of North Africa, the aggressiveness and expansionary momentum of the Arab advance seem so striking. There was no apparent threat to the recently established Arab dominance in the former Visigothic Septimania to be expected from the Aquitanians. Eudo was entirely taken by surprise in this unlooked for attack on his principal southern city, and had to assemble an army in haste to relieve it.

The initial reverse in front of Toulouse in 720 may have slowed down the Arabs' expansionary ambitions, in that the chronicler of 754 records that during the tenure of office of the next governor, 'Anbasa, only a series of small scale incursions were carried out under the conduct of his deputies.[20] However, the governor himself was preparing a major expedition into Frankish territory and had assembled a large army for such a purpose at the time of his death, from natural causes, in 725. The thirteenth-century Arab author Ibn al-Athīr here reports a rather more notable Arab success than the account of the Spanish chronicler seems to suggest. He records the capture by 'Anbasa of the strategically vital town of Carcassonne, probably in the year 724.[21] This effectively cut Aquitanian access from the north into the coastal region of western Provence. Following this initial success 'Anbasa was also able to occupy Nîmes without resistance. A less permanent achievement but an even more telling indication of the nature of the Arab threat was the capture and sack of Autun on 31 August 725. This was recorded in the nearest thing to a contemporary Frankish source, the *Chronicle of Moissac*, which in present form was put together in the very early ninth century but much of which

[20] *Chronicle of 754*, 74, p. 88.
[21] Ibn Al-Athīr, p. 57.

is genuinely mid-eighth century.[22] Such a raid into the heart of Burgundy is impressive testimony of the striking power of the Arab armies, and it is probably the news of this great raid that reached the Venerable Bede in Northumbria and was included by him in the closing pages of his *Historia Ecclesiastica*.[23] Why no word of it was mentioned in the *Chronicle of 754* is hard to explain, in that the chronicler shows no traces of any anachronistic pan-Christian sympathy that might have led him to suppress it, and he was apparently as hostile to the Franks as any of his Visigothic predecessors. In reconciling the Arab and Frankish accounts with the brief and admittedly ambiguous mention of 'Anbasa's expedition in the *Chronicle of 754*, it is reasonable to assume that his death occurred in the course of the operation that culminated in the sack of Autun, and that it was his appointee 'Udra who conducted the return of the army to Spain.

It was not until the second governorship of 'Abd ar-Raḥmān al-Gafīqī that Arab campaigning on the marches with Aquitaine was renewed. In part this may have been due to various internal difficulties already alluded to which the governors had to face in the peninsula itself, but in general the almost untamed aggressiveness of the earlier 720s never seems to have reasserted itself. The causes of the conflict that was to culminate in the battle of Poitiers are rather more likely to be found in actions taken by the Aquitanian duke Eudo. The frontier area in the eastern Pyrenees was controlled by a series of Berber garrisons established in the principal towns under the command of a certain Munnuza.[24] He was led, around 731, to plan a Berber uprising against the Arabs in Spain, because of the way his people were being treated by the Islamic 'judges' (probably here implying local administrators) in North Africa, and apparently in the interests of achieving this made an alliance with 'the Franks', or more exactly the Aquitanians under Duke Eudo. 'Abd ar-Raḥmān, reappointed governor in 731, was alerted to the threat and able to strike before Munnuza was ready.

[22] *Chronicle of Moissac*, s.a. 725, ed. G. Pertz, *MGH SS*, I, p. 291. On the chronicle see W. Levison and H. Löwe, *Deutschlands Geschichtsquellen im Mittelalter*, vol. II (Weimar, 1953), pp. 265–6.

[23] *Baedae Venerabilis Historia Ecclesiastica*, V. xxiii, ed. C. Plummer (Oxford, 1896), p. 349. This is entered under the year 729, but no such devastation is otherwise known at that time.

[24] For this episode see *Chronicle of 754*, 79, pp. 94–8.

An expedition sent to the eastern Pyrenees besieged Munnuza in 'the city of Cerdanya', possibly the fortress of Llívia, and when he escaped tracked him into the mountains, where he killed himself.[25] In the captured city the victors found his wife, the daughter of Duke Eudo and symbol of their alliance, who was then sent via Spain as a present to the Caliph. The 754 chronicler was unashamedly delighted to record Munnuza's downfall, which he regarded as just retribution for the latter's killing of a bishop 'Anambadus', probably to be identified with Bishop Nambaudus of Urgel.

In these circumstances the ensuing Arab attack on Aquitaine can hardly be seen just as an act of unprovoked aggression.[26] With the elimination of Munnuza, some retribution was likely to be directed at his confederate, the duke of Aquitaine. 'Abd ar-Raḥmān launched a major raid across the western Pyrenees, which defeated the army of Duke Eudo of Aquitaine across the river Garonne. The Arab army continued its northwards advance, sacking churches as it went, with the city of Tours as its objective. However, at a site somewhere to the south of the latter city and north of Poitiers, the Arabs encountered the forces of the Frankish Mayor of the Palace Charles Martel. In the ensuing battle 'Abd ar-Raḥmān was killed, and the Arab army used the strategem of appearing to prepare to resume battle the following day whilst actually making a hasty retreat under the cover of darkness. It withdrew to Spain without further conflict.[27]

The significance of the Battle of Poitiers can be exaggerated.[28] In itself it did not put an end to Arab raids across the Pyrenees into Frankish territory. These were to continue for some while longer, and were ultimately terminated by internal divisions and civil war inside the peninsula. It would be thus most unwise to see the battle itself as marking a decisive turning point in the European expansion of Arab power and the extension of Islam. As has been suggested, the real dynamism in this direction might have expired in the early 720s. On the other hand, the very fact of 'Abd

[25] M. Delcor, 'Llívia, antiga capital de la Cerdanya', in his *Estudis historics sobre la Cerdanya* (Barcelona, 1977), pp. 35–51.

[26] J. Deviosse, *Charles Martel* (Paris, 1978), pp. 159–62.

[27] *Chronicle of 754*, 80, pp. 98–100.

[28] R. Collins, *Early Medieval Spain: Unity in Diversity, 400–1000* (London, 1983), pp. 167, 254.

ar-Raḥmān's victory over Eudo and his march through the full length of Aquitaine from south to north might suggest that the duchy's continued existence was in serious jeopardy. In the event it was to be the northern Franks who reaped the benefit of Aquitaine's weakness, though it was to take them nearly 40 years to achieve undisputed mastery over the region. Hostile Frankish chronicles portrayed the Aquitanians as conspiring with the Arabs, which is a travesty of the truth of these events, and there seem no reasons to doubt that instead it was Eudo, militarily humbled by 'Abd ar-Raḥmān, who had to call on his former adversary Charles Martel for assistance.[29]

There exist a number of chronological problems to be faced in giving a precise date to the Battle of Poitiers, and that generally accorded it, October 732, seems most likely to be wrong by either one or two years.[30] Later Arab traditions supply the precision in respect of the month.[31] In so far as the chronology of the *Chronicle of 754* has to be accepted, as being the only text which in present form is even nearly contemporary with these events, the governorship of 'Abd ar-Raḥmān must be seen as starting between March and December of 731 and lasting for a period of 'nearly three years'.[32] The appointment of his successor, in the 116th year 'of the Arabs' (i.e. Year of the Hegira) was made by the Caliph Hishām, and must therefore have taken place between February and December of 734.[33] The accompanying regnal dates given for both the

[29] M. Rouche, 'Les Aquitains ont-ils trahi avant la bataille de Poitiers?', *Le Moyen Age*, 1 (1968), pp. 5–26.

[30] See the arguments of Deviosse, *Charles Martel*, pp. 315–22; Ibn 'Abd al-Ḥakam places the death of 'Abd ar-Raḥmān in the year of the Hegira 115, which lasted from February 733 to February 734, see Ibn 'Abd al-Ḥakam, p. 33.

[31] Ibn Khaldūn, cited by Al-Maqqarī, II, p. 37; however, not as much weight should be placed on this as often has been. Al-Maqqarī quotes chronological opinions from Ibn Bashquwāl (d. 1183) that are both mutually contradictory and opposed to the dating given by Ibn Khaldūn (d. 1406). The precise month must remain uncertain. See Al-Maqqarī, II, p. 36. Ibn al-Athīr (p. 58) places the second expedition and death of al-Gafiqī in 732. Ibn 'Abd al-Ḥakam, p. 33, the earliest of the Arab references, puts the defeat and death of 'Abd ar-Raḥmān in A.H. 115 (February 733 to February 734). He immediately contradicts himself by having 'Ubayda, the governor of *Ifrīqīya* appoint a successor and then himself leave for Syria in Ramadān of 114 (October 732). This latter notice may lie at the root of the common but ill-founded belief amongst later Arab and modern historians that October 732 was the date of the battle.

[32] *Chronicle of 754*, 79, p. 96.

[33] Ibid., 81, p. 102.

Byzantine emperor Leo III and the Caliph may not be accurate in terms of absolute chronology, in that the 754 chronicler starts the reign of Leo in the year 720 rather than 717, a fault he shares with the source of the Byzantine *Chronicle of Theophanes*, and he also initiates the Caliphate of Hishām in 723 rather than January 724 as in later Arab tradition.[34] However, in terms of his own relative chronology both of these regnal dates agree with the 'Year of the Arabs' and Spanish era years that he assigns to this appointment. It must be asumed that some time lapsed before the news of the battle fought in northern Aquitaine reached the Caliph in Syria and he could despatch a new governor. From the chronological parameters of the chronicler's information it is possible to believe that the battle was fought in late 733, though not earlier, or at almost any point up to about October in 734. However, as the next governor is said to have held office for nearly four years and yet to have been replaced in 737 it is likely that his appointment was made early in 734, and that therefore the battle of Poitiers should be placed in late (October?) 733.

After the death of 'Abd ar-Raḥmān the governors of *Al-Andalus* seem rarely to have taken to the field in person in the raiding and fighting on the frontier with the Franks. This latter had been extended in the 720s to include not only all of the old Visigothic Septimania but also to take in all of the coastal region between the eastern Pyrenees and the Rhone valley. All of the major cities of the area appear in the meagre Frankish and Spanish sources as being in Arab hands. The *Chronicle of Moissac* records that in the year after the battle of Poitiers a new subordinate governor was appointed to control this marcher zone from Narbonne. This Yūsuf ibn 'Abd ar-Raḥmān took Arles in 735, and apparently 'depopulated and devastated Provence for four years'.[35] He had a long and dramatic career ahead of him.

Just as the establishment of the Berber presence in the eastern Pyrenees had seemed to open up possibilities of diplomatic manoeuvre and military co-operation for the then ruler of Aquitaine, either against the growing threat of Frankish intervention in his

[34] Ibid., 71, p. 861 Theophanes, *Chronographia*, ed. C. de Boor (Leipzig, 1883), s.a. 6212, p. 401.

[35] *Chronicle of Moissac*, s.a. 734, p. 291. N.B. the dates given are not those of the original chronicler.

duchy or against the then perhaps less menacing Arabs, so too in the 730s those in the south of France who feared the consequences of the mounting power of Charles Martel were able to look to the Arabs as a potential counterweight. It would be quite anachronistic to assume that the Provençal aristocracy or those whose primary interests lay in the south would welcome the extension into their region of the authority of the eastern Frankish Mayors of the Palace, or that a sense of Christian solidarity should mean more than the dictates of *realpolitik*.[36] For that matter it was not with any sense of obligation to free formerly Christian lands from Islamic rule that Charles Martel launched a raid into western Provence in 737. He took Avignon, but clearly did not retain it, and advanced to beseige Narbonne, the centre of Arab control of the March. The Frankish chronicles record his victory over a relieving force sent by the governor 'Uqba, but their uniform silence makes it clear that despite this he failed to take the city itself. In withdrawing he ordered the destruction of (the defences of) the city of Maguelonne and of the amphitheatre of Nîmes.[37]

A second raid by Charles in 739 was directed not so much against the Arabs as against the most prominent of their local allies, the Duke Maurontus of Marseille. Having taken Avignon for a second time, he advanced on Marseille, causing the duke to flee to a fortified island.[38] The further history of Maurontus is not known, but it is unlikely to be coincidental that the year following the raid of Charles Martel and his successful gaining of power in Marseille saw the launching of the first major expedition of a governor of *Al-Andalus* against the Franks since 733.[39] In fact it did not lead to anything in that the news of a major Berber revolt in Africa was brought to the governor when he had only reached as far as Zaragoza, but it is legitimate to speculate that the operation had been intended to restore Arab prestige and the local authority of their allies in the region of the lower Rhône valley. Another

[36] J. Deviosse, *Charles Martel*, pp. 207–11 rightly stresses the lack of appeal of Carolingian hegemony in the south. Charles's propagandist self-presentation is to be seen in the Continuations of the *Chronicle of Fredegar*, ed. J.M. Wallace-Hadrill, pp. 93–6.

[37] *Chronicle of Moissac*, s.a. 737, p. 292. Continuations of the *Chronicle of Fredegar*, 20, ed. J.M. Wallace-Hadrill, pp. 93–5.

[38] Ibid., 21, pp. 95–6.

[39] *Chronicle of 754*, 82, p. 104.

interesting sidelight on these campaigns that needs to be noticed is the statement of the Lombard historian Paul the Deacon to the effect that Charles Martel proposed joint action against the Arabs to the Lombard King Liutprand (712–44). According to Paul, a Lombard army was then sent to Provence, most probably in relation to the campaign of 737, but perhaps unsurprisingly the Frankish sources make no mention of this outside assistance.[40]

The governor sent by the Caliph to take the place of 'Abd ar-Raḥmān al-Gafīqī was a certain 'Abd al-Malik ibn Qaṭan al Fihrī, a member of the most prestigious of the Arab tribes, that of Quraysh, whose first tenure of office was to last into 737. According to the *Chronicle of 754* he was an exceedingly wealthy man of noble family. Here as elsewhere the chronicler's words seem ambiguous or hard to interpret, but they suggest that the new governor and the judges (here probably to be taken to include a variety of administrators and civil officials) he appointed proved to be highly extortionate. So much so that the land 'rich in many good things after so many and so great dangers' and seeming to be on the point of recovery – 'fully in flower after so many sorrows' – was in danger of being ruined completely and beyond hope of recovery.[41] However, Ibn Qaṭan was suddenly replaced on the orders of the governor of *Ifrīqīya* and put in chains. This would make sense in the context of what seems to be a more widespread practice, employed elsewhere in the Arab Empire in the time of Hishām, of successful regional governors being suddenly replaced by personal or factional opponents and forced by often dubious legal means to disgorge their wealth to the greater benefit of the caliphal treasury.[42] Ibn Qaṭan's subsequent career may reinforce belief in some such interpretation.

Of the details of his first governorship the *Chronicle of 754* records tantalizingly little. He does not seem to have undertaken any new expeditions against the Franks, and this apparently was by direct caliphal command. Instead he led a major expedition into the Pyrenees, but achieved nothing, and was forced by the resistance of the indigenous Christian inhabitants to retire to the plains with

[40] *Pauli Historia Langobardorum*, VI.liv, ed. G. Waitz, *MGH SRG*, p. 237.
[41] *Chronicle of 754*, 81, p. 102.
[42] P. Crone, *Slaves on Horses: the Evolution of the Islamic Polity* (Cambridge, 1980), pp. 42–5.

the loss of many of his troops.[43] This vaguely delineated operation has been taken by a number of Spanish historians as representing 'an echo of the victory of Covadonga', that is to say the battle by which in Asturian tradition Pelagius was able to secure a decisive victory over the army of one of the Arab governors, which effectively insured the independence of his tiny Christian kingdom.[44] Such a view needs to be treated with some scepticism. The chronicler mentions the Pyrenees specifically, and there are no good grounds for believing that he either did not know what he was talking about or that for him the Pyrenees extended from the Mediterranean to Galicia.[45] That there is no other account of an unsuccessful attempt to penetrate the mountains at this time needs no necessary explanation in view of the very limited nature of the sources available for the knowledge of almost any event in the peninsula at this time.

The governor sent from North Africa to replace Ibn Qaṭan was 'Uqba ibn al-Ḥajjāji as-Ṣalūli, who as well as imprisoning his predecessor also penalized his appointees.[46] This may have involved banishing them from Spain. 'Uqba was the son of the greatest of the Umayyad governors of Iraq, and may have owed his appointment to the then governor of Egypt, who was the descendant of a freedman of his family. The five years assigned to his period of office, following the chronology of the *Chronicle of 754*, must have extended from late in 737 to some point before November in 742.[47] His rule also saw the making of a new census and a more rigorous collection of the ensuing tax. It is interesting that this should not have attracted the chronicler's censure in the way that the self-enriching activities of the previous governor and his cronies had. Once again, a purely Spanish approach to these events can obscure their wider context. As has been mentioned, Hishām's regime in Syria was noted in later Arab accounts for its

[43] *Chronicle of 754*, 81, p. 102.

[44] J. Pérez de Urbel, in *Historia de España*, ed. R. Menéndez Pidal, vol. VI (Madrid, 1956), p. 29.

[45] Al-Maqqarī, II, p. 37, is categoric that the expedition was directed against the Basques.

[46] *Chronicle of 754*, 82, p. 104; Ibn 'Abd al-Ḥakam, p. 34.

[47] *Chronicle of 754*, 82, p. 104. Most of the Arab sources would place the end of his governorship in 739, which would contradict the evidence relating to his part in opposing the Berbers; see Lafuente's discussion in *Ajbar Machmua*, appendix III, p. 237. Ibn al-Athīr, p. 69 puts his death into the year of the Hegira 123 (25 Nov. 740–13 Nov. 741).

fiscal rapacity, which on occasion could lead to regional revolts, and it is likely that 'Uqba was responding to pressures from the caliphal court, transmitted via his immediate superior in *Ifrīqīya*.

One short statement in the *Chronicle of 754* has long gone unnoticed and uncommented on, but indicates a vital stage in the normalizing of relations between the Arabs and their indigenous non-Muslim subjects in the peninsula. Of 'Uqba the chronicler writes that 'he condemned no one except by the justice of his own law' (*iustitia legis propriae*).[48] As its use in other contexts indicates, the term *lex propria* indicates personality of the law, that is to say each man would be judged according to the rules of the law of his own particular people. This was a standard practice under the Carolingians, who ruled over a large number of disparate peoples, ranging from Lombards and Visigoths to Saxons and Frisians, as well as various types of Frank, and each man was entitled to judgement under the law of his particular *gens*.[49] In the same way, it seems, the Arabs in Spain guaranteed the continued application of the rules of the Visigothic law code, the *Forum Iudicum* to their indigenous Christian subjects.[50] Indeed, it is hard to see how they could have done other, in that the norms of Muslim law, as enshrined in the Koran, could have hardly been applied to non-believers. However, the survival of an independent body of indigenous law could play a vital role in the maintenance of a sense of separate group identity.

The preservation of substantial pockets of local self-government, as evidenced by the treaty made with Theodemir, and the large measure of continuity that clearly existed in such areas as law and administration between the Visigothic and Arab regimes as far as the bulk of the population of the peninsula was concerned indicate the considerable distancing that existed between conquerors and conquered in the first four decades of Arab rule in Spain. A

[48] *Chronicle of 754*, 82, p. 104; here J. E. López Perreira translates *neminem nisi per iustitiam legis propriae damnat as* ' No castiga a nadie, as no ser de acuerdo con la justicia'.

[49] On personality of law see R. Büchner, *Die Rechtsquellen*, supplementary volume to Wattenbach–Levison, *Deutschlands Geschichtsquellen im Mittelalter* (Weimar, 1953), p. 5 and n. 12; see the use of 'legem propriam' in the text quoted.

[50] R. Collins, 'Visigothic law and regional custom in disputes in early medieval Spain', in *The Settlement of Disputes in Early Medieval Europe* (Cambridge, 1986), pp. 85–104, especially pp. 96–7, analysing a legal text from Muslim-ruled Lérida.

number of garrison towns had been created by the Arab and Berber troops, including both Córdoba and Narbonne and perhaps also Zaragoza.[51] In the case of Narbonne at least this had been preceded by the slaughter or enslavement of the indigenous population.[52] Such centres of military control and supervision existed elsewhere in the Arab world, as for example at Baṣra and Kufāh in Iraq and Kairouan in *Ifrīqīya*. They testify to the initial, purely military nature of the Arab occupation of their newly-conquered territories, but, as with the other parts of the Arab Empire, this had to give way in a short passage of time to a more complex set of interrelationships between the conquerors and their subject populations.

Arab versus Berber, Arab versus Arab

Some consideration has already been given to the reasons for the Arabs' initial success in Spain, and how the elimination of the central institutions of the previous Visigothic monarchy effectively prevented the resurgence of any form of centralized resistance. The treaties made with towns and local potentates, together with the salutary examples made of those who did resist, played a vital part in dissuading those who might have contemplated it from essaying a purely localized opposition. Yet when this was attempted, in the Asturias in 718 or 722, it proved completely successful, and, very surprisingly, after the initial revolt the Arabs made no serious effort to eliminate the minute Christian kingdom that thus came into being in the north of the peninsula. It almost looks as if in the period of the rapid expansion of the Arab empire continuity in the process of conquest was more important than the consolidation of the conquerors' hold on the territories thus acquired. It is probably worth looking back over the period of the first two decades of the Arab presence in the Iberian peninsula to form some impression of the role and functioning of their military forces during those crucial years.

It is not now possible to know with certainty the size of the Arab and Berber armies that took part in the conquest of the Iberian peninsula; the figures given by some of the Arab sources

[51] *Chronicle of 754*, 64, 69, pp. 80, 84; Al-Maqqarī, II, p. 37.
[52] *Chronicle of Moissac*, s.a. 721, p. 290.

do not command respect.[53] However, it is unlikely that very large numbers are involved or were required. To take parallels from an earlier but not dissimilar period, for the conquest of Vandal Africa in 533 a Byzantine army of 15,000 sufficed, and a force exactly half that size was sent to Italy in 535, though this proved too small for the task to be undertaken.[54] An assumption that the Arab and Berber forces operating in Spain around the year 712 totalled no more than 15,000 men would seem to be realistic. This concurs with the figure of 12,000 ascribed to the army commanded by Ṭāriq given in the entry on Mūsā ibn Nuṣayr in Ibn Khallikān's biographical dictionary.[55] Problems of commissariat alone would make a larger army very difficult to maintain.

The precise composition of the armies, at least two of which seem to have been functioning in 711, is equally difficult to determine. The role of the Berbers was probably crucial, but subsequent racial and cultural antagonisms between Arab and Berber have led to the underplaying or distortion of their part in these proceedings in the later Islamic accounts, which were all written from an Arab perspective.[56] Not until the work of the fourteenth-century historian Ibn Khaldūn did the Berbers find a significant voice of their own, and even he was totally dependent on the work of Arab predecessors. Once again the traditions used by Ibn Khallikān take us closer to the realities of the early eighth century than some of the Spanish Arab accounts. He records that not only was the composition of Ṭāriq's army almost exclusively Berber but also that Ṭāriq himself was a Berber, attached by clientage to an Arab tribe.[57]

No reinforcements had been sent from the heartlands of the Caliphate to Africa at the time of the apparently unpremeditated invasion of Spain in 711. Nor, it is clear enough, could the newly-established province of *Ifrīqīya* have been denuded of its

[53] E.g. the figure of 100,000 given by Al-Maqqarī, I, p. 269 for the size of the Visigothic army. However, the traditions he reports as to the composition of the invaders' forces, which range from 7,000 to 12,000 if mutually contradictory, are much closer to the realm of the probable. Ibid., pp. 266–7.

[54] Procopius, *History of the Wars*, III.xi.2, V.v.2, ed. H.B. Dewing, vol. II, p. 102, vol. III, p. 42.

[55] Ibn Khallikān, tr. J. MacGuckin de Slane, vol. III, (Paris, 1868), p. 476.

[56] H.T. Norris, *The Berbers in Arab Literature* (London and Beirut, 1982), especially chs 3 and 4.

[57] Ibn Khallikān, tr. J. MacGuckin de Slane, vol. III, p. 476.

Arab garrisons in the interests of promoting the venture in the Iberian peninsula. Thus the belief that the Berbers, recruited from a small number of the most powerful of the tribes in North Africa, provided the greater proportion of the manpower for the conquest seems eminently reasonable. The impression must be that the Arabs, having after a hard struggle defeated the indigenous peoples of North Africa, quickly used them to attack the next victim, in this case the Visigothic kingdom.[58] Thus it could be argued that they were taking an important step in the consolidation of the conquest of Africa in undertaking the invasion of Spain. Might the same process have begun to be applied in the Iberian peninsula with the rapid extension of fighting and conquest across the Pyrenees? This is at least plausible, and would assume some degree of the use of elements of the indigenous population of Spain in the attacks on Aquitaine.

However, as has been seen, with the exception of the campaign that culminated in the battle of Poitiers, the further expansion of Arab control north of the Pyrenees seems to have lost much of its impetus in the 720s. There is a phenomenon to be encountered elsewhere on the fringes of the Arab empire in the first half of the eighth century which may help to explain this. As can be seen in the cases of the Taurus Mountains, the Atlas and the Hindu-Kush, Arab armies which were masters of warfare on the plains, proved much less effective in mountainous terrain.[59] In general the Arabs proved incapable of extending their control into new territory divided from their main bases by major mountain chains. They could, as with a series of annual incursions into Asia Minor, make successful raids into such areas, but these never developed into territorial conquests.

Another factor that needs at least contemplation in the case of conditions in Spain before the Arab conquest is the absence of a social organization easily adaptable by the Arabs for military mobilization. Apart from the armed following of the kings, the *comitatus*, probably a quite small body, which provided the nucleus of necessary trained manpower for any military operation, the Visigothic army consisted of local levies under the control of

[58] For the Arab conquest of North Africa see P. Hitti, *A History of the Arabs* (8th edn, London, 1964), pp. 213–14.

[59] Ibid., pp. 206–13.

the nobility. Major military undertakings were rare in the late seventh century, and certainly one king complained about the non-appearance on campaign of those supposed to turn out.[60] The royal *comitatus* was almost certainly destroyed in the course of the fighting in 711/12, and the system of military recruitment existing in the Visigothic kingdom was not suited to the kind of long distance campaigning typical of the wars conducted by the Arabs. Thus, unlike the Berbers, the army of the Visigothic state could not be easily turned into a new source of military manpower for the conquerors in extending their power into new areas. It is notable that such treaties as that made by 'Abd al-Azīz ibn Mūsā with Theodemir do not envisage military assistance being given by the indigenous inhabitants to the Arab governors. Whilst the tribal structures of Berber society in North Africa made recruitment of whole units relatively easy, especially if under the command of leaders of indigenous origin, the mobilization of Spanish resources of manpower, as in the case of those from many other parts of the Arab Empire, would have required a more complex form of integration into the society of the conquerors. Once the initial and really quite short period of continuing military activity and expansion up to and beyond the Pyrenees was over, the character of the Arab occupation of the peninsula was bound to change.

There has been a powerful tendency in the Spanish historiographical tradition over the last few generations towards minimizing the impact of the Arab conquest on the indigenous society of the peninsula.[61] To put the argument simply, the proponents of such a view would rather see the Arabs Hispanized than the peninsula Arabized. To some degree such a view has depended on a prior ideological commitment to belief in a quality of 'Spanishness' or *Hispanidad* that proved able to impose itself on all conquerors and inhabitants of the peninsula from the earliest times. This represents a kind of cultural-geographical determinism of a peculiarly Ro-

[60] *Leges Visigothorum*, IX.ii.8, ed. K. Zeumer, pp. 370–3; see also E.A. Thompson, *The Goths in Spain* (Oxford, 1969), pp. 262–7.

[61] This underlies the arguments of C. Sánchez-Albornoz, *España un enigma histórica* (2 vols, Buenos Aires, 1956). A variant approach would see a mass conversion to Islam having taken place amongst the indigenous population rather than an invasion: this reached its most extreme form in I. Olagüe, *Les Arabes n'ont jamais envahi l'Espagne* (Paris, 1966); see the riposte of P. Guichard, 'Les Arabes ont bien envahi l'Espagne: les structures sociales de l'Espagne musulmane', *Annales E.S.C.*, 29 (1974), pp. 1483–513.

mantic kind. However, some of the particular arguments of those who would minimize the discontinuities of the impact of the Arab conquest have more serious foundations. Not least amongst these would be various interpretations that stress the rapid breakdown of traditional Arab social structures in the aftermath of their establishment in the peninsula.

Such approaches have recently been countered by a study that has been able to demonstrate continuity in the use of tribal labelling amongst the various Arab sectors of the population in the peninsula during at least the first three centuries following the conquest.[62] At the same time it has proved possible to show how far distinctive forms of social organization were retained amongst the Berbers, who made up the other major and non-indigenous component of the population.[63] With the latter part of the argument there is little need to quibble, in that it has never been suggested that Berber society was permeable, and what may be called the nationalist historiography has tended to visualize the Arabs as being assimilated and hispanized whilst the Berbers remained isolated and irrevocably alien. The question of the survival of tribal organization and nomenclature amongst the Arabs, however, is not a self-evident solution to the particular problem at issue. This is because the significance of tribal identities amongst the Arabs in the century following the establishment of the Caliphate has become a subject of considerable debate. The argument thus becomes one that needs to be placed in a wider context than just that of eighth-century Spain.

Contemporary Arab sources of evidence are as much lacking for the principal areas of the Arabs' conquests and settlement in the Near East and the eastern Mediterranean as for their territories in the West. Thus for much of the history of the period of the ascendancy of the Umayyad dynasty (661–750) recourse has to be made to the narrative of the great history of the Persian writer al-Ṭabarī (839–922/3).[64] Valuable as his presentation of the events in Syria, Egypt and Iraq in the early eighth century may be, it is

[62] P. Guichard, *Tribus arabes et berbères en Al-Andalus* (Paris, 1973); Spanish tr. *Al-Andalus: estructura antropológica de una sociedad islámica en occidente* (Barcelona, 1976).

[63] Ibid., pp. 365–409 of the Spanish tr.

[64] On whom see the article by R. Paret, 'al-TABARI', in *Shorter Encyclopedia of Islam*, eds H. A. R. Gibb and J. H. Kramers (Leiden/London, 1961), pp. 556–7.

inevitably coloured by the perceptions and expectations of the period in which he was writing. Simply put, the picture that is presented of the politics of the late Umayyad state in the works of Ṭabarī and other later Arab authors is one of factional conflict, centring on two more or less evenly balanced tribal confederacies, those of the Qays and the Kalb. Fluctuations in the Caliphal support for or use of these two groupings appear to constitute the dynamics of the politics and power struggles of the later Umayyad state.

Taking the Arab accounts at face value has led some historians to postulate the existence of a great traditional feud between the tribes of southern Arabia, known collectively as the Yemenis (or the Kalb), and those of the north, represented by the Qays.[65] Such an interpretation is not only inherently improbable, but finds no substantiation in the materials relating to Arab society in the lifetime of Muḥammad, let alone earlier. Rightly dissatisfied with an explanation that had both acquired the status of orthodoxy and failed to be intellectually satisfying, other scholars have sought to interpret the evidence relating to factional conflicts in the period of the 720s to 740s in terms of divergences over policy. Thus one view makes the conflict one between those anxious to preserve the momentum of conquest and the distinctions between conquerors and conquered and those concerned to achieve a consolidation and assimilation of the two elements.[66] More recently still it has been suggested that what was taking place was no more than a naked power struggle between two rival military factions anxious to monopolize the routes to wealth and influence, for whom tribal labelling provided a convenient way of articulating group identity.[67]

In other words the modern interpretations of the important, if evidentially obscure, military and political conflicts of the late Umayyad state depend upon a belief that the nature of the tribal organization of Arab society altered significantly in the century following the beginning of the period of the conquests in the 630s. The tribes themselves were in composition, though not in structure, transformed from what they had been in the time of Muḥammad. Such a conclusion is perhaps less surprising than the one

[65] J. Welhausen, *Das arabische Reich und sein Sturz* (Berlin, 1902), Introduction, section 9.
[66] M.A. Shaban, *Islamic History*, pp. 120–4.
[67] P. Crone, *Slaves on Horses*, pp. 42–8.

inherent in the older view, which implicitly postulates the conquest and subsequent occupation of an enormous swathe of territory, extending in this case from just north of the Pyrenees to the fringes of India, by a numerically small body of men. Theoretically, the initial achievement of such a conquest might be conceivable on such basis, but its subsequent longevity and the effective absorption of so many new cultural elements by the conquered population is not.

This brief synopsis of the historiographical debate will at least have made it clear that these are not questions that can expect to be answered satisfactorily in an exclusively Spanish context. Equally obvious must be the fact that in the present state of the argument no clear resolution can be seen. Indeed, such are the problems of the evidence, that one may never emerge that commands universal assent. However, the existence of powerful challenges to older certainties and orthodoxies of dubious worth is an important advance in its own right. As far as the Spanish dimension of the argument is concerned, the extreme 'Hispanization' view is flawed even in some of its initial premises and may be discarded. The reply that stresses almost a total impermeability on the part of Arab tribal society to elements of the indigenous culture of the peninsula is probably equally extreme, though its value in demonstrating the fundamental divisions between Arab and Berber social structures and the particular tenacity of the latter should not be underestimated. There did exist ways in which elements of indigenous society could be assimilated fairly rapidly into that of the conquerors, or at least the politically dominant if numerically small Arab sector of it.

The techniques of assimilation from the Arab point of view were limited but effective. The consequences of conquest over such large areas of territory included the assimilation of a substantial body of slaves. This could include men trained in or capable of fighting. Certainly in the East the limited resources of Arab manpower in the *junds* or armies were reinforced by the addition of individual former slaves, who as freedmen were attached to the different tribes of their former masters and still bound by a number of formal ties to their particular previous owners. As has been mentioned quite a number of the most prominent of the Arab generals of the early eighth century were either freedmen or the immediate descendants of them. In the case of Mūsā ibn Nuṣayr, his grandfather had been a Syrian townsman captured and enslaved in the course of one of the earliest of the Arab campaigns. His son, Mūsā's father, had been emancipated by his master the Umayyad Caliph Mu'āwiya (661–81), the commander of whose personal guard he became.[68] The nature of the ties of personal dependency involved in the *mawali* or client relationship made him peculiarly fitted for such a sensitive task. His son in turn could become initially at least, a trusted viceroy of the Umayyads in a vital frontier region.

The relationship itself was obviously direct in terms of the man freed and his former master, but it also created less legally definable but socially powerful bonds of obligation between their descendants.[69] Thus, 'Ubaydallāh ibn al-Ḥabab, the governor of Egypt appointed by the Caliph in 734, is said to have immediately offered the choice of either of the two great dependent governorships under him, those of *Ifrīqīya* and of *Al-Andalus* to 'Uqba ibn al-Ḥajjāji. The latter, already rather elderly, was the son of the great al-Ḥajjaj, who had been governor of Iraq from 695 to 714 and the most powerful man in the eastern Arab territories for most of that time. However, his family had subsequently fallen from grace and trust. The appointment of 'Uqba, by his own choice to *Al-Andalus*, was made solely on the grounds that his father had manumitted 'Ubaydallāh's grandfather. 'Ubaydallāh is also said to have denounced his own sons for criticizing his decision.[70] Despite the current low standing of 'Uqba and the prominence of that of the new governor of Egypt, the former ties of clientage remained sacred to 'Ubaydallāh, if not his sons.

These bonds, particularly in the first generations of a clientage relationship were obviously very important in the making of military command structures, not least for the Caliphs themselves. Their initial tendency to give viceregal and army commands to members of their own family or of their tribe of Quraysh increasingly gave way to the selection of *mawalis* of the Umayyad house instead.[71] To what extent such relationships were important in the building up of what may be called the rank and file of the Arab

[68] Ibn Khallikān, tr. J. MacGuckin de Slane, vol. III, p. 475.
[69] On clientage see P. Crone, *Slaves on Horses*, pp. 49–57.
[70] *Akhbar Machmua*, pp. 37–8.
[71] P. Crone, *Slaves on Horses*, pp. 32, 39.

armies at this time is not so easy to say, as the sources concentrate almost exclusively on the doings of the leaders rather than of the led. There does not seem to have been any use of slave soldiers *en masse* at this time. That was to be essentially a ninth-century development.[72] The stress still placed on the tribal organization of warfare meant that only full members of tribal society or those integrated into it by bonds of clientage or emancipation from slave status would be expected to fight, and to obtain the rewards of so doing.

The system of clientage has been thought to show many traces of continuity with practices current in the Late Roman Empire.[73] Indeed the same similarities can be detected between the Arab form of clientage and the legal relationship that existed between freedmen and their former masters in the Early Medieval West, where the imprint of Roman ideas and procedures also remained strong. In particular a substantial amount of evidence relating to the ties between freedmen and those who had manumitted them can be found in the legal and also the hagiographical texts of Visigothic Spain.[74] Thus in themselves the clientage relationships introduced into the peninsula by the Arabs harmonized closely with a pre-existing form of social relationship. On the other hand, however, the acceptance of Islam looks to have been a necessary pre-condition to the making of such a clientage relationship based on the emancipation of slaves.

Unfortunately there are no ways of knowing quantitatively the extent to which such forms of assimilation were being practised in the Iberian peninsula in the period of the rule of the governors. Certainly a substantial number of *mawalis* or clients of the Umayyad house were to be found in Spain in 756.[75] It is possible that

[72] M.A. Shaban, *Islamic History. A New Interpretation, 2, A.D. 750–1055* (Cambridge, 1976), pp. 63–6, doubts its existence even then, but see P. Crone, *Slaves on Horses*, pp. 74–81.

[73] P. Crone, *Roman, Provincial and Islamic Law* (Cambridge, 1987), argues for its essential rooting in 'the indigenous law of the Near East as it developed after Alexander' (p. 99); something that in other contexts might be called Roman 'vulgar law'.

[74] On the obligations of freedmen see Title 7 of Book V of the *Forum Iudicum* in *Leges Visigothorum*, ed. K. Zeumer, pp. 235–45; also Canons 67–74 of IV Toledo, ed. J. Vives, *Concilios*, pp. 30–3, and Canons 11–16 of IX Toledo, pp. 7–9. For a hagiographical text see *Vitas Patrum Emeretensium*, V.xiii.4–7, ed. J.N. Garvin (Washington, 1946), pp. 248–50.

[75] Al-Maqqarī, II, p. 62, which reports that there were 4000–5000 of them enrolled in the Arab *jund* in *Al-Andalus* in 756.

many of these had been sent into the peninsula from the eastern Mediterranean or North Africa in the course of the fighting that took place in Spain in the 740s. On the other hand, the story of Theodemir's visit to the Caliph to obtain confirmation of the treaty made with 'Abd al-Azīz ibn Mūsā, indicates that the making of personal ties of dependency between Spaniards and the Arab ruling house was not inconceivable.[76]

The treatment of Narbonne in 720 is, however, revealing. The slaughter of the men and the enslavement of the women and children would seem to indicate that the Arabs' priorities, at least in that area and at that time, were different.[77] They either did not want or could not use the adult male population. Slave children could in due course have been expected to provide additional resources of military manpower, but the enslavement of the women is particularly interesting. An over-great concentration on the tribal organization of Arab society and on the doings of the menfolk has left unasked the rather obvious but neglected question of whether the Arab conquerors of Spain, or most other parts of the Arab world for that matter, had brought wives and families with them. The speed of movement of the Arab armies, as well as the fighting practices of modern desert Arab societies, might suggest they had not. Thus the probability must be that a substantial proportion of the conquerors would be interested in the acquisition of local women. In view of the limited nature of the evidence in general it is perhaps not surprising that information on such domestic details is hard to come by. In the only known case relating to the family arrangements of one of the Arab leaders, that of 'Abd al-Azīz ibn Mūsā, one of the conquerors rapidly took an indigenous wife.[78]

Towards the end of his five-year governorship, which lasted from 737 to 742, 'Uqba planned a major expedition into Frankish territory, probably the first large scale operation since the disaster of 733, and to be connected with the after effects of Charles Martel's campaigning in the lower Rhône valley in 739.[79] However, when he was advancing with his forces into the Ebro valley,

[76] *Chronicle of 754*, 87, p. 114; ibid., 56, p. 74 reports that Mūsā took many of the Spanish nobles back with him to Syria in 712 to be presented to the Caliph. See also J.B. Vilar, *Orihuela musulmana* (Murcia, 1976), pp. 40–1.

[77] *Chronicle of Moissac*, s.a. 721, p. 290.

[78] *Chronicle of 754*, 59, p. 78.

[79] See above pp. 92–3.

he was informed at Zaragoza of a major Berber revolt in Africa, which led to his immediate withdrawal to Córdoba. In fact so menacing did conditions in Africa become that he launched his army, via the mysterious 'Transductine Promontories', which had seen the defeat of Roderic, into Africa instead. The chronicler's account of the campaign is tantalizingly brief, but seems to suggest that initial Arab attacks on the Berber fortresses were unsuccessful, but subsequently the governor was able to slaughter all the 'traitors and double dealers or workers of evil and those heretics who are called the *Arures*' whom he encountered. He then secured the crossing points into Spain, in the form of the equally mysterious 'Trinacrios portus', before returning to his own governorship, where soon after he was to die from natural causes.

The account of the earliest Arab history to deal with events in North Africa and Spain, that of Ibn 'Abd al-Ḥakam, written *c*.850, usefully complements the *Chronicle of 754* in its version of this episode, which was in fact to be but the start of a series of complicated and bloodthirsty events.[80] It is necessary to try to make sense of them here because of their role in determining the political development of *Al-Andalus* in the second half of the eighth century. Ibn 'Abd al-Ḥakam records a major Berber revolt under the leadership of one Maṣayra in the region of Tangiers in the year 740/1. Interestingly, amongst other prominent supporters of the revolt was a certain 'Abdallāh ibn Ḥodayj, described as being a Greek, which is to say of Byzantine origin, and a former freedman of Mūsā ibn Nuṣayr, the conqueror of Spain. He was made governor of Tangiers by Maṣayra. The army sent against them by the governor of *Ifrīqīya* was destroyed, and the revolt spread, even though its initial leader Maṣayra was soon killed by his own followers. Another army under Ḥabīb ibn Abi 'Ubayda, grandson of 'Uqba ibn Nāfi', the founder of Kairouan and pioneer of Arab expansion in North Africa, was unable to advance further west than Tlemcen.[81]

[80] On Ibn 'Abd al-Ḥakam see D.M. Dunlop, *Arab Civilisation to A.D. 1500* (London and Beirut, 1971), pp. 116–17, and C. Sánchez-Albornoz, *En torno a los orígenes del feudalismo, 2, Fuentes de la historia hispano-musulmana del siglo VIII* (2nd edn, Buenos Aires, 1977), pp. 64–8.

[81] Ibn 'Abd al-Ḥakam, pp. 34–5. Also Ibn 'Idhārī, I, pp. 50–6; Ibn al-Qūṭiyya, pp. 11–12; Ibn al-Athīr, pp. 63–6.

These events in Africa in the early 740s were soon to make a dramatic impact on Spain. Berber discontent there and the close links between the Berbers in Africa and those in the peninsula were demonstrated in the episode of Munnuza's putative revolt in the Pyrenees in 731. The problems of racial conflict in Africa and the treatment of the Berbers by the numerically inferior Arabs look to have been exacerbated by the remarkably rapid acceptance of Islam by many of the former.[82] In itself Islam was a totally egalitarian religion, but its particular genesis and its linking with the extraordinary military conquests of the Arabs made it hard for many of its proponents not to regard it as a purely Arab preserve. In general the rate of conversion to Islam amongst the subject peoples of the Arab empire looks to have been slow, and certainly little pressure to convert was explicitly directed towards them.[83] In this, however, the Berbers may have been a major exception.

In part the tribal basis of Berber society may have made mass conversion not only easier, but also socially the only acceptable form of major religious change. This had certainly been the case with the Arabs in the earliest days of Islam. Doubtless, Christian and even pagan Berber tribes still existed in parts of North Africa, but it is important to note that the great Berber revolt of the early 740s was in no sense an anti-Islamic movement. According to the Arab sources Maṣayra proclaimed himself Caliph, and after his murder another Berber leader was to do likewise at Tunis.[84] That is to say they were naming themselves to be the true leaders of the Islamic community. In addition, the 'heretics' or *Arures* mentioned by the *Chronicle of 754* are probably to be identified with the Ibadites, members of an Islamic fundamentalist movement amongst the Berbers.[85] The religious dimension to the revolt was thus largely centred around a set of variant forms of Islam, rather than constituting an attempt to overthrow it.

[82] On the speed of Berber conversion, here possibly exaggerated, see Ibn 'Abd al-Ḥakam, p. 29; in general, M. Sadok Bel Ochi, *La conversion des Berbères à l'Islam* (Tunis, 1981).

[83] On conversion see R.W. Bulliet, *Conversion to Islam in the Medieval Period: an Essay in Quantative History* (Cambridge, Mass., 1979); for Africa and Spain see pp. 99–103, 114–27.

[84] Ibn 'Abd al-Ḥakam, pp. 34, 39; *Akhbar Machmua*, p. 39–41.

[85] *Akhbar Machmua*, p. 39 identifies them as Ibadites, on whom see the articles, 'KHARIDJITES' and 'IBADIYA' in the *Shorter Encyclopedia of Islam*, pp. 246–8, 143–5. Also Ibn al-Athīr, p. 63 for Maṣayra as a Kharijite.

Whether or not it was due to the failure of his lieutenants to suppress the Berber insurrection, the Caliph removed 'Ubaydallāh ibn al-Ḥabab from control in Egypt and Africa in 741, and sent out a new governor called Kulṭum with an army made up of detachments drawn from the various units of the Syrian army, the principal fighting force of the Umayyad state. To Kulṭum and his deputy and nephew Balj ibn Bishr were subordinated the various local Arab leaders in North Africa, with the primary task of confronting and destroying the Berber rebels in Tangiers. According to the Arab accounts, Kulṭum's misplaced disdain for and refusal to benefit from the local knowledge of the leaders of the Arab communities in North Africa led to disaster. His army was routed by the Berbers in the vicinity of Tangiers, and he and many others, including the African veteran Ḥabīb ibn Abi 'Ubayda, were killed.[86]

Not surprisingly, this new success led to a series of further Berber revolts all along the North African coast as far as Tunis, and Kairouan itself was threatened. At the same time the Berber military colonies in Spain broke out into an anti-Arab revolt. The remnants of the Syrian army, now under the leadership of Balj, had managed to take refuge in Ceuta, and had resisted successive Berber attacks, but were clearly cut off from hope of withdrawing towards Kairouan.[87] It was in these circumstances that they came to play a role in the increasingly disorderly events in Spain. Probably early in 742 the governor of *Al-Andalus*, 'Uqba ibn al-Ḥajjāji had died. The *Chronicle of 754* reports variant accounts of what happened next.[88] At one point the chronicler states that the dying 'Uqba designated his own successor in the person of 'Abd al-Malik ibn Qaṭan, the very man he himself had replaced and imprisoned, but only a few lines later he describes ibn Qaṭan as having taken power in Spain again 'by election of the Arabs'. Certainly, some of the Arab sources state that Ibn Qaṭan seized power illegally and not by appointment of either the Caliph or his

[86] *Akhbar Machmua*, pp. 42–5, Ibn 'Abd al-Ḥakam, pp. 36–7; Ibn al Athīr, pp. 64–5; Ibn 'Idārī, I, pp. 52–6.

[87] Ibn 'Abd al-Ḥakam, p. 37, *Chronicle of 754*, 84–5, pp. 106–10, *Akhbar Machmua*, pp. 45–7.

[88] *Chronicle of 754*, 84, p. 106: *consensu omnium*, cf. 82, p. 104: (Uqbah) *Abdilmelic prefato regnum restaurans*.

viceroy in Africa.[89] However, as his resumption of office looks to have coincided with both the killing of the new viceroy and the breaking of communications with the East as a result of the Berber revolt, such niceties were hardly practicable. It did, though, leave him in a constitutionally weak position.

He was also faced with the Berber risings in the peninsula itself, which according to one later Arab account had already led to the flight of the Arabs from much of the north of the peninsula other than the Ebro valley.[90] The Berbers were then threatening Toledo. In these circumstances a mutually beneficial agreement was reached between Ibn Qaṭan in Córdoba and Balj ibn Bishr stranded in Ceuta. The former agreed to provide the ships to transport the latter and his much needed army across to Spain in return for their military aid against the Berbers in the peninsula. However, Ibn Qaṭan, whose own standing seems to have been far from clear, was obviously unwilling to envisage Balj and his Syrians subsequently remaining in *Al-Andalus*, and, according to the Arab accounts, he required them to agree that they would not remain in the country after the end of the campaign.[91]

He was right to be concerned, if ultimately powerless to enforce his allies' removal. The Syrian and Andalusī Arab forces proved capable of eliminating the Berber threat in Spain fairly rapidly. The Berbers had divided their forces into three columns: one was intended for the capture of Toledo, another to kill Ibn Qaṭan in Córdoba, and the third to take the defences of the Straits of Gibraltar from the north and then to cross to link up with the Berber forces threatening Ceuta. All three of the columns met with disaster. Twelve miles from Toledo the main Berber force, which had been besieging the city for a month, was defeated by an army under Ibn Qaṭan's son. The column advancing on Córdoba, perhaps from Mérida, was driven back, though with the loss of the Arab general, whilst Balj's Syrian and North African forces, transported from Ceuta, eliminated the final Berber army near Algeciras. When, with the Berber threat removed, Ibn Qaṭan required

[89] *Akhbar Machmua*, p. 41. Ibn al-Athīr records both traditions, pp. 65 and 69, without resolving the conflict.

[90] *Akhbar Machmua*, p. 48.

[91] *Akhbar Machmua*, pp. 47–8. Ibn al-Athīr, p. 70 records two different versions of Ibn Qaṭan's dealings with Balj; in one of them he agrees to admit the Syrians to Spain for the space of no more than one year; see also Ibn 'Idārī, I, p. 56.

Balj to honour the agreement and return to Africa, the latter, not surprisingly perhaps in view of the fact that the fighting there was far from over, immediately marched on Córdoba, and captured and killed Ibn Qaṭan, whose own troops were still with his son in the vicinity of Toledo.[92]

Balj is not treated as a governor or 'king' of Spain in the *Chronicle of 754*, although he does feature as such in the later Arab accounts.[93] What his ultimate intentions may have been cannot be gauged, in that within a month of his killing of Ibn Qaṭan he faced the latter's army under the command of his son 'Ummaya, reinforced by North African troops led by 'Abd ar-Raḥmān ibn Ḥabīb, who blamed the Syrians for his father's death. In the ensuing battle Balj was killed, but his opponents failed to win an outright victory. A certain Ṭalāma ibn Salāma, one of Balj's lieutenants, took over the leadership of the Syrians, and effectively a full scale civil war seems to have ensued between them on the one hand and the Andalusī Arabs and their African allies on the other.[94]

This was only terminated by the restoration of order in North Africa. In the aftermath of the destruction of Kulṭum the Berbers had seemed on the point of completely overthrowing the Arab hold, but under rival leaders and without a co-ordinated strategy they lost their opportunity. The Arabs in Kairouan were able to defeat two threatening Berber armies that failed to act together, and thus held the city until the arrival late in 742 of a new governor sent from the East with reinforcements. This was Ḥanẓala ibn Safwān, recently appointed governor of Egypt.[95] Within a year he was able to suppress the Berber revolts in Africa, and what is more to despatch a new legitimate governor into *Al-Andalus*. His appointee, Abu al-Ḳattar, was in turn able with the threat of his superior's power behind him to impose a settlement on the warring

[92] Cf. *Akhbar Machmua*, pp. 49–50. Ibn 'Abd al-Ḥakam, p. 37, gives an alternative tradition to the effect that Balj as the deputy of Kulṭum, who had been the Caliph's appointee, successfully required Ibn Qaṭan to surrender the governorship of *Al-Andalus* to himself, and then executed him. *Chronicle of 754*, 86, p. 110, the work of a contemporary observer and historian of these civil wars, provides the outline given here. Ibn al-Athīr, p. 71 states that it was the prospect of being sent back to fight the Berbers that led the Syrians to attack Ibn Qaṭan.

[93] Ibn 'Abd al-Ḥakam, pp. 37–8; Al-Maqqarī, II, p. 43.

[94] *Chronicle of 754*, 86, p. 112 (and 94, p. 126 for Ṭalāma); *Akhbar Machmua*, pp. 52–4; Al-Maqqarī, II, pp. 43–5.

[95] Ibn 'Abd al-Ḥakam, pp. 38–9; Ibn al-Athīr, p. 73.

factions in Spain, and to ship Ṭalāma and some of his Syrians back to Africa. He also arranged for the removal of 'Abd ar-Raḥmān ibn Ḥabīb and at least some of the African Arabs, who had been using Spain as a theatre for their revenge on the Syrians.[96]

Thus, in both Africa and Spain the end of the year 743 should have seen the end of nearly three years of constant and savage fighting, and the restoration of control over these regions of the distant Umayyad Caliphs. Unfortunately for the latter, it also saw the death of the Caliph Hishām and the succession of his nephew Walīd II. Within a year the latter's supposedly unorthodox and un-Islamic lifestyle, and more significantly his mishandling of factional politics in Syria had led to a military insurrection and the murder of the new Caliph in one of his palaces.[97] With this subversion of authority in the centre the all too recently closed wounds in the periphery were re-opened. A major revolt broke out in Africa led now by the indigenous Arabs of the region under the leadership of 'Abd ar-Raḥmān ibn Ḥabīb, the great-grandson of 'Uqba ibn Nāfi'. Without caliphal support Ḥanẓala was forced to evacuate *Ifrīqīya*. At the same time the news of the murder of Walīd II led to a revolt in 744 against Abu al-Ḳattar, his appointee in Spain.[98]

The instigator of the revolt was a certain Ismā'ȳl, one of the leading members of the Spanish Arab community in Córdoba, the principal residence of the governors. Warned of what was happening, Abu al-Ḳattar was able to kill the rebel leader, but was forced out of the city. There followed yet another civil war that lasted for most of two years before the rebels were finally able to eliminate the former governor and his supporters, leaving the way open for the proclamation in 746 of Ṭawāba ibn Yazīd, one of the original leaders of the revolt, as the new *wali*.[99] On his death from natural

[96] Ibn 'Abd al-Ḥakam, p. 39; *Akhbar Machmua*, p. 54; Al-Maqqarī, II, p. 45 (here quoting Ibn Khaldūn); *Chronicle of 754*, 88, p. 114.

[97] P. Crone, *Slaves on Horses*, pp. 43–8; for some of the posthumous defamations that have until now provided the basis for the traditional view of this Caliph see P. Hitti, *History of the Arabs*, pp. 227–28.

[98] *Chronicle of 754*, 88, pp. 114–16; Ibn 'Abd al-Ḥakam, p. 41; Ibn 'Idhārī, I, pp. 62–5; Ibn al-Athīr, p. 74 records that Ibn Habīb landed back in Africa from Spain on 19 February, 744.

[99] *Chronicle of 754*, 88, pp. 116–18; Al-Maqqarī, II, pp. 45–9, an account with too much detail and reported speech in it to be trustworthy; Ibn al-Athīr, pp. 84–6, who makes Ṭawāba a deposed former governor of Seville.

causes in the following year authority passed to Yūsuf ibn 'Abd ar-Raḥmān, military commander in the region of Narbonne in the later 730s and most probably another leading figure in the revolt against Abu al-Ḳattar. Significantly too, he seems to have been another of the descendants of the redoubtable 'Uqba ibn Nāfi', and thus also a relative of the new *de facto* ruler of *Ifrīqīya*.[100] As in North Africa in 744, the revolt in Spain of the indigenous Arabs, allied to one of the Syrian Arab factions, marked the breaking of direct Umayyad control over these peripheral regions. It was, however, to be resumed in the peninsula over a decade later in a new and unexpected fashion.

[100] *Chronicle of 754*, 91 p. 122. For the revolt in Africa and the seizure of power by Ibn Ḥabīb see Ibn 'Abd al-Ḥakam, pp. 41–2; Ibn 'Idhārī, I, pp. 62–75. For the relationship of Yūsuf to 'Uqba, see Al-Maqqarī, II, p. 79.

5

The Rise of an Adventurer

The Making of a Dynastic Legend

The middle decades of the eighth century saw the Arab empire facing the greatest series of crises of its still relatively short existence.[1] The Umayyad regime in Syria seems to have come under considerable strain during the reign of the Caliph Hishām (724–43). In part this manifested itself in a fiscal policy that seemed oppressive and increasingly burdensome. How far references to this represent an actual stepping up of exactions on the part of the caliphal administration and how far a gradual change in attitude on the part of those obliged to pay is now impossible to gauge. All of the available sources post-date the Umayyad period, and are inevitably informed by the prejudices of hindsight and of the great revolt that was soon to overthrow the first caliphal dynasty.

There existed a number of opposition groups within the Arab empire, taking either the form of rival claimants to political authority, such as the descendants of Muḥammad's cousin and son-in-law 'Alī or the heirs of his uncle 'Abbās, or of those such as the Kharijites who were fundamentally opposed to the present constitution of the Islamic state. These various individuals or factions provided the nuclei around which other elements of discontent could coalesce. In particular the growing body of non-Arab Muslims in the former territories of the Persian Empire, who played an important part in the Arab campaigns on the eastern fringes of their land, seem to have become increasingly discon-

[1] See in general M.A. Shaban, *The 'Abbāsid Revolution* (Cambridge, 1970).

tented with the Syrian dominance of the Umayyads, and the failure of the caliphs to ensure genuine equality of status as between Arab and non-Arab Muslims.[2] Other manifestations of regional disquiet leading to active opposition can be seen in first the Berber revolts and then the seizure of power by the long-established Arab settlers in North Africa. In both cases these developments produced parallel results in Spain.

The account of the Spanish *Chronicle of 754* testifies to the reality of both the fiscal exactions of the Syrian Umayyad regime and the growth of regional discontent. The dynasty itself was at the time dangerously disunited, not just because an uncertain system of inheritance of power had left a number of potentially competitive heirs on the death of Hishām, but more significantly because there existed factions within the ranks of the close military following of the Umayyads able to manipulate the rivalry of the various aspirants to the Caliphate. As has been seen the resulting instability in the years 743 and 744 led to a loss of effective control over Spain and North Africa. In Syria Walīd II, Hishām's designated heir, was speedily murdered at the instigation of one faction, which, however, saw its own appointee to the Caliphate die, probably of natural causes, within a matter of months, leaving the throne effectively vacant for the third claimant and his supporters.[3]

The new caliph, Marwān II, whose power base was clearly both much narrower and less stable than that of most of his predecessors, may, according to a later but reasonable tradition, have sought to regularize the position in respect of *Al-Andalus* at least by recognising the *de facto* ruler Ṭawāba as his designated governor.[4] If so, such recognition may not have been extended to Ṭawāba's successor Yūsuf. Contrary to modern historiographical practice, which divides the earliest period of Muslim rule in Spain into two sections: that of the governors notionally or actually dependent on the Caliphs, and that of the independent Umayyad Amirs, with the division coming in 756, the Spanish Christian

[2] Ibid., pp. 138–63. J. Lassner, *The Shaping of 'Abbāsid Rule* (Princeton, 1980), pp. 3–16, and n. 3 on p. 255.

[3] P. Crone, *Slaves on Horses: the Evolution of the Islamic Polity* (Cambridge, 1980), pp. 46–8.

[4] *Historia de al-Andalus, de Ibn al Kardabuš*, ed. F. Maillo (Madrid, 1986), p. 76.

authors, who in the late ninth century drew up lists of the Arab rulers, make Ṭawāba the last of the governors and Yūsuf the first of the independent 'kings'.[5] Whether or not the last of the Ummayad Caliphs of Syria recognized the *de facto* rulers of Spain can have mattered little in practice. Within five years of his accession Marwān II was faced by a major revolt fostered by another branch of the lineage of Muḥammad, the 'Abbāsids, who succeeded in manipulating a number of the other non-Umayyad claimants together with a large body of discontented Persian *mawallads* into a great alliance against the Caliphs and their Syrian troops. Within a year Marwān had been driven from his capital, and died in a last ditch resistance in Egypt, whilst possibly seeking to escape to North Africa.[6] With him perished the Umayyad caliphate, and the 'Abbāsids may have attempted to ensure that the change of dynasty was permanent by slaughtering all members of the rival family who fell into their hands in 750.[7]

Traditionally, amongst the few members of the line who managed to escape was one of the grandsons of the Caliph Hishām, called 'Abd ar-Raḥmān ibn Mu'āwiya, who then made his way to North Africa and ultimately to Spain, where he was able to establish a independent base of power for himself and his descendents. The detailed and dramatic story of his flight, his evasion of murderous pursuers by swimming across the Euphrates, subsequent adventures, and ultimate triumph in a new land is found in a number of the Arab histories of *Al Andalus*. As usual, the tradition comes in Russian doll form, that is say as an excerpt within a story within an account. The fullest form of it may be found in the latest of available sources, the great compilation of al-Maqqarī. He in turn avers that for at least some of his information he is quoting from the *Muqtabis* of Ibn Ḥayyān, a historian of the mid-eleventh century, and within the extract then quoted Ibn Ḥayyān himself states that the story came ultimately from 'Abd ar-Raḥmān

[5] *Chronica Albeldensia*, XVIII, ed. J. Gil, *Crónicas asturianas*, p. 185.

[6] M.A. Shaban, *'Abbāsid Revolution*, p. 167.

[7] Those sources relating to *Al-Andalus* that record this 'Abbāsid massacre of the Umayyads also report the continued existence of several members of the latter family in the East around the year 756: Al-Maqqarī, II, pp. 75–6; *Akhbar Machmua*, p. 90. The 'Abbāsid Caliph As-Saffāh was either considerably less efficient than is made out or the whole episode has been much exaggerated!

himself.[8] Indeed the text here cited takes the form of a first person narrative.

Unfortunately, the passage in Al-Maqqarī comes from one of those parts of the work of Ibn Ḥayyān that is otherwise lost, and so it not possible to see how far the seventeenth-century compiler was being faithful to his eleventh-century predecessor. However, in general there are no grounds for doubting Al-Maqqarī's assertion that he was here using Ibn Ḥayyān. There are considerably fewer reasons for trusting the assertion of Ibn Ḥayyān that what he had quoted was the autobiographical narrative of 'Abd ar-Raḥmān. For one thing, as previously explained, the current state of scholarly opinion on the development of Arabic literature would not allow for the existence of such a composition at this period. Equally significant may be the evidence for the existence of yet another version of the same set of adventures, but this time cast as the autobiographical narrative of 'Abd ar-Raḥmān's freedman Badr, who played a key role in some of the episodes.[9] This work, which does not now exist, may have lain behind the version of the story to be found in the eleventh-century compilation known as the *Akhbar Machmua*, which varies from that in the Ibn Ḥayyān–Al-Maqqarī tradition in a number of respects.[10]

In that these stories of the escape, adventures and triumph of 'Abd ar-Raḥmān represent the founding legends of the Umayyad dynasty in its Spanish manifestation, it is not unexpected that they should have received increasingly sophisticated literary elaboration during the course of the dynasty's rule in *Al-Andalus*. That these might take the form of the pseudo-autobiographical accounts of the principal participants is again more a reflection of their intrinsic literary interest than of their historical reliability. Autobiographical narrative, which had become a feature of Arabic composition in the peninsula by the late eleventh century could not be looked for

[8] Al-Maqqarī, II, pp. 58–61; Ibn al-Athīr, pp. 97–8. The essential reliability of this set of stories is taken at face value by E. Lévi-Provençal, *Histoire de l'Espagne musulmane* (Paris/Leiden, 1950), vol. I, pp. 95–101.

[9] C. Sánchez-Albornoz, *En torno a los orígenes del feudalismo*, 2, *Fuentes de la historia hispano-musulmana del siglo VIII* (2nd edn, Buenos Aires, 1977), pp. 18–22 argues that Ibn 'Idārī, amongst others, is excerpting this supposed work by Badr.

[10] *Akhbar Machmua*, pp. 58–62.

in the mid-eighth.[11] If then, as with the legendary surrounds of the original Arab conquest of *Al-Andalus*, the elaborate narrative of the adventures of 'Abd ar-Raḥman needs to be treated with the greatest reserve, which elements if any may be relied on?

The termination of the account of the *Chronicle of 754* in that year is particularly to be regretted. Its author was writing under the period of the rule of Yūsuf, and had clearly no idea of the dramatic changes that were to be brought about in Spain so soon after the ending of his work. The next extant historical composition to be produced in the south of the peninsula was the work of Aḥmad ar-Rāzī, written in the mid-tenth century but now only extant in a Portuguese translation dated *c.*1300.[12] The treatment in this of the movement that led to the overthrow of Yūsuf and the substitution of 'Abd ar-Raḥmān is extremely brief, but states that, far from being a fugitive, the latter had actually been sent by the Caliph, whose favourite he had been.[13] As the date specified here was the Year of the Hegira 138, that is to say AD 756, acceptance of this story would make of 'Abd ar-Raḥmān a collaborator with the 'Abbāsids, who subsequently betrayed his masters. Intriguing as this possibility is, it would be unwise to pursue it when it remains unsupported by any other evidence. Ar-Rāzī was also the only one of the historians whose extant works deal with this episode who actually lived under Spanish Umayyad rule.

A little earlier in date, at least in its original form, is the account of Ibn 'Abd al-Ḥakam, whose principal concern here was with North African affairs. Once again this is a text that is both fragmentary and likely to have suffered interpolations since its first composition *c.*850, and in this particular case in his use of it Al-Maqqarī only paraphrases the account rather than citing extracts from it.[14] However, it does seem to confirm the essential truth of the outline of the more detailed and romantic version of 'Abd ar-Raḥmān's African sojourn given by Ibn Ḥayyān. In

[11] See the 'memoirs' of the Zīrid ruler of Granada, 'Abdallāh, in *El siglo XI en la persona*, tr. E. Lévi-Provençal and E. García Gómez (Madrid, 1980). However this is unaccompanied by any study of the autobiographical *genre* in Arabic literature.

[12] *Crónica del Moro Rasis*, ed. D. Catalán and M. Soledad de Andrés (Madrid, 1975). See C. Sánchez-Albornoz, *En torno a los orígines*, 2, pp. 115–58.

[13] *Crónica del Moro Rasis*, ch. clx, p. 371.

[14] Al-Maqqarī, II, p. 62.

particular it corroborates the five-year period spent by the fugitive amongst the Berbers, and the hostility displayed towards him by Ibn Ḥabīb, the ruler of *Ifrīqīya*. The former feature in particular may corroborate the tradition that 'Abd ar-Rahmān's mother was herself a Berber.[15] Such a family tie would explain Berber willingness to support an otherwise friendless fugitive. The elements of the fully developed story that would seem to command a measure of credence appear to be the following: that after the overthrow of the Umayyad regime in Syria, 'Abd ar-Raḥmān, a grandson of the Caliph Hishām did arrive in North Africa. It is possible, if the story in Ar-Rāzī, is to be credited, that he did so at the direction of the fugitive Marwān II, who was himself seeking to withdraw to *Ifrīqīya*, to make it the base for his continued resistance to the 'Abbāsids. The death of the last Umayyad Caliph in Egypt, however, left 'Abd ar-Raḥman isolated. The ruler of North Africa, Ibn Ḥabīb, who does not seem to have fully recognized the 'Abbāsids, proved unwilling to countenance the presence of an Umayyad pretender, who also threatened his own position, and it was only by taking refuge with various Berber tribes that 'Abd ar-Raḥmān was able to remain secure.

Various features in the accounts dealing with the creation of the Umayyad state in Spain help to explain how it came into being when it did. In 755 Ibn Ḥabīb was murdered, and North Africa returned to political orthodoxy by recognizing the rule of the 'Abbāsid Caliphs.[16] That 'Abd ar-Raḥmān found it expedient to make his move into Spain in 756 is thus less fortuitous than is usually assumed. His original appearance in Africa in 750/1 is mentioned in respect of there being available there a potential body of support for his line.[17] In practice this does not seem to have

[15] Ibn al-Athīr, p. 99.

[16] Ibn 'Idhārī, I, 75–8 for the events in Africa in the years 755–7. According to Ibn al-Athīr, Ibn Ḥabīb had recognized the authority of the 'Abbāsid Caliph As-Saffāh (750–4), but had broken with his successor Al-Manṣūr. This in turn contributed to his own murder at the hands of two of his brothers, the dominant one of whom, Elyas, then took power and restored 'Abbāsid suzerainty. He was overthrown by Ibn Ḥabīb's son, who in turn fell in 757 fighting his late uncle's Berber allies. The latter took Kairouan, and it was not until 761 that direct caliphal rule was restored in *Ifrīqīya* by an army sent from Egypt: pp. 77–83. These problems may have delayed the first 'Abbāsid moves against the Umayyads in Spain until 763, giving 'Abd ar-Raḥmān I an extra six years in which to establish his hold in the south of the peninsula.

[17] Al-Maqqarī, II, p. 61.

materialized. On the other hand, a more reliable Umayyad faction does seem to have existed in Spain. There are references to a substantial body of clients of the former caliphal house existing in the peninsula, and, as previously, discussed, this kind of bond was an extremely powerful one.[18] In addition the relatively secure information about 'Abd ar-Raḥmān's time of refuge amongst the Berbers suggests another set of links. Initially he was able to live amongst the Nafsa Berbers, who were his mother's people, but he was subsequently forced to take a more secure refuge amongst the Zanata, who had long been opponents of Ibn Ḥabīb.[19] However, the Zanata, who were amongst the most powerful of the Berber confederacies, may have taken little part in the original conquest of *Al-Andalus*, where despite the defeats of the early 740s the Berbers still constituted a major military element in the peninsula. Thus some degree of Berber support for 'Abd ar-Raḥmān existed in Spain, if less than that he had acquired in Africa.

In 756 Yūsuf had ruled for nearly a decade. His African ties seem to have been broken by the murder of his relative Ibn Ḥabīb, and he had also fallen out with some of his own local supporters. These may have included some of the Berber leaders. However, he retained the backing of the most significant of the Qays or Banu Muḍar Arab military commanders, As-Ṣumayl, who had played a vital role in the war against the last Umayyad appointed governor, Abu al-Ḳattar in 744/5. His reward has been to be entrusted with control of the frontier regions of firstly Toledo, and subsequently the Ebro valley and the city of Zaragoza.[20] There are suggestions that As-Ṣumayl was briefly involved in the conspiracy to bring 'Abd ar-Raḥmān to Spain, but this is no clearer to us than it was to Al-Maqqarī, writing in the seventeenth century, who had to record quite opposed traditions on the matter in the various accounts available to him.[21] Whatever his initial contacts with the Umayyad

[18] Al-Maqqarī, II, p. 62. P. Crone, *Slaves on Horses*, pp. 49–57.

[19] Ibn 'Abd al-Ḥakam, pp. 42–3.

[20] He was credited with the final defeat and execution of Abu al-Ḳattar in 746 according to Ibn Ḥayyān, quoted by Al-Maqqarī, II, p. 50. Ar-Rāzi stated that he was responsible for the nominating of Yūsuf to succeed Tawāba in 747, ibid., p. 54; ibid., p. 63 for his control of Zaragoza from 750–56, and *Akhbar Machmua*, p. 67; Ibn al-Athīr, p. 91 for As-Ṣumayl as governor of Toledo in 753/4.

[21] Al-Maqqarī, II, pp. 63–4 (accounts with much reported, i.e. invented, conversation); *Ajbar Machmua*, pp. 70–6, is equally unreliable.

may have been, in practice As-Ṣumayl remained unwavering in his support for Yūsuf. One feature that does seem common to many of the sources, though, is that the nucleus of the revolt against Yūsuf was to be found in the south-east, particularly around Elvira, the latter Granada. Traditionally, it was at Almuñecar that 'Abd ar-Raḥmān landed, probably in the late Spring of 756.[22] Although it is not safe to be categoric on the matter, this still seems to have been a region with a strong concentration of Syrian Arab garrisons.[23]

Traditional accounts of the creation of a body of support for 'Abd ar-Raḥmān tend to concentrate upon the supposed conflict between the rival Arab confederacies of the Qays or Banu Muḍar and the Kalb or Yemenis, mirroring the role usually assigned to them in the central politics of the Umayyad state in the East in the early eighth century. However, as previously mentioned, modern interpretations of the latter now tend to see the supposedly ancient feud of the Qays and the Yemenis as little more than a way by which later generations of Arab historians were able to rationalize processes and conflicts the real significance of which had been lost to them.[24] It is particularly important to note that some of the labels used are quite deceptive. By 'Syrians' should probably be understood the central standing army of the Umayyad state, largely based in Syria, but drawn from a number of Arab tribes, elements of which were available to be sent to various parts of the empire in times of crisis, as with the Berber revolts in Africa. Within the greater Syrian area particular tribal elements controlled or were entrusted with different territorial divisions. Access to the increased opportunities for wealth and power that emanated from the caliphal court led to the growth of factional rivalries between these different military groupings, and civil wars between rival Umayyad claimants or between the latter and non-Umayyad aspirants to the Caliphate provided opportunities for the military commanders to establish the dominance of their particular faction. It has been suggested that in the process the tribal labels of the rival

[22] Al-Maqqarī, II, p. 66.

[23] P. Guichard, *Al-Andalus* (Barcelona, 1976), p. 344. Ibn al-Athīr, p. 99 reports that the governors of the regions (quras) of *Rayyā* (Malaga), *Chidouna* (Sidona), and *Mouron* (Morón) declared for 'Abd ar-Raḥmān on his arrival in Spain.

[24] See above p. 101.

elements came to be nothing more than identifying tags.[25] Thus exclusive recruitment from the tribe whose name was being used would be no more to be expected than in the relationship between some of the regiments of the British army and the counties whose names they employ.

This may be an extreme view, but is a useful corrective to the over-literalness that used to be current in the approach to the accounts of the Arab sources. Certainly within these 'Syrian' tribal or military forces a number of sub-groupings can be detected in the later Syrian Umayyad period. The most significant of these indeed were on the one hand the Yemenis and on the other the Qays and the Banu Muḍar.[26] The former are peculiarly confusing in the sense that the name implies a direct southern Arabian origin, whereas in fact it is vital to appreciate that what are being discussed are the Yemeni elements amongst the forces in Syria. Their tribal labels and the ancestors of many or even most of them may have originated in the Yemen and adjacent areas, but they had been established in Syria in some cases since the 630s, and certainly before the 680s. It is the non-appreciation of this distinction that caused the long-standing belief in a grand ancestral feud between the Arab tribes of the north and of the south of the Arabian peninsula.[27]

In general, then, the 'Syrian' regiments were the traditional adherents and defenders of the Umayyad house, although divided by the factional politics of the last decade of that dynasty's rule. The despatch and apparent non-return of what had been a large army of these men to quell the Berber revolts in North Africa may well have weakened the subsequent and unsuccessful Umayyad resistance to the 'Abbāsids, and it is likely to have been their presence there that had led Marwān II to try to escape to the west. Although the short-lived governor Abu al-Ḳattar is reported to have sent at least some of the Syrians in *Al-Andalus* back to Africa, later traditions suggest that a substantial body remained, and that both the south-eastern and south-western corners of the peninsula in general became their stronghold.[28] Thus with the presence of

[25] For this interpretation see P. Crone, *Slaves on Horses*, pp. 29–48.
[26] Ibid., pp. 42–8.
[27] Classically expressed in J. Welhausen, *Das arabische Reich und sein Sturz* (Berlin, 1902), Introduction, section 9.
[28] P. Guichard, *Al-Andalus*, pp. 344–8.

these Syrians, amongst whom may have been a body of the freedmen of the Umayyad house, and some measure of Berber support, 'Abd ar-Raḥmān's agents and followers were clearly able to rely on sufficient backing for his bid to seize power in Spain.

On the other hand just as he might be able to call upon the resources of a significant body of support on largely *a priori* grounds and irrespective of his own personal qualities, so too would 'Abd ar-Raḥmān be faced with a substantial opposition. Yūsuf, like Ṭawāba before him, had been able to seize power largely on the basis of a combination of different strands of opposition to Umayyad caliphal rule.[29] As has been seen, in his own person he represented what may be called the 'indigenous' Arabs of North Africa and Spain, those established in the regions for two, three or more generations.[30] In addition, the Syrian forces sent by Hisham in 741 may well have been split by the implication of the factional struggles that erupted in the east after that caliph's death. His tendency in the last years of his reign to favour the Yemeni units amongst the Arab armies was reversed by his successor Walīd II. The intensity of factional polarization led to the latter's murder. The Yemeni confederacy amongst the Syrian tribal forces set up their own candidate in the person of Yazīd III, but his premature death allowed power to pass quickly into the hands of Marwān II, who like Walīd II had the backing of the Qays and Muḍar grouping.[31]

It is significant that the Arab accounts of 'Abd ar-Raḥmān's struggle with Yūsuf isolate Syrian and Berber forces as providing the most important elements in the fighting strength of both of the participants.[32] In general the Syrian troops who joined 'Abd ar-Raḥmān came from the Yemeni units, whilst those who remained loyal to Yūsuf were their Muḍar and Qays rivals, amongst

[29] Al-Maqqarī, II, p. 46, following Ibn Ḥayyān and others, presents it as a reaction to an overly partial judgement given in a dispute. Such a reduction of complex issues to personal confrontations is typical of the Arab sources in general. Ibn al-Athīr, p. 85 has a variant of the same story. More sensible may be Ibn al-Athīr's assertion, p. 88, that Yūsuf was selected to succeed Tawāba, because he was a Qurayshi, that is to say a member of the tribe of the Prophet, and attached to neither the Qays or the Yemeni factions.

[30] *Chronicle of 754*, 86, p. 112, the only contemporary witness, presents it as a conflict between 'easterners' and 'westerners', or those Arabs longer established in Spain and the newly-arrived Syrians.

[31] P. Crone, *Slaves on Horses*, pp. 43–8.

[32] *Akhbar Machmua*, pp. 81–2, 84–5.

whom As-Ṣumayl was particularly prominent. The more recent conflicts were additionally fuelled by the memories and obligations of feuds deriving from some of the earlier civil wars of the Umayyad period. Thus one account of the principal battle between 'Abd ar-Raḥmān and Yūsuf has the former reminding his followers of the Battle of Marj Rāhiṭ (684) in which one of his ancestors, similarly supported by a Yemeni army, had defeated the Qays adherents of a rival aspirant to the Caliphate.[33] Such memories and the requirements of vengeance helped to perpetuate divisions and factional loyalties. The later Umayyad caliphs had deliberately manipulated and played off such conflicts for their own interests, very much in the way 'Abd ar-Raḥmān was to do in 756.

It is also advisable not to be too monolithic in the presentation of such groupings. 'Abd ar-Raḥmān is also reported to have been backed by some Qays tribesmen. Admittedly only three of them were said to have done so, thus duplicating the three Qays said to have joined the victorious Umayyad army in the battle of Marj Rāhiṭ.[34] Such figures are hardly worthy of trust; the implications rather than the precise details are what matter here. To take a generally sceptical view of the matter, it is quite conceivable that far too much weight has been put on such supposedly deep-rooted divisions. To take Spanish examples alone, both Yemenis and Qays are reported fighting in the armies of the rival sides in 756, and Yemenis who had supported 'Abd ar-Raḥmān in that year appear fighting for Yūsuf in the following one.[35] A high degree of fluidity seems indicated rather than a pattern of rigid, traditional and long-lasting allegiances.

Interestingly, such manipulation of what may seem like ancient history, for the Battle of Marj Rāhiṭ was some 70 years in the past, may have been particularly significant in the Spanish context in involving those Arabs who were much longer established in the peninsula in the conflict.[36] Their own links to and participation in the recent events in Syria and the east were slight or non-existent, but the ancestors of many of them will have taken part in the civil wars of the 680s, and traditional allegiances could be revived by the

33 Al-Maqqarī, II, p. 71.
34 Ibid.
35 *Akhbar Machmua*, pp. 91–2.
36 On the Battle of Marj Rāhiṭ see P. Crone, *Slaves on Horses*, p. 35.

manipulation of old feuds. It is in this sense particularly interesting that the conflict of 756, unlike those of the 740s, did not seem to involve a polarization of the participants as between the longer-established Arabs and the relative newcomers. Some caution is needed here in that the perspectives of the Arab historians and of the Christian author of the *Chronicle of 754* were very different, and the generic differences in the sources for the two periods may also help explain the apparent change of emphasis. Certainly, too the scars of more recent conflicts, particularly between those who supported and those who had opposed the last Umayyad appointed governor in the mid-740s, also provided ready-made factional interests. In addition to honouring the dictates of blood feuds created in that fighting, the adherents of the defeated Abu al-Ḳattar could hope to reverse their loss of local power by abetting this challenge to their rivals.

The time of ʻAbd ar-Raḥmān's crossing into Spain was fortunately or carefully chosen, in that Yūsuf had set off on campaign early in 756 to relieve Zaragoza, which was being besieged by pro-ʻAbbāsid rebels.[37] Thus when ʻAbd ar-Raḥmān arrived from Africa he had time to occupy Elvira, and to gather and consolidate his forces before advancing on Córdoba. He may also have gained control of Seville. In the north Yūsuf had in the meanwhile re-established control over Zaragoza, but a detachment of his army sent against the Basques had been annihilated. According to an invented dialogue in the anonymous *Akhbar Machmua* this seriously weakened Yūsuf's ability to resist the Umayyad revolt, when news of it reached him and he hastened back to Córdoba.[38]

Another problem for him, if the *Ajbar Machmua* is to be believed, was the status of his opponent. For ʻAbd ar-Raḥmān was a leading member of the Umayyad family, which not only drew its distinction as much from its closeness to the lineage of the Prophet as from its former caliphal authority, but its members had also on various occasions been benefactors to Yūsuf's own ancestors. Although in no sense an Umayyad client and himself a member of a sub-section of the Prophet's own tribe of Quraysh, Yūsuf was in a

[37] *Akhbar Machmua*, pp. 68–9; Al-Maqqarī, II, pp. 66–7. Two previous pro-ʻAbbāsid risings are reported as occurring during the rule of Yūsuf in Ibn al-Athīr, pp. 90–1.

[38] *Akhbar Machmua*, p. 77.

difficult position morally in respect of 'Abd ar-Raḥmān's claim to a superior authority in *Al-Andalus*, and seems to have responded by first offering a compromise.[39] By this 'Abd ar-Raḥmān would marry one of Yūsuf's daughters but clearly not acquire the power he sought during the latter's lifetime. When this was rejected the issue was settled by a battle fought close to Córdoba in which Yūsuf was defeated. Although able to escape to Mérida and to continue the fighting for some months longer he was forced to submit to 'Abd ar-Raḥmān before the end of 756.[40]

It has been necessary to consider this episode of the seizure of power in *Al-Andalus* by 'Abd ar-Raḥmān in some detail, not only because its inherent drama makes a good story, but also because of the source-critical problems that are so easily overlooked in the normal narrative presentation of it. Moreover, an analysis of the elements involved, in so far as they can now be isolated, helps to explain some of the many and serious residual problems 'Abd ar-Raḥmān was to find himself facing during his thirty-year reign as first independent Amir of *Al-Andalus*. It is an extraordinary affair, not so much because of the inherent romance of the events, which anyway was clearly much embroidered and exaggerated in the various Arab accounts, as because of the light it sheds on conditions in Muslim-ruled Spain in an otherwise rather dark period.

It is notable that the coming to power of 'Abd ar-Raḥmān broke or rather radically transformed the nature of the ties between the peninsula and North Africa. For the first four and a half decades of Arab rule in Spain *Al-Andalus* was in many respects a dependency of *Ifrīqīya*. Although nominally by command of the Caliphs, most of the governors had been nominated and held office at the pleasure of their immediate superior in Kairouan. Even the earliest forms of Arabic coinage in the peninsula, before a standard pattern was adopted throughout the Islamic world, were of African rather than indigenous Spanish type. When the western regions went their own way, free of caliphal control, in the mid-740s, the family relationship of Yūsuf and the African dictator Ibn Ḥabīb suggests that earlier ties between Spain and North Africa continued much as

[39] *Akhbar Machmua*, pp. 79–81. Ibn al-Athīr, p. 99 suggests other motives.

[40] *Akhbar Machmua*, pp. 83–90; Al-Maqqarī, II, pp. 70–3. The particular details of these long and overly circumstantial accounts should be treated with the utmost caution.

before.[41] It is interesting in this context to note the possibility that Ibn Ḥabīb's father, who died fighting the Berbers, had been one of the principal counsellors of 'Abd al-'Azīz ibn Mūsā in Seville, and also directly implicated in his murder.[42] Yet in the middle 750s a fundamental political break occurred with the return of Africa to a recognition of the secular authority of the Caliphs, now of the 'Abbāsid line, whilst Spain accepted the rule of one of the surviving Umayyads.

The Umayyad Coup d'état

To a certain extent what has often been a purely insular approach to the history of Islamic Spain, concentrating on that to the exclusion of its wider setting, has obscured the full significance and complexity of the Umayyad seizure of power in *Al-Andalus*. On the other hand it has also tended to maximize the significance of the events of 756 and minimize that of those of the mid-740s.[43] Although 'Abd ar-Raḥmān's deposition of Yūsuf led to nearly three centuries of his family's rule in the peninsula, it is questionable how different it was to Yūsuf's own taking of power a decade previously. He also had several sons who played prominent parts in his later campaigns and he doubtless envisaged some form of hereditary succession. Although not quite as distinguished in lineage as the Umayyads his own Fihrī descent and the achievements of his ancestors in Africa gave him considerable status. As far as the evidence now can indicate, the Christian chroniclers of the late ninth century were thus probably right to class him with his Umayyad successors as one of the independent kings of *Al-Andalus*.[44]

This, together with the Umayyad coup of 756, pose some significant questions about the nature of the Caliphate. In itself this may not be a matter of direct concern for the history of early

[41] Although never explicitly stated, it is possible that Yūsuf was actually the son of 'Abd ar-Raḥmān ibn Ḥabīb; Al-Maqqarī, II, pp. 53–4 on the family's movements between Spain and Africa.

[42] Ibn 'Abd al-Ḥakam, p. 27.

[43] E. Lévi-Provençal, *Histoire de l'Espagne musulmane*, vol. I devotes 20 pages to 'Abd ar-Raḥmān I's seizure of power, and a mere 10 to the years 732–56.

[44] See above, p. 114f.

Islamic Spain, but the relationship between *Al-Andalus* and the rest of the Islamic world is of relevance, and this relates directly to the nature of the only universal institution in Islam. The office of Caliph or successor to the Prophet has proved no easier for modern scholars to define than for Arab society in the Umayyad and early 'Abbāsid periods.[45] The complex internecine struggles in the ranks of the conquerors of so much of the Near East and Mediterranean in the period *c.* 650–750 can be presented as largely depending on rival views of the nature and exercise of spiritual and political authority in the Islamic community. Not only were there clashes between aspirants to the Caliphate, but the contrasting views of the nature of the office themselves fuelled and gave direction to several of the conflicts.

What might be termed the orthodox view amongst Islamic scholars is that under the Umayyads the Caliphate became little more than a secular political office, the Islamic equivalent to that of the Byzantine emperor or the recently extinct Sassanian shah.[46] Thus much of the opposition to them, especially in the final phase of Umayyad rule, can be presented as being essentially directed against this exclusively secular nature of their conception of and exercise of their responsibilities. What may be termed the religious dimension of their function could by this approach be seen as being reduced to the titular headship of the Islamic community, manifested publically in the mention of the Caliph's name in prayers every Friday in all of the principal mosques throughout Muslim-controlled territory. This in turn can be seen as little more than a form of declaring political allegiance. Thus, for 'Abd ar-Raḥmān I to omit the name of the 'Abbāsid Caliph from the Friday prayers in the mosque in Córdoba from 757 onwards was tantamount to a unilateral declaration of independence, but nothing more than that.

This is a simple and undemanding way of looking at the issue, but whether it is an accurate one is another matter. It is very difficult to re-create early Islamic ideology, but if current studies of both late Roman and Sassanian Persian equivalents are anything to

[45] Article 'KHALIFA' in *Shorter Encyclopedia of Islam*, pp. 236–41, especially pp. 239–41 on the theory.

[46] P. Hitti, *A History of the Arabs* (8th edn, London, 1964), pp. 185–6 – 'the Caliphate a pre-eminently political office'.

go by such a view of the nature and manifestation of authority in seventh- and eighth-century Arab society is bound to seem naive. Moreover, if the caliphal title was so ambiguous why did neither 'Abd ar-Raḥmān nor any of his successors for nearly two centuries claim it for their own? On the other hand, if it did represent an exclusive claim to authority within the Islamic community, what was signified by 'Abd ar-Raḥmān's refusal to acknowledge the 'Abbāsids' right to it, as indicated by his excluding mention of them from the Friday prayers?

The implications here would seem to be that the title and office of Caliph were unique, and represented an authority that could not be duplicated. Had the significance been purely secular there was nothing to stop 'Abd ar-Raḥmān from proclaiming himself Caliph in Spain, in the way that various aspirants and pretenders had taken the Roman imperial title in Italy and Africa in the course of the seventh century. Instead, he contented himself with the titles of *Amir* and *Malik* (king). The claim thus made was to exclusively secular political and military authority over other Muslims.[47] On the other hand his treatment of the 'Abbāsids implied that the Caliphate itself was from his point of view vacant. This status, though, could not be claimed by him on the basis of power in *Al-Andalus* alone. What may be called the Umayyad criteria for the achieving of caliphal office cannot now be defined with certainty. They probably had very little to do with the kind of arguments put forward by those writers who concerned themselves with the theory of caliphal authority, and whose works first appear in the eleventh century. By this time the institution had existed for some 400 years, and had been substantially modified in the process.

In particular the dynastic succession to the Caliphate achieved by the Umayyads might and generally has been taken as no more than the shoddy manoeuverings of a family determined to obtain and then cling on to power. This is tied directly to the view of the Umayyad concept of the Caliphate as being just a secular office. On the other hand the equally clear but materially less successful dynasticism of their 'Alīd opponents is seen as being at the heart of the growth of the unorthodox Shī'ite form of Islam and thus a

[47] E. Lévi-Provençal, *Histoire de l'Espagne musulmane*, vol. I, pp. 132–3 on 'Abd ar-Raḥmān I's titles.

powerful ideological force. Recent suggestions that the earliest forms of the orthodox Sunni Caliphate, as manifested in the Umayyads as well as their four 'Rightly Guided' predecessors, were much closer to the Shī'ite model of the Imāmate than it later became possible to admit or recognize, indeed deserve some serious attention.[48]

In the case of 'Abd ar-Raḥmān, he lacked one of the main requirements for the transmission of authority, which was designation by his Umayyad predecessor. Admittedly, this procedure had broken down absolutely in the upheavals of 744, but the reminiscence in Ar-Rāzī that he had been the favourite of the Caliph may be an echo of such a claim. Equally, in *Al-Andalus* he was far removed from control of the principal holy places of Islam. Election in Medina had served the purposes of one of the most serious of the opponents of the Umayyads in their hey-day. In so far as 'Abd ar-Raḥmān wanted to revive the claim of his ancestors to a universal authority over the Muslim community and a unique spiritual authority within it, this could only be achieved within the central heartlands of the Islamic world. That this might not be attained by military conquest from *Al-Andalus* must soon have been clear enough, but as late as 780 'Abd ar-Raḥmān was planning an invasion of Syria.[49] In his person he continued to present a major alternative to the 'Abbāsid monopoly of the Caliphate after 750. Never before can a ruler of Spain have been so personally interested in developments in the Near East.

Like the distinctly less successful 'Abd al-Azīz ibn Mūsā, 'Abd ar-Raḥmān I's creation of an independent state in Spain may have benefited from the previous existence of a Spanish monarchy, but the interests of the first Umayyad ruler of *Al-Andalus* were far from bound by the limits of the Iberian peninsula. His successors came increasingly to accept the reality of the geographical limitations of their power, and by the early tenth century a Caliphate that was confined to Spain and a small part of North Africa proved credible enough to be created. In fact 'Abd ar-Raḥmān III's self-proclamation as Caliph in 929 represented a substantial diminution of the aspirations of his namesake and ancestor. In part this

[48] P. Crone and M. Hinds, *God's Caliph* (Cambridge, 1986).
[49] Al-Maqqarī, II, pp. 84; Ibn al-Athīr, p. 128, who gives the year as A.H. 163, which began on 16 September 779.

was due to significant changes that had taken place both in the nature of the Caliphate itself as perceived by the orthodox Islamic community as a whole and also in the fortunes of the ʻAbbāsid dynasty since the middle of the eighth century.[50]

However, whatever the aspirations of ʻAbd ar-Raḥmān I may have been, his first practical requirement was clearly the securing of his position in *Al-Andalus*. Both in the achieving of this and with an eye to a future restoration of the status of his family on the wider stage the building up of a secure body of support was clearly essential. There seem no reasons for doubting the traditions that have him making *Al-Andalus* a place of refuge for other members of the Umayyad line and for their remaining adherents.[51] In the process, however, and for reasons that are far from clear, he succeeded in alienating some of those elements who had supported him in 756. In part this further demonstrates the fluidity of alliances and to some degree the essential irrelevance of traditional factional allegiances at this time. Amongst the reasons given by the Arab historians for this particular change of adherence were the refusal of ʻAbd ar-Raḥmān to allow his Yemeni supporters to loot Córdoba after the first defeat of Yūsuf, and the increasing favour he subsequently showed to the defeated Qays, a necessary step in the ensuring of a broader base for his regime.[52] But with expansionary warfare on the frontiers at a standstill for over a decade, it is not surprising that what amounted to standing armies should try to profit by manipulating internal divisions.

The Arab *junds* or armies, particularly the elements introduced into Spain in the early 740s, were the most obvious manifestations of a society still prepared for a state of permanent warfare.[53] It is quite probable that many of the Arabs who were longer established in *Al-Andalus* had created a more settled lifestyle for themselves in the peninsula, particularly in Córdoba and those other towns under direct Arab rule. The various Syrian detachments, though, should perhaps be envisaged as still being full-time soldiers. That is to say they anticipated making their profits in the form of payments and land from warfare. In that no further expansion of Arab

[50] H. Kennedy, *The Early ʻAbbāsid Caliphate* (London, 1981).
[51] *Akhbar Machmua*, p. 90; Al-Maqqarī, II, pp. 75–6.
[52] *Akhbar Machmua*, pp. 91–2.
[53] P. Guichard, *Al-Andalus*, pp. 315–38.

rule was practical or seems even to have been envisaged after the 740s, the question of political favour became increasingly important. If one group of the conquerors was to be rewarded it would have to be at the expense of another. It is notable that on few occasions, and for this we have both contemporary Christian and later Arab testimony, do the Arab rulers seem to have resorted to unjust and oppressive measures against their non-Muslim subject populations in the interests of solving such problems. However the political realities be envisaged, it is also important not to overlook the additional impact of ideological considerations.

'Abd ar-Raḥmān I was faced by a number of rebels and opponents in the course of his lengthy reign. That the various conflicts are generally classed as rebellions by modern historians does less than justice to the realities of a complex situation.[54] As has been seen the constitutional nature of 'Abd ar-Raḥmān's power is very hard to define. He was self-proclaimed, and patently at odds with the 'Abbāsids. The formal system of the caliphal appointment of governors had broken down fatally in the 740s, since when *de facto* power, based on the strength of local military support looks to have been the only basis for authority in *Al-Andalus*. There has been a tendency to accept 'Abd ar-Raḥmān I at his own valuation; that is to believe that his self-proclamation, validated by his victory over Yūsuf, legitimately vested him with a peninsula-wide authority.[55] In fact his period of rule is probably better seen as one of the gradual transformation of this ideal into reality, and as being marked by fierce conflicts between different and rival sources of power.

Inevitably, the Arab sources that deal with the early history of *Al-Andalus* do so from an Umayyad perspective. If not actually written during the tenure of power of that dynasty or depending on such works, they can not avoid the reality of its three centuries of rule. Thus they present a sense of the inevitability and even the legitimacy of 'Abd ar-Raḥmān's right to rule, things which were far from clear in the second half of the eighth century.[56] It is hard

[54] E.g. by E. Lévi-Provençal, *Histoire de l'Espagne musulmane*, vol. I, pp. 108–14: 'la lutte contre les rebelles'.

[55] Ibid., pp. 104–8.

[56] *Historia de al-Andalus de Ibn al-Kardabuš*, ed. F. Maillo (Madrid, 1986), section 24, p. 80. This, twelfth-century, author states that all of *Al-Andalus* gave obedience to 'Abd ar-Raḥmān after his first defeat of Yūsuf.

also not to suspect that details of particular episodes have been strongly coloured by this distortion of perception. The nature of Yūsuf's treaty with 'Abd ar-Raḥmān in 756 may be a case in point. It is not well described by the Arab accounts, but one salient feature of it that is clear was Yūsuf's, and his ally As-Ṣumayl's, insistence that they be permitted to reside in Córdoba.[57] Had this been 'Abd ar-Raḥmān's stipulation, enabling him to keep a closer eye on his defeated foes, it would occasion no surprise. However, in this context, it may rather indicate that the treaty represented more of a compromise than is usually thought, and that even some form of joint authority was created by it. It is significant that 'Abd ar-Raḥmān's repudiation of the 'Abbāsids did not take place until 757, after he had once again had to fight and defeat Yūsuf.

Whatever the nature of the agreement made in 756, it broke down the following year. Yusuf withdrew from Córdoba to Mérida, where he raised a Berber army said to be 20,000 strong. No trust should be placed in such figures; more significant is the location of this support. The pattern of the ensuing events is by no means clear, and the surviving accounts are mutually contradictory on a number of points.[58] However, it seems that Yūsuf made an attempt to march on Seville, but was defeated by the forces commanded by the governors of that city and of Morón, and forced to withdraw to Toledo, then held for him by his cousin Hishām ibn 'Urwa.[59] What happened to As-Ṣumayl is less clear, but he seems to have been imprisoned in Córdoba, where he was later strangled.[60] Yūsuf may have held out in Toledo for another two or three years before being murdered by some of his own men.[61] An alternative tradition has him defeated and killed while conducting his retreat to the city in 757.[62]

It is hard to know where to place the greater reliance in such contradictory accounts, but the implications of both versions are

[57] *Akhbar Machmua*, pp. 89–90.

[58] *Akhbar Machmua*, pp. 91–4; Al-Maqqarī, II, pp. 78–80; Ibn al-Athīr, pp. 102–3.

[59] *Akhbar Machmua*, pp. 93–4 states that he was intercepted and killed before he reached the city. See also J. Porres Martín-Cleto, *Historia de Ṭulayṭula* (Toledo, 1985), pp. 20–1. Ibn al-Athīr, p. 103 also has him killed near Toledo, but gives the date as 27 October 759.

[60] Al-Maqqarī, II, pp. 79–80, here probably following Ibn Ḥayyān.

[61] Ibn al-Athīr, p. 101, has him dying in 757, 759 or *c*.761.

[62] Al-Maqqarī, II, p. 79.

clear in so far as Toledo is concerned. It was a major centre of support for Yūsuf, and whether under Yūsuf himself or under his cousin Hishām ibn 'Urwa it remained free of Umayyad control until the early 760s. In 761 Hishām is reported to have revolted and to have been besieged in the city by 'Abd ar-Raḥmān. In reality the notion of this as a revolt may be quite anachronistic. It is equally probable that this siege represented a bid by the ruler of Córdoba at last to bring Toledo under his authority. Such a view may be corroborated by the outcome, which was the making of a treaty when 'Abd ar-Raḥmān's forces failed to take the city, whereby Hishām retained control of Toledo but gave one of his sons as a hostage.[63] In fact he continued his defiance of the Umayyad Amir as soon as the latter withdrew his army, and a renewed siege proved equally fruitless. The hostage son was decapitated and his head catapulted into the city. Only a further campaign in 764 led to the fall of Toledo, not by assault but by a faction in the city seizing Hishām and his principal lieutenants and handing them over to the besieging army commanded by 'Abd ar-Raḥmān's freedman Badr.[64]

The captive leaders were then subjected to public humiliation in a triumphal entry into Córdoba before being executed by crucifixion. The incidental details of these procedures provide an extraordinarily revealing light on unexpected continuities from Late Roman and Visigothic practices. The men were shaved or quite possibly scalped and led into the city mounted on donkeys before being put to death.[65] 'Decalvation' – the precise significance of this in terms of shaving or scalping remains debatable – was a standard form of punishment in the Visigothic period. The whole procedure of public humiliation, often involving the victims being mounted on peculiar or particularly shameful beasts, was standard in the Late Roman Empire, and its roots could be found in the earlier Roman Triumph.[66] In the particular context of the events of 764 the only original contribution of the Arabs would seem to be the linking of this with execution by crucifixion, an ancient practice but one otherwise suppressed by the establishment of Christianity

[63] *Akhbar Machmua*, p. 95; Ibn al-Athīr, p. 105.
[64] *Akhbar Machmua*, pp. 97–8; Ibn al-Athīr, pp. 106–7.
[65] *Akhbar Machmua*, p. 98.
[66] M. McCormick, *Eternal Victory: Triumphal Rulership in Late Antiquity, Byzantium and the Early Medieval West* (Cambridge/Paris, 1986), especially pp. 35–111, 313–15.

as the religion of the Roman Empire. It is possibly as a deliberate affront to Christianity that the Arab rulers used it so frequently, at least in *Al-Andalus*, though this was generally done in a context, such as the present one, in which no Christians were involved.

Even after the elimination of Hishām ibn 'Urwa and the imposition of Umayyad control on the city, Toledo seems to have retained a sympathy for the heirs and followers of Yūsuf al-Fihrī. His last surviving sons Abu al-'Aṣwad and Qasim ibn Yūsuf raised a revolt there against 'Abd ar-Raḥmān I in 785, only to be swiftly defeated.[67] With their subsequent elimination the opposition centred on the family of the former governor (or if preferred the first independent ruler of *Al-Andalus*) was finally extinguished, but what is so striking is that this took nearly thirty years to achieve. It is not easy to say what the precise sources of support for Yūsuf and his sons actually were. As a member of the tribe of Fihrī he had a considerable prestige and some natural tribal allies. His own achievements when governing the frontier area around Narbonne may have added to his personal following, as well as the role he played in ejecting the last governor imposed on *Al-Andalus* from outside.[68] However, where he seems to have been peculiarly effective was in marshalling both Syrian Arab and Berber support. His alliance with As-Ṣumayl seems to have been particularly important in the securing of Qays Syrian military aid both during his period of independent rule and in his struggle with 'Abd ar-Raḥmān.[69] On the other hand, what little is known of Toledo at this time would suggest it still retained an important indigenous Christian population, and at the same time there is no suggestion that it ever became a base for any of the various Syrian units who entered the peninsula in the 740s. Thus it is possible that Yūsuf was able to appeal to the interests of both some of the non-Muslim elements and to the

[67] E. Lévi-Provençal, *Histoire de l'Espagne musulmane*, vol. I, pp. 109–10; Ibn 'Idārī, II, pp. 57–8; Ibn al-Athīr, pp. 131–2, who states that Abu al-'Aṣwad lived on in a fortress in the vicinity of Toledo until 786/7, and that command of this revolt then passed briefly to his brother Qāsim, who being foolish enough to meet 'Abd ar-Raḥmān without safe conduct was seized and executed.

[68] Al-Maqqarī, II, pp. 53–4 gives Ar-Rāzī's account of the origins and career of Yūsuf.

[69] As-Ṣumayl had been one of the commanders of Kulṭum's forces in the disastrous conflict with the Berbers, and had subsequently been a follower of Balj ibn Bishr. His own status and these involvements gave him a particularly high standing amongst the Syrians of the Qays faction: Al-Maqqarī, II, p. 80.

longer established Arabs, as well as those Syrians who had backed the revolt against the last Umayyad governor in 744.

Whilst the threat of Umayyad involvement in developments in the Islamic heartlands remained theoretical, that of the 'Abbāsids in Spain took practical shape. In 763 a certain al-'Ala' ibn Mughiṭ arrived in *Al-Andalus* as the 'Abbāsid appointed governor. He established himself in Beja, and proclaimed the 'Abbāsid cause.[70] This again is treated as a revolt, but should rather be seen as the conflict between rival sources of authority. The 'Abbāsids, as well as actually holding the office, had a powerful claim to the Caliphate, through the relationship of their eponymous dynastic founder 'Abbās to the Prophet. It was, by such a criterion, a somewhat stronger one than that of the Umayyads.[71] All too often in the modern historiography of early Islam it has been felt necessary to shy away from ideological explanations for group or individual motivation and to prefer arguments based on notions of *realpolitik* or self-interest. However, it would be quite anachronistic to believe that there was no-one in Spain who accepted the legitimacy of the 'Abbāsid Caliphate, or that when the Caliph al-Manṣūr wished to put that authority to practical effect by sending a governor he would only be able to rely on the support of those who were dissatisfied with Umayyad rule for purely material reasons.

This bid to bring *Al-Andalus* once more under the rule of the Caliph through his own appointed deputies proved unsuccessful, but it may have been more of a near-run-affair than is often appreciated. For one thing 'Abd ar-Raḥmān, unlike in his conflict with Yūsuf, did not attempt to face al-'Ala' and his forces in open battle, nor does he seem to have felt able to await them in Córdoba. Instead he located himself inside the fortress town of Carmona and prepared to sit out a siege. In the event this was to last for two months before he was able to effect a sortie when his opponents were unprepared and disperse the besieging army. In the fighting al-'Ala' and other 'Abbāsid leaders were killed, and 'Abd ar-Raḥmān is reported to have had their heads secretly transported to Kairouan to serve as a warning to other potential 'Abbāsid

[70] Ibid., pp. 80–1; *Akhbar Machmua* pp. 95–7; Ibn al-Athīr, p. 106.

[71] B. Lewis, art 'ABBASIDS' in *Encyclopedia of Islam* (2nd edn, Leiden, 1954), but see P. Crone and M. Hinds, *God's Caliph* for a more convincing interpretation of the nature of the Umayyad Caliphate.

invaders.[72] Later traditions make Mecca the site of the depositing of the heads, but Kairouan is more credible.[73] In general the tradition of sending the heads of defeated usurpers or overthrown emperors was one long established in Late Roman political practice and the ceremonial of victory, so a ritual element in this episode should not be overlooked.[74] That the 'Abbāsids were thinking of Africa as the starting point of their recovery of authority in *Al-Andalus* is not surprising in view of the previous relationship between the two regions. Their next would-be governor, sent in 777, was called 'Abd ar-Raḥmān ibn Ḥabīb al-Fihrī, and the tribal identity and similarity of name would make the idea of his being both North African and a relative of the earlier Ibn Ḥabīb, and thus of Yūsuf al-Fihrī, perfectly credible.

The nature of the fighting in 763 is particularly interesting. The size of the armies involved can hardly have been considerable, at least on the Umayyad side, in that the number of men who could have been supported within the defences of Carmona for the course of a two-month siege would have to be relatively small. Nor does this length of siege seem to have led to any significant interventions in the conflict by other parties. It looks as if the rest of Muslim-ruled Spain sat back to await the outcome, ultimately decided by the careful timing of 'Abd ar-Raḥmān's surprise attack. The role of siege warfare in the determining of such major conflicts is also demonstrated by the next threat that the Umayyad ruler had to face.

In 766 a revolt, and this seems to have been just that, broke out in the region of Niebla, headed by Sa'īd al-Maṭarī, who was then able to make himself master of Seville. When threatend by 'Abd ar-Raḥmān I he, like the Umayyad in 763, preferred to face his opponent from within a fortress, and established himself in Alcalá de Guadaira. In the course of the ensuing siege he attempted a sortie, but on this occasion it was the besiegers who were better prepared, and Sa'īd was killed and his supporters routed.[75] Clearly, as an alternative to immediate battle, such a form of warfare had advantages, particularly if the two sides were unequally matched.

[72] *Akhbar Machmua*, p. 97.

[73] Al-Maqqarī, II, pp. 81. Ibn al-Athīr, p. 106 has heads sent to both Kairouan and Mecca.

[74] M. McCormick, *Eternal Victory*, pp. 18, 36, 46, 48, fig. 6 on p. 57.

[75] Ibn al-Athīr, p. 107; *Akhbar Machmua*, p. 98; Ibn al-Qūṭiyya, pp. 25–6.

Everything depended on the maintenance of vigilance on the part of besieger. A lapse could provide the opportunity for the besieged to redress the odds, and a surprise attack from within the fortress could disperse a larger force. Also, much may have depended on the fates of the individual commanders, and it is notable that in both of these episodes the leaders of the defeated sides fell in the fray. It is also clear that in this type of fighting cavalry can have played only a limited role, and this may support the views of those who wish to underplay the role of the horse in the whole process of the Arab expansion and the nature of warfare used in it.[76]

Probably in the same year that saw the collapse of Sa'īd al-Maṭarī's bid to seize power in Niebla and Seville, 'Abd ar-Raḥmān executed one of the most prominent of his own former supporters, the Yemeni leader Abu as-Ṣabbāh.[77] Whether these events were coincidental may be doubted, but no explicit testimony links Abu as-Ṣabbāh's death to the failed revolt. In itself, though, it did create the necessary conditions for a feud. This may be the cause of yet another revolt some years later. According to one version, in 774 Yemeni Arabs led by 'Abd al-Ghaffar, a cousin of the late Abu as-Ṣabbāh, revolted in Seville, but when they marched on Córdoba they were defeated by the Amir's forces under his own cousin 'Abd al-Malik ibn 'Umar, who pursued the remnants across the Sierra Morena and decisively routed them on the river Bembezar.[78] The same Umayyad commander is also credited with the defeat of Yūsuf in 757.[79]

In fact it is both significant and depressing to see that no two of the various Arab accounts of this episode agree in almost any of the major points of detail. A variety of dates are available, ranging from 771 to 774, and there exists no unanimity as to the principal participants or to the location of the single or various battles that resulted. The same is true of so many aspects of the history of the

[76] This is the main line of argument of the 3rd vol. of C. Sánchez-Albornoz, *En torno a los orígenes del feudalismo* (2nd edn, Buenos Aires, 1977), and in theory the *raison d'être* for the whole work.

[77] *Akhbar Machmua*, p. 98; Ibn al-Athīr, p. 109.

[78] Ibn al-Athīr, p. 120, followed by E. Lévi-Provençal, *Histoire de l'Espagne musulmane*, vol. I, p. 112. Ibn al-Qūṭiyya, p. 23 links this revolt with the need to avenge Abu as-Ṣabbāh.

[79] *Akhbar Machmua*, p. 100; for other variants see A. Arjona Castro, *Anales de Córdoba musulmana (711–1008)* (Córdoba, 1982), docs. 14 a-c, pp. 22–3. For 'Abd al-Malik's supposed role in 757 see *Ajbar Machmua*, pp. 92–3. This text credits the Amir himself with the victory on the Bembezar.

reign of the earliest Spanish Umayyads. In this particular case there is enough consistency to allow for no more than a measure of belief that a revolt did break out in the early 770s, in which a man called 'Abd al-Ghaffar played a prominent part. The centre of the revolt was to be found in Seville, and the rebels were subsequently defeated in battle somewhere in the general area of the Guadalquivir valley by forces loyal to the Umayyad Amir. The enormous confidence in the details of the stories that they are relating is all too commonly to be found in the works of the medieval Arab historians, and their modern counterparts who now have to make sense of their accounts tend to do so either by taking one of the opposed variants as being reliable or by trying to create a composite picture out of elements taken from all of the versions. In neither procedure is there a great deal of methodological virtue. It has to be admitted that the fictive or elaborating tendency in medieval Arab historiography has not been sufficiently remarked on, and modern historians have tended to be far too optimistic in respect of the degree of reliance that they think they can place upon such sources. In general it may be advisable to reduce the variants to their lowest common denominators (and not place a great deal of reliance on those either!). It has to be borne in mind that for virtually every feature of the history of the reign of 'Abd ar-Raḥmān I the extant sources date from no earlier than the eleventh century. Moreover, a variety of other factors had by that time intruded upon the historiographical tradition to colour and distort the significance of particular episodes.

This suppression of the revolt in the early 770s marked the end of the so-called Yemeni opposition to 'Abd ar-Raḥmān I. The common feature of the revolts (and in that they involved groups who had previously accepted 'Abd ar-Raḥmān's authority this is a fair description of them) was a location in the south-west of the peninsula. Al-'Ala' had raised his 'Abbāsid standard at Beja. Sa'īd al-Maṭarī had begun his operations in the region of Niebla, and 'Abd al-Ghaffar had based himself in Seville. Indeed, this last city, which had received 'Abd ar-Raḥmān himself even before his first encounter with Yūsuf, seems to have been the centre or a main point of support for all of these movements. [80]

Why the Yemeni element in particular was associated with all of these movements of opposition is not easy to explain. The degree

[80] J. Bosch Vila, *La Sevilla islámica, 712-1248* (Seville, 1984), pp. 24–42.

to which contact was still maintained by them with their parent bodies in the East cannot be known, but it is significant that of all the Syrian armies in the aftermath of the overthrow of the Umayyads it was the Yemenis who collaborated most closely with the victorious ʿAbbāsids.[81] Their own power had been considerably checked by Marwān II, whose rival they had backed in 744.[82] The new caliphal dynasty never came to trust them or treat them with especial favour, but Yemeni support for the intended ʿAbbāsid governor of *Al-Andalus* may be a reflection of the realignments taking place in Syria at this same time. The revolt of al-Maṭarī may have been similarly motivated, and certainly the supression of both movements inevitably created blood feuds and the requirements of revenge, as was almost certainly the case with ʿAbd ar-Raḥmān's execution of Abu as-Ṣabbāh.

One more than theoretical difficulty that is to be encountered, not only in these cases but also in the analysis of other episodes in the early history of *Al-Andalus*, is the problem of anachronistic antiquarianism in the extant sources. By the tenth century if not before an enormous social premium was placed amongst the upper levels of Andalusi society on being able to claim a pure Arab descent, especially from a distinguished lineage. This could be utterly at variance with genealogical realities, but much effort was put into locating particular tribal elements and drawing up lists of who settled where in the period of the conquest. An English parallel, though a much less powerful phenomenon, would be the kind of emphasis once placed upon families that could show they had 'come over with the Conqueror' in 1066. In this context it is thus necessary to be on the look out for the invention of suitable histories for the various tribal or family units in the period between the Arab conquest of Spain and the tenth and eleventh centuries. Thus Ibn Ḥazm, writing in the mid-eleventh century, and himself a dubious claimant to high descent, drew up lists of the Yemeni and other families settled in Seville and other major centres in the peninsula.[83] There is thus a danger that the Arab historians perpetuated in the interests of the cultural requirements of their own society classifications that had lost the basis for their reality long in the past.

[81] J. Lassner, *Shaping of ʿAbbāsid Rule*, pp. 103, 107.
[82] Ibid., pp. 149–50.
[83] Ibn Ḥazm, *Kitāb Yamharat ansat al-ʿarab*, ed. E. Lévi-Provençal (Cairo, 1948).

In the case of the supposed Yemeni opposition to 'Abd ar-Raḥmān I, the groupings and rivalries of the 740s were probably still capable of making themselves felt, alongside of recent developments in the East. But it may be questioned for how much longer this was to last. It is notable that the various revolts were concentrated largely in the area of the lower Guadalquivir valley. Other areas of possible Yemeni settlement contributed nothing to these conflicts, and it becomes open to question to what extent it makes sense to see them exclusively in such terms.[84] To some extent sense can also be made of these shifts of allegiance by seeing them in terms of rivalry between Seville and Córdoba. Situated on the same river the two cities were natural competitors, something that may have been exacerbated by shifts in the location of the centre of government from one to the other in the course of the first half century of Arab rule in the peninsula. Seville had given way to Córdoba soon after the murder of 'Abd al-Azīz ibn Mūsā, and the early adherence of Seville to the cause of 'Abd ar-Raḥmān might have been expected to lead to reversal of Córdoba's pre-eminence. The desire of 'Abd ar-Raḥmān's Yemeni followers to sack Córdoba is significant in more than terms of immediate gratification of a hunger for loot.[85]

If, instead of assuming that 'Abd ar-Raḥmān took over a unitary state, it be accepted that the establishment of Umayyad authority in *Al-Andalus* was a gradual process, it is possible to see just how that power spread. From a limited base in the Guadalquivir valley and the south-east 'Abd ar-Raḥmān was only able to make his control of Toledo a reality after 764, whilst, although notionally accepting him from the beginning of his reign, Seville took up to eight years longer to be brought to heel. It is noteworthy that he only seems to have started minting coins in 763. It is significant too that it is only after this period that information becomes available relating to areas further north, particularly the Ebro valley. As the actual rather than the claimed authority of the Amir of Córdoba began extending itself into more distant parts, so it was to encounter new elements of resistance, not least that of the tiny Christian kingdom established in the Asturias.

[84] P. Guichard, *Al-Andalus*, pp. 338-52 for the settlements.
[85] J. Bosch Vila, *Sevilla islámica*, pp. 15–34.

6

A Dynasty of Opportunists

Pelagius and the Asturian Revolt

The Asturian kingdom presents a set of evidential and historiographical problems all of its own. The Christian Latin authors writing in the centre or the south of the peninsula in the middle of the eighth century make no mention of their co-religionists in the north, and unsurprisingly the treatment afforded the kingdom in the Arab sources is both limited in scope and highly partisan in character. Thus the short chronicles written in the Asturias in the late ninth century become the principal and in many cases the only fount of information for the history of this Christian kingdom. They can be supplemented, but only to a limited degree, both by the occasional notices in the Muslim texts and by other forms of evidence, above all charters. These latter become relatively numerous from the ninth century, but hardly survive at all from the eighth. Only fifteen Asturian charters are known that purport to date from earlier than the year 800. Of these only six can be regarded as being genuine, whilst another two may be given the benefit of the doubt and be classed as having been interpolated.[1]

A full enquiry into the origins and character of the late ninth-century Asturian chronicles will have to be conducted in relation to the period of their actual composition. For present purposes what matters is the nature and credibility of the information they

[1] *Diplomática española del periodo astur*, ed. A.C. Floriano, 2 vols (Oviedo, 1949/51), nos 7, 9, 12, 13, 14, 15 are the only ones the editor was prepared to trust fully. Nos 11 and 16 he regarded as interpolated.

have to offer in respect of the eighth century. The chronicles themselves have generally been thought of as comprising three separate works, but the most recent editors have rightly reduced this number to two.[2] The earliest in date of composition is the one known as *The Chronicle of Albelda*, which received its first form around the year 881.[3] It takes its name from the Riojan monastery of Albelda, where the primitive text received a brief continuation in 976. To this core text should also be added a series of lists, regnal tables and also a prophecy as to the limited future extent of Muslim domination in the peninsula, which once was treated as a separate work under the title of *The Prophetic Chronicle*.[4] The second chronicle is that known as *The Chronicle of Alfonso III*, because of the probable composition of at least the first form of the text by the Asturian king of that name, who reigned from 866 to 910. This now exists in two distinct versions, containing separate expansions of the original, made in the early tenth century. It is quite possible that the first form of the text consisted of no more than a history of the reign of Alfonso III's father King Ordoño I.[5]

Not surprisingly, the information contained within these two basic chronicles with their variant or expanded versions relating to the eighth century is relatively slight, at least up to the reign of Alfonso II (791–842). On the other hand this period was also the one in which was situated what may be termed the dynastic foundation legend. The ruling line of the kings of the Asturias traced their descent from Pelagius, who led the successful revolt that freed the region from Arab domination. If their continued rule needed an ideological justification it was here that it would have to be found. Thus, not surprisingly, the revolt and the victorious battle fought against the Arabs at Covadonga occupy a quite disproportionate amount of the space allotted to eighth-century events in both of the chronicles.[6]

[2] J. Gil, J.L. Moralejo and J.L. Ruiz de la Peña, *Crónicas asturianas* (Oviedo, 1985).

[3] Ibid., pp. 80–90 for discussion of this text; pp. 91–105 for its sources.

[4] Edited as such in R. Menéndez Pidal, 'Las primeras crónicas de la Reconquista', *Boletín de la Real Academia de la Historia*, 100 (1932), pp. 622–8.

[5] Suggested by J. Gil, *Crónicas asturianas*, p. 75. Another excellent edition of the *Chronicle of Alfonso III*, with two later versions of the text and a full introduction, may be found in J. Prelog, *Die Chronik Alfons' III* (Frankfurt/Bern/Cirencester, 1980).

[6] *Adefonsi Chronica*, sections 8–11 of both versions, pp. 122–31; *Chronica Albeldensia*, 15, section 1, p. 173.

Various attempts have been made to analyse the sources of information at the disposal of the late ninth-century chroniclers, and it has even been suggested that the *Chronicle of Alfonso III* can be divided into three component parts: the final section deriving from the work of the Asturian king, a middle section dating to the reign of Alfonso II, and an opening reproducing an otherwise lost Toledan chronicle of the early eighth century.[7] As has been suggested previously, none of this is very convincing. The supposed Toledan chronicle should be consigned to oblivion, and from the reign of Alfonso II the only certain piece of historical composition is no more than a regnal list of his predecessors.[8] Thus it seems unlikely that the extant Asturian chronicles contain texts of earlier date subsumed into themselves. Their perspective is therefore strictly that of their own day, and thus may tell us more about late ninth-century perceptions than about eighth-century realities.

A comparison of the information relating to the final stages of the Visigothic kingdom to be found in the two versions of the *Chronicle of Alfonso III* and the much briefer *Chronicle of Albelda* is very revealing.[9] In both recensions of the former the reputation of Wittiza is very black, whilst no general comment is made on him by the Albelda text. The latter, however, but in only two of its three principal manuscripts, gives an account of how Egica had installed Wittiza as his co-ruler with his seat at Tuy in Galicia, how Wittiza had there killed Duke Fafila 'on account of his wife', and how this led in turn to Wittiza expelling Fafila's son Pelagius from Toledo when he succeeded Egica as sole king. All three texts agree in assigning ten years to the rule of Wittiza and three to that of Roderic, who according to the Alfonsine chronicle was elected king by all of the Goths. The Albelda chronicle makes no comment on the means of his coming to power.

Only one of the two versions of the *Chronicle of Alfonso III* provides any genealogical information about Roderic. In the one known as the 'B' or, from its principal manuscript, 'Roda' text, he is made out to be the grandson of the Visigothic king Chinda-

[7] *Crónica de Alfonso III*, ed. A. Ubieto Arteta (Valencia, 1971), pp. 12–15; M. Stero, 'El latín de la crónica de Alfonso III', *Cuadernos de Historia de España*, 4 (1946), pp. 125–35.

[8] Preserved in the 13th-century MS Madrid, Bibl. Univ. 134, fol. 2.

[9] *Adefonsi Chronica*, sections 4–7 of both versions, pp. 118–23; *Chronica Albeldensia*, 14, sections 32–4, p. 171.

suinth.[10] His father, like Pelagius's in the Albelda chronicle, is said to have suffered at the hands of Wittiza, this time in Córdoba, where he was blinded by order of this arch-villain. The sons of Wittiza also partake of the infamy of their father in the Alfonsine chronicles. They betray Roderic at a crucial juncture in his encounter with the invading Arabs and cause his defeat. According to the other version of the Chronicle, known as the 'A' or Sebastian text they were also responsible for inviting the Arabs into the kingdom in the first place.[11] These sons of Wittiza and their treason do not feature in the Albelda chronicle at all.

It is not too much of a burlesque to say that the traditional approach to these sources is to take all of the variant pieces of information therein contained and try to make a composite picture from them. Methodologically this is quite unacceptable. If even the two versions of the *Chronicle of Alfonso III* cannot agree, then the supplementary material has to be regarded as not even belonging to the late ninth-century core text and must be classed as late traditions. Similarly, variants within the Albelda corpus, such as the story of Wittiza's rule at Tuy, need to be treated with the utmost suspicion. It has been fashionable amongst some scholars to look upon such cautions with scorn and to denounce what they see as 'hypercriticism', but the alternative is to write fiction and fantasy rather than history.

In addition to these discrepancies, there exist a number of clear anomalies in these accounts. The scheme of dating may well be inaccurate, and the supposed role in the conquest of the sons of Wittiza is open to serious doubt. The 'B' or Roda version of the *Chronicle of Alfonso III* states that Egica married a daughter of his predecessor Ervig (680–87) but subsequently repudiated her. This is true enough, and derives from information to be found in the acts of the Fifteenth Council of Toledo in 688.[12] According to the chronicle, Wittiza was the product of this short-lived union, and this must place his birth at some point in the early 680s; at his death he can have been no more than thirty years old and was

[10] *Adefonsi Chronica – Rotensis*, 6, p. 120.

[11] *Adefonsi Chronica – Ad Sebastianum*, 6, p. 121. This version takes its name from the prefatory letter from Alfonso III to a certain Sebastian, often thought to be a bishop of Astorga. In the edition by Prelog (see n. 5 above) this is the 'A' text.

[12] XV Toledo, section V, ed. J. Vives, *Concilios visigóticos e hispano-romanos* (Barcelona and Madrid, 1963), pp. 464–6.

probably younger.[13] Thus it is quite impossible for him to have had sons of sufficient age to play the kind of roles in the Arab conquest attributed to them in the Asturian tradition.

These worries about the historical reliability of the information contained within these chronicles, especially the most substantial Alfonsine texts, can only be accentuated by an examination of their accounts of the revolt of Pelagius and the establishment of the Asturian kingdom. In the 'A' version Pelagius is said to be of Visigothic royal stock: no such claim is made for him in the 'B' text, where instead he is described as the sword bearer of the last two kings.[14] The 'B' text contains a story about the desire of Munnuza the (Berber) governor of Gijón for Pelagius' sister and Ṭarīq ordering him to capture Pelagius and send him in chains to Córdoba.[15] Both versions of the *Chronicle of Alfonso III* concur in having the army sent to supress the rebels commanded by an Arab general called 'Alkama' and a Christian bishop Oppa, one of the omnipresent sons of Wittiza. The 'A' text makes him bishop of Seville, and the 'B' that of Toledo.[16] Both then concur in the location of the resulting conflict at the place later known as Covadonga ('in monte Asevua'), and provide a dramatic dialogue between Pelagius and Oppa before the battle. The 'B' text form of this is longer than that in the 'A'.[17] Their accounts of the outcome of the battle, and subsequent brief statements of the length of reign of Pelagius present no major discrepancies.

The *Chronicle of Albelda*'s version of these events is both substantially briefer and less florid.[18] It does, however, seem to substantiate the bare outlines of the accounts to be found in the two texts of the *Chronicle of Alfonso III*. There is no mention of Pelagius as a man with royal connections, but his expulsion from Toledo by Wittiza is referred to, and in this case by all of the manuscripts. He is said to have rebelled against the Arab rule, and defeated a punitive expedition in a battle fought 'in monte Libana', in which the Arab general Alkama was killed and a bishop Oppa, of no stated see, was captured. The subsequent killing of Munnuza

[13] *Adefonsi Chronica – Rotensis*, 4, p. 118.
[14] Ibid., 8, p. 122; *Ad Sebastianum*, 8, p. 123.
[15] *Rotensis*, 8, pp. 122–4.
[16] Section 8 of both versions, pp. 123, 124.
[17] Section 9 of both versions, pp. 124–7.
[18] *Chronica Albeldensia*, 15, section 1, p. 173.

the governor of 'Iegione' (Gijón or León) is also referred to, and the length of reign ascribed to Pelagius is effectively the same as that provided by the Alfonsine tradition. One worrying element is the location of the date of the revolt in the period of Yūsuf's rule in Córdoba, which occured in the years 747–56, and at the same time recording the date of Pelagius's death as being in the year 737, something which is corroborated by the *Chronicle of Alfonso III* and all other evidence relating to the Asturian regnal succession.[19]

In that Pelagius's own descent in the male line died out with his son Fafila in 739, a certain ambiguity had to exist in respect of the founding figures of the dynasty of the Asturian kings. In strictly patrilineal terms the later rulers all traced their descent from the third king Alfonso I (739–56), who married Pelagius's daughter Ermesinda. Thus in the two versions of the *Chronicle of Alfonso III* he is made out to be of Visigothic royal descent, and in the 'A' text this is specified to be from kings Leovigild and Reccared, themselves the effective founding figures of that monarchy.[20] That Alfonso's father was a Duke Peter 'of Cantabria' was agreed, but his Visigothic royal descent is not suggested in the Albelda chronicle.[21] In general, later Asturian interest in linking the dynasty with a Visigothic royal past had to concentrate on the person of Alfonso I, and, apart from his one battle with the Arabs, the rest of the reign of Pelagius is left empty in all of the chronicles. Only the Albelda text specifies that he ruled from and was buried at Cangas in the Asturias.[22]

What may be termed the ideological content is much higher in the two versions of the *Chronicle of Alfonso III* than in that of Albelda. The concern with linking the dynasty to one form of a Visigothic past and at the same time the repudiation of another, that of the sons of Wittiza, is a marked feature of the former work, especially in the 'B' text. This 'neo-Gothic' ideology was, in its earliest form, a product of the reign of Alfonso II (791–842) and most fully articulated in later periods, and thus probably no

[19] See the regnal lists from the MSS of the Albelda Chronicle, ibid., p. 177. MS Madrid Real Academia de la Historia 78 gives an absolute chronology, which starts the reign of Pelagius in 718.

[20] *Adefonsi Chronica – Ad Sebastianum*, 13, p. 131.

[21] *Chronica Albeldensia*, 3, p. 173 for this reign.

[22] Ibid., 1, p. 173.

reflection of actual early eighth-century concerns.[23] This dimension as a whole, together with the numerous discrepancies on points of detail, requires much of the content of the chroniclers' accounts of Pelagius' revolt and rule in the Asturias to be regarded as later accretions. Moreover, not even the most fervent believer in the activities of the sons of Wittiza has been prepared to believe in the dialogue between Pelagius and bishop Oppa as a piece of accurate reporting.

Stripped of its many dubious features, the historical tradition relating to the successful revolt of Pelagius becomes very bald indeed. That Pelagius was a noble of Visigothic origin and that his father's name was Fafila would seem to be unexceptionable enough statements. That he was forced to withdraw from the court at Toledo in the time of Wittiza is possible, but this may be a contamination resulting from the later historical reputation of Wittiza in the Asturian tradition, the causes of which were suggested in an earlier chapter. This story would enable the Asturian chroniclers to keep their founding figure clear of the evil associations of the reign of this king and its supposed moral responsibility for the subsequent fall of the kingdom. In fact the *Chronicle of Albelda* has him located in the Asturias before the destruction of the Visigothic realm, whilst the Alfonsine texts make of him a fugitive in the aftermath of the overthrow of Roderic.[24]

This again is a significant opposition in the historiographical tradition. The Albelda story would make of Pelagius a more firmly Asturian figure; someone whose natural place of resort was the Asturias. The implication of the Alfonsine chronicle is that he was a legitimate representative of the ruling line of the Visigothic kingdom as a whole, forced by political circumstances to take refuge in a particular part of the peninsula. In that the expansions of the core text of Alfonso III's work were probably made outside of the Asturias proper and after the moving of the capital to León, such a divergence from the more regional emphasis of the Albelda chronicle is quite comprehensible. Moreover the ideological presuppositions of the expanded Alfonsine chronicle required just such a view of Pelagius.

[23] See in general C. Sánchez-Albornoz, *Los Orígenes de la nación española: el Reino de Asturias*, vol. II (Oviedo, 1974), pp. 623–39: 'la restauración del orden gotico'.

[24] *Chronica Albeldensia*, 1, p. 173; *Adefonsi Chronica*, 8 (both versions) pp. 122–4.

On the other hand, the impression given by the *Chronicle of Albelda* that the roots of Pelagius's family's wealth and status were to be found in the north-west of the peninsula, in the Asturias and Galicia, makes far more sense of the revolt that he led in its actual eighth-century context. There is no suggestion to be found that he or any of his immediate successors saw themselves as reviving the Visigothic kingdom of *Hispania*, or even beginning a process that might lead to it. Pelagius's actual objectives remain totally opaque to us. The *Chronicle of Albelda* speaks of the birth of the kingdom of the Asturias and sees this as resulting from the victory over 'Alkama', but this is the view of hindsight.[25] This is what happened in terms of the perspective of a later century; not what the participants intended to achieve.

The roots of Asturian independence are not easy to uncover. To a very large degree the creation and even more so the survival of the tiny kingdom in the northern mountains depended upon factors outside of its inhabitants' own control, above all the limited nature of the Arab response. To view what happened, as has often been done, from the perspective of the later process and ideology of *Reconquista* is quite anachronistic. To a considerable extent regional revolts and the establishment of short-lived local rulers were perennial phenomena in the Visigothic kingdom, above all in periods of the transfer of power. For Pelagius and the Asturians to challenge the newly-established authority of the Arab rulers was generically little different to Paul and the nobles of Septimania testing the strength of the recently installed Wamba in 673.[26]

To view the episode as a Christian stand against Muslim rule may be tempting, but is dangerous. If this is how the participants saw it, what was a Christian bishop doing amongst the leaders of the Arab army? That he was present is common to all three of the Asturian accounts, and the actual existence of a bishop Oppa at this time may be deduced from a list of incumbents of the see of Seville. He was third in line after a bishop Faustinus, who signed the acts of the Seventeenth Council of Toledo in 693.[27] In that the sons of Wittiza must be regarded as a rather debased currency in

[25] *Chronica Albeldensia*, 1, p. 173.

[26] For an example of the traditional view see J. Pérez de Urbel, *España cristiana, 711–1038*, vol. VI of *Historia de España*, ed. R. Menéndez Pidal (Madrid, 1956), pp. 21–31.

[27] *CSM*, I, pp. xvii–xviii, n. 10, for edition of the list.

respect of the realities, as opposed to later interpretations, of the period of the Arab conquest, there are no necessary grounds for believing with the Alfonsine chroniclers that this Bishop Oppa was one of them.

A revolt and a battle become almost the only certain features of the stories relating to Pelagius. That it is presented as a revolt and that a Berber governor of the region with his seat at either Gijón or León is a common element in all indicate that Arab rule over the Asturian region had previously been established.[28] This was not a case of prolonged resistance. In many respects it is probably helpful to see Pelagius in the light of Theodemir, and to envisage him as another local noble forced by the collapse of central authority to take responsibility for his own region. That he, like Theodemir, had been responsible for agreeing terms with the conquerors is a reasonable guess. If so, he subsequently repudiated them for reasons that are unknown. Conflict with the Berbers established in garrisons in various parts of the north of the peninsula is a possible explanation. The creation of a self-proclaimed kingship, based upon a form of election by local leaders, was in the circumstances the only alternative source of authority for Pelagius, whose former masters had been dethroned and present ones defied. A victory over the punitive force sent against him turned aspiration into reality.

It is regrettable that neither the Arab historians nor the author of the *Chronicle of 754* seem to have known about or recorded the Asturian revolt and the defeat of the Arab army under 'Alkama'. In that Muslim reverses were as fully recorded as successes in the period of the governors, there seem to be no grounds for saying that the episode was deliberately suppressed. Its significance, however, may not have been as great at the time as later interpretations made of it. The matter of dating has not yet been alluded to. The chronology of the kings of the Asturias is, for once, a fairly uncontroversial matter, in that the regnal lists are generally in accord as to the length of reign to be assigned to each monarch, and by the later ninth century at least these can be effectively corroborated by a substantial body of dated charters.[29] That Pelagius died in

[28] *Chronica Albeldensia*, 1, p. 173 ('Iegione' could stand for either León or Gijón); *Adefonsi Chronica – Rotensis*, 8, p. 122, *Ad Sebastianum*, 11, p. 131.

[29] For the regnal lists see *Crónicas asturianas*, p. 172.

737 would seem credible. His length of reign is given as nineteen years in the 'B' text of the *Chronicle of Alfonso III*, and eighteen in the Albelda chronicle. The discrepancy is probably explained by the statement in the 'A' text that he died in his nineteenth year of rule.[30] The other two authors thus recorded this uncompleted year in different ways. This therefore places the commencement of his rule in 718 or 719. An alternative line of argument that places the date of the revolt and the battle a little later, in 722, has been considered previously and not found sufficiently strong to require adjustment of this traditional chronology.[31]

Should the commencement of the revolt be associated with the date of the battle of Covadonga?[32] It is by no means certain that the regnal list compiled in the time of Alfonso II shared the presupposition of the late ninth-century chroniclers that the beginning of the reign should date from the victory rather than from Pelagius's proclamation or election as king. In which case the issue would turn on the speed of the Arab reaction. It is unlikely that this was long delayed, and in the absence of more precise information this is no reason not to place both revolt and battle in or close to the year 718/19.

The failure of the Arab governors to pursue the issue after the defeat of their first army appears possibly less surprising when the general pattern of events both in the south of the peninsula and across the Pyrenees be considered. In particular, the great Berber revolt of 741 seems both to have removed most of the occupying forces from the north-west of the peninsula, and to have led subsequently to a permanent abandonment of Berber settlement in those regions. Moreover, judging by the total lack of information relating to the rest of the reign of Pelagius and that of his son Fafila, the tiny kingdom seems to have presented no threat to any of the other areas of Arab domination. In many ways the most obvious period for a successful Asturian rebellion and a truncated Arab riposte to have occurred would be in the troubled 740s. Intellectually it would thus be quite satisfying to be able to place reliance on the tradition in the *Chronicle of Albelda* that associates Pelagius's revolt with the period of Yūsuf's rule, but this would

[30] *Chronica Albeldensia*, 1, p.173; *Adefonsi Chronica – Rotensis*, 11, p.130, *Ad Sebastianum*, 11, p. 131.

[31] See above p. 82f.

[32] See the discussion in Sánchez-Albornoz, *Los Orígenes*, vol. II, pp. 41–155.

foreshorten the chronology of the Asturian monarchy by over 20 years, and none of the other evidence would allow for such a contingency. Failing this, a chronology that places the revolt in the period between the governorships of Al-Ḥurr and As-Sāmh, which is to say around 718, makes sense in the light of the latter's involvement in eliminating the vestigial Visigothic kingdom of Narbonne and initiating the war with the Aquitainians.

The Kingdom's Opponents: Muslims and Christians

The only other reasonably secure tradition relating to Pelagius is his establishment of his capital at Cangas. This, together with the location of the crucial battle in the vicinity of nearby Covadonga, places the centre of the kingdom in the eastern section of the Asturias.[33] If Gijón rather than León was the principal Berber fortress in the region it is not known when it was abandoned. Quite possibly it remained in occupation until the period of the Berber revolt. This would reinforce the eastwards facing aspect of Pelagius' interests, as further testified to by the marriage of his daughter to the son of the *Dux* ('Duke') of Cantabria.

Argument has continued since at least the eighteenth century as to the precise geographical definition of this latter region.[34] At its widest this looks as if it could have been extended in the Visigothic period to include not only the area of the Cantabrian mountains but much of the upper Ebro valley and the Rioja as well.[35] Nothing so extensive is likely to have been implied in practice in the present context, in that most of the Rioja and the western Pyrenees seem to have been under some form of submission to Arab rule in the period of the governors. As for Duke Peter, there is no indication as to whether he was alive or dead at the time of his son's marriage or whether or not he had retained an independent territorial power in the area to the east of the emergent Asturian kingdom.

[33] For the location see *Adefonsi Chronica*, 9 (both versions), pp. 124–5, and Sánchez-Albornoz, *Orígenes*, vol. II, pp. 12–9, 25–6; also A. Ballesteros Beretta, 'La batalla de Covadonga' in *Estudios sobre la monarquía asturiana* (2nd edn, Oviedo, 1971), pp. 43–87 for a reconstruction of the battle.

[34] See E. Flórez, *La Cantabria*, with introduction and commentary by R. Teja and J.M. Iglesias-Gil (Santander, 1981).

[35] R. Collins, *The Basques* (Oxford, 1986), pp. 92, 139, 148.

Pelagius's son Fafila was killed by a bear in 739, an end which earned him the unanimous rebuke of all of the Asturian chroniclers, who regarded him as being too much given up to 'levity'.[36] This is perhaps hard, in that the role of the hunt, which in the mountainous parts of Spain certainly also encompassed bears, had a political as well as a recreational function, in that it helped express and maintain the group solidarity of the ruler's household and close following.[37] However, as in this case, such things could be obtained at too high a price. The only other recorded activity of Fafila in his brief reign was the foundation of a church of the Holy Cross, probably in Cangas.[38] His replacement by his brother-in-law Alfonso is interesting for a number of reasons. As previously mentioned, it is by no means clear whether the latter had been a permanent member of Pelagius's court or had inherited some regional authority in Cantabria from his father. In so far as his succession was determined by his having married Pelagius's daughter, this seems to indicate a far greater concern for dynastic continuity in the Asturian kingdom than was ever the case with its Visigothic predecessor. This was, indeed, to be a marked feature of its kingship throughout the whole of its existence.

With the reign of Alfonso I (739–57) a slightly more three-dimensional picture of the Asturian kingdom can begin to be drawn from the brief statements of the later chroniclers. The *Chronicle of Albelda* records of him that 'he often waged war with God's help' and that he captured the towns of León and Astorga. He also laid waste the area of the *Campos Góticos* as far as the river Duero.[39] This information is amplified by the accounts in the two versions of the *Chronicle of Alfonso III*.[40] Both texts emphasize that his brother Fruela played an important part in his campaigns, and, rather than just the simple 'León and Astorga' of the Albelda chronicle, they provide much more extensive lists of the towns that he captured. These are not quite mutually consistent, but include Lugo, Braga, Tuy, Salamanca, Zamora, Simancas, Avila and Sego-

[36] *Chronica Albeldensia*, 2, p. 173; *Adefonsi Chronica*, 12, pp. 130–1.

[37] J. Jarnut, 'Die frühmittelalterliche Jagd unter rechts- und socialgeschichtlichen Aspekten', *Settimane di studio del Centro italiano di studi sull'alto medioevo*, 31 (1985), pp. 765–808.

[38] *Adefonsi Chronica – Rotensis*, 12, p. 130.

[39] *Chronica Albeldensia*, 3, p. 173.

[40] *Adefonsi Chronica*, 13 (both versions), pp. 131–3.

via. In practice virtually all of the major settlements of the northern Meseta, Galicia, and the north of the later area of Portugal are mentioned in these lists.

The question of just how much reliance should be placed upon them is not easy to determine. In addition to recording the names of towns captured, both versions of the chronicle concur in stating that Alfonso repopulated a number of regions in the north of the peninsula, including the coastal parts of Galicia, and 'Vardulia, which is now called Castille'.[41] They also state that the regions of Vizcaya, Alava, Pamplona, and the Berroeza valley were always in the possession of their inhabitants. In other words they never submitted to Arab rule. This latter claim is totally unfounded as far as the eighth century is concerned. Pamplona only freed itself from Muslim tutelage in the early ninth century and the same is true of most, though not all, of the other regions here mentioned.[42] Therefore at least one section of this account is inaccurate and misleading. Thus, it would be unwise to place absolute reliance on all of the details provided by the *Chronicle of Alfonso III*, whilst noting the general resemblance of its record of the reign to the more restrained one of the *Chronicle of Albelda*.

More significant than the question of precisely which towns Alfonso I did manage to capture is the matter of the general pattern and intention of his campaigns. What all the chronicles agree upon is that he created a desolate and uninhabited zone to the south of the Asturian kingdom. The *Chronicle of Albelda* would locate this between the mountains and the Duero valley, whilst the Alfonsine accounts would extend it much further south. According to their versions the towns listed as being captured were then depopulated: the Arabs being slaughtered and the Christian inhabitants taken back to the Asturias.

This makes sense in the wider context of events in the peninsula as a whole at this time. Within a year of Alfonso's accession the Berber revolt had broken out. Although successfully suppressed, this and the ensuing civil wars of the period 741–46 seem to have led to an abandonment of previous areas of Berber occupation in

[41] Ibid., 14 (both versions), pp. 132–3.

[42] This will be discussed more fully in the next volume in the series. The order and significance of the events in question are highly controversial, but no interpretation of them would allow this claim by the Asturian chroniclers to be correct; see Collins, *The Basques*, pp. 123–2.

the northern Meseta and Galicia, areas that had once been garrisoned by the Roman army against threats perceived as coming from the northern mountains. This obviously created something of a vacuum as far as the exercise of more than local power was concerned. Rather than attempting to fill this by an inevitably short-lived extension southwards of the Asturian kingdom into the open plateau of the Meseta, Alfonso's actions were remarkably far-sighted. The removal into the north of the inhabitants of some or most of the towns of the Meseta enormously enhanced his resources of manpower, and at the same time the creation of a *cordon sanitaire* along the Duero valley both provided a demarcation of the zones of authority of the Arab rulers in the south and the Christian king in the north and also made the whole frontier more easily defensible.[43]

Paradoxically, an extension of Asturian rule into the Meseta at this point could have led to the rapid collapse of the kingdom. It would have been impossible to rule the long-established and relatively sophisticated urban settlements of the Duero valley and the Meseta from what was no more than a village in the northern mountains. On the other hand to have moved his capital to León or Astorga would have placed the court in a vulnerable and exposed position militarily, as subsequent campaigns would reveal. Moreover, it may be questioned to what extent the Asturian kingdom was actually ideologically or economically capable of absorbing towns into itself at this point in its existence.

Unfortunately little or no archaeological traces of the earliest centres of royal government in the Asturias, at Cangas de Onis and Pravía, have come to light. But there is no sense in which these could be called towns. They would seem to have been little more than ceremonial centres in which the kings were inaugurated, where they occasionally resided, and where they were buried. Even Oviedo, which came to replace Pravía as the capital in the reign of Alfonso II, was no more than this for most of the ninth century.[44] It is reasonable to assume that the kings drew much of their revenue from their royal and private estates, and were gener-

[43] The nearest equivalent to this would seem to be the attempt made by the Huns in the 430s and 440s to create an uninhabited frontier region along the Danube.

[44] For Oviedo see J. Fernández Buelta and V. Hevia Granda, *Ruinas del Oviedo primitivo* (Oviedo, 1984).

ally peripatetic between their various villas. If Gijón had been the residence of the Arab governor before the revolt of Pelagius, and perhaps the nearest thing to a town in the Asturias, it is notable for its subsequent absence from any mention in the chronicles.

The enhancement of the population of the Asturias as the result of Alfonso and his brother's military activity opened the way to the repopulation of other regions adjacent to the original nucleus of the kingdom. This again is a matter over which some disquiet has been expressed in respect of the evidence of the *Chronicle of Alfonso III*.[45] An extension of Asturian rule into both Castille and the western regions of Galicia would seem hard to credit at this point. If the Duero valley was being abandoned then the creation at the same time of a salient of territory to the east and south of it makes little sense. Similarly, it is not clear that Asturian rule had yet extended itself as far as the river Miño in Galicia, let alone across it to the coast.

There is a danger here that Alfonso I, the patrilineal founder of the dynasty, was credited with a series of achievements that were actually those of some of his successors. Such a tendency can be paralleled elsewhere. Additionally, the coincidence of the territorial extent of Alfonso I's activity with that of Alfonso III and his sons may indicate a further ideological slant to the chroniclers' information.[46] By suggesting that the principal towns of the kingdom as it existed in the late ninth and early tenth centuries had been conquered by the dynastic founder, the legitimacy of his heirs' reimposition of their authority on them might be more easily justified. It may also have reinforced more specific proprietorial rights claimed by the kings over those who had re-occupied these settlements in the intervening period. Whatever the *de facto* power of the Asturian kings the ideological basis of their rule over ever increasing areas of territory from the mid-ninth century onwards clearly worried them, and led to the elaboration of claims to descent from the Visigothic rulers and the presentation of their kingdom as the successor state to that of the Goths.

Whatever the extent of Alfonso I's forays into the Arab and Berber controlled regions to the south of his kingdom, they do not

[45] C. Sánchez-Albornoz, *Los Orígenes*, vol. II, pp. 223–37.
[46] See in general A. Cotarelo, *Historia crítica de la vida de Alfonso III el Magno* (Madrid, 1933).

seem to have been sufficient to have led to action being taken against him. This could certainly have been undertaken once order had been restored in the south under the domination of Yūsuf. As in the case of the original revolt in 718/19, Alfonso's activities neither made a mark in Arab historiography nor earned him any military reprisals.[47] The impression must be that the Arab rulers did not take the threat that he and his kingdom posed very seriously. This needs to be set against the triumphalist tone of the Asturian chronicles.

To some extent it is probably fair to say that the rulers of *Al-Andalus* were not interested in what was happening in the north of the peninsula, other than in the Ebro valley and the Pyrenees. In terms of hindsight this may seem foolishness on their part, but it is really a question of perspective. Although the Iberian peninsula may seem a natural geographical and political unit, a view reinforced by the traditions of the Visigothic monarchy, it was from the Arab point of view merely on the fringes of the Islamic world. In the period of almost continuous expansion of Arab power the principal thrust was directed across the Pyrenees. The north-west of the peninsula was just a *cul de sac*. Additionally, it is clear enough that the Arabs found campaigning in mountainous terrain both difficult and uncongenial. Thus there was little reason for them to be concerned about the degree to which they were able to control the northern Meseta, Galicia and the Asturias. Even the advent of 'Abd ar-Raḥmān I made little difference to this perspective, in that his first concerns were with establishing his authority in areas much closer to Córdoba than the Asturias.

In these circumstances Alfonso I was able to expand his royal power in the north, and possibly just as much at the expense of previously autonomous communities in the Basque regions and Galicia as at that of the Arab and Berber garrisons of the Meseta. He is reported by the *Chronicle of Alfonso III* to have 'built many churches', but none of these are named.[48] A miracle was reported to have occurred at his death bed. He died in the course of the night and while the officers of the court were maintaining a ceremonial watch over the body, angelic voices sang a text from

[47] Ibn al-Athīr, p. 104, records his death, but assigns the conquests to his son 'Firowilia' (i.e. Fruela).

[48] *Adefonsi Chronica – Ad Sebastianum*, 14, p. 133.

Isaiah, in the form in which it was used as an antiphon for the Vigil of Easter in the Visigothic antiphonary.[49] From this may have come his later epithet of 'the Catholic', used to distinguish him from the numerous other kings called Alfonso.

His son and successor Fruela 'the Cruel' (757–68) enjoyed a somewhat different reputation. His nickname in later tradition derived from one of the last of his acts, which was to murder with his own hands his brother Vimara. He in turn was soon after murdered himself at Cangas by some of his own men.[50] The root causes of these human dramas remain veiled, but Fruela was able to achieve successes in other directions in the course of his reign. Although the *Chronicle of Albelda* contents itself with just saying that he gained many victories, more detail is provided by the Alfonsine chronicle. Both versions concur in attributing to Fruela a great victory over the Arabs, in which 54,000 of them were killed and their leader 'Umar captured and executed, but only the 'A' text seeks to identify this 'Umar as the son of an 'Abd ar-Raḥmān ibn Hishām.[51]

The silence of the 'B' text has not prevented historians from believing this particular detail and, moreover, identifying the unfortunate Arab leader as an otherwise unknown son of 'Abd ar-Raḥmān I, although the latter was ibn Mu'āwiya not ibn Hishām. The question of his identity must at best remain open, and obviously the figure given for the Muslim casualties will command no respect whatsoever, but the fact of the victory itself can be accepted. This would seem to be the first serious punitive action directed against the tiny Christian kingdom, now some forty years old. This battle, however, made no mark in the later Arab historiographical tradition. The latter, as represented by Ibn al-Athīr and the work of Al-Maqqarī, here following Ar-Rāzī, attributes the capture of Lugo, Oporto and Segovia to Fruela as opposed to his father.[52] The only other item that might have been thought to relate to these conflicts is the report of a treaty supposedly made in 759 between 'Abd ar-Raḥmān I and the men of

[49] Ibid., 15 (both versions), pp. 132–5; the antiphon (for the vigil of Easter Saturday) will be found on fol. 170v of *Antifonario visigótico-mozárabe de la Catedral de León*, eds L. Brou and J. Vives (Madrid/Barcelona/León, 1953).

[50] *Adefonsi Chronica*, 16 (both versions), pp. 134–5.

[51] Ibid., *Ad Sebastianum*, 16, p. 135.

[52] Ibn al-Athīr, p. 104; Al-Maqqarī, II, p. 85, cf. p. 261.

Castille.[53] The difficulties in accepting this as it stands have long been recognized. The later County of Castille did not exist in the mid-eighth century, and, additionally, it could be noted that the authority of ʻAbd ar-Raḥmān I in 759 did not even extend as far north as Toledo, then in the hands of Yūsuf or his supporters.

Other opponents of Fruela were to be found closer to home. Both versions of the *Chronicle of Alfonso III* record that Fruela was faced by revolts of the Basques and the Galicians.[54] It must be asked, though, to what extent the chroniclers were here again being tendentious. The 'B' text reports that during this reign Galicia was repopulated as far as the river Miño, thus implicitly denying the previous statement made in relation to the supposed conquest of the maritime regions by Alfonso I. In what sense, it must be asked, did Galician opposition to Fruela constitute rebellion? Was this, rather, resistance to the extension of Asturian royal authority over the region?

The impression to be gained from the chronicles is that Galicia, like the Duero valley and northern Meseta after the campaigns of Alfonso I, had become depopulated, and that successive Asturian kings in the mid-eighth century were busy restocking it with new inhabitants. This is a peculiar assumption: no reliable evidence exists to show that Galicia ever had been denuded of its human occupants. The only elements of population known to have left the area are those of the Berber garrisons established there in the opening phases of the Arab conquest of the peninsula.[55] That these had occupied the former fortresses of Braga, Lugo, León, and Astorga is a reasonable guess, if no more than that. If Alfonso and Fruela were introducing new population into Galicia, it may have been in the shape of military manpower to replace the former garrisons. It is important to appreciate that for the indigenous inhabitants of Galicia there may have been no greater preference initially for Asturian over Arab rule. Both were equally alien.

[53] E. Lévi-Provençal, *Histoire de l'Espagne musulmane* (Paris/Leiden, 1950), vol. I, pp. 116–17.

[54] *Adefonsi Chronica*, 16 (both versions), pp. 134–5.

[55] *Akhbar Machmua*, pp. 66–7, which here suggests that some of the (Berber) garrisons became Christians under pressure of Asturian attacks and the great famine of 749/50. The author reports that they then became tributary to the Christian ruler. In that Berber adherence to Islam was no more than half a century old and relations with the Arabs had been so bad, this is a quite credible scenario.

The same was undoubtedly true of the Basques, also said to have rebelled against Fruela I. In the case of the Galicians, the evidence seems to imply that they were resisting conquest rather than throwing off existing rule. For the Basques the argument is more complicated. It is clear enough that not all of the Basques or *Vascones* are being referred to in the chroniclers' remarks. Most of the Basque speakers lived well outside of the area of influence of the Asturian monarchy, in Navarre, the Aragón valley, and to the north of the Pyrenees.[56] However, the westernmost limits of the Basque territories are less easily delineated, especially in the area of the headwaters of the Ebro. Equally vague are the eastern frontiers of the Asturian kingdom in the mid-eighth century. In particular, it is possible that if the Duchy of Cantabria once possessed by the father of Alfonso I had survived the Arab conquest, then an area occupied by Basque speakers may have come under direct Asturian rule in 739.

By the early tenth century the kingdom of Asturias-León and the Navarrese monarchy based upon Pamplona were competing for dominance in the regions of the later provinces of Vizcaya and Alava.[57] What is not clear is the degree to which the former had established its control over the western parts of these regions as early as the eighth century. As in the case of the Galicians, the fact that by the time the chroniclers were writing in the later ninth and early tenth centuries both the whole of Galicia and an area of Basque territory were firmly included within the boundaries of the Asturian kingdom, may have led to their regarding previous Basque opposition as rebellion rather than resistance.

The report that, once the so-called rebellion had been put down, Fruela married a Basque lady called Munia might support such a view, in that this is more the act of a conqueror looking for acceptance than of an outraged overlord whose legitimate authority had been flouted.[58] It would be interesting indeed to be better informed about Munia, and the nature of her previous status in the

[56] Collins, *The Basques*, pp. 134–8.

[57] Ibid., pp. 138–40.

[58] *Adefonsi Chronica*, 16 (both versions), pp. 134–5; the *Ad Sebastianum* text offers a variant detail in stating that she was carried off by Fruela as part of his loot, as a slave, and that he subsequently married her. Such a rise parallels that of the Frankish queen Balthildis. See J. Nelson, 'Queens as Jezebels' in *Medieval Women*, ed. D. Baker (Oxford, 1978), pp. 31–77.

Basque area brought under Asturian domination, but nothing more is known of her. Their son, the later king Alfonso II, was on occasion able to take refuge amongst his mother's people, and his long reign of over fifty years was probably responsible for the real integration of this distinctive Basque element into the Asturian kingdom.

His succession, however, was to be delayed for some twenty-three years. The murder of his father might alone have caused such a hiatus, but as Alfonso was only a few years old power passed instead to his father's cousin Aurelius. This latter was the son of Fruela the brother of Alfonso I.[59] The nature of the succession practices of the Asturian kingdom were subtly different to those of the preceding Visigothic monarchy.[60] For one thing dynastic continuity seems to have played a part largely lacking in the earlier period. Despite occasional crises, that included the murder or deposition of rulers and a militarily disputed succession, those who held the kingship, or were thought eligible so to do, came from the ranks of the descendants of Pelagius and Duke Peter of Cantabria, or were married to them. The strength of this attachment to the rule of a single dynasty could, however, allow considerable flexibility in the pattern of succession actually followed within it.

The *Chronicle of Albelda*, which presents its information in the form of an expanded regnal list, contents itself with the simple formula 'X ruled for Y years' in commencing its brief treatment of each reign.[61] The two versions of the *Chronicle of Alfonso III* are more informative. In general they both state that each king in turn 'succeeded' the previous one, almost implying a natural process of succession determined on *a priori* grounds. In that this is used of the way that Aurelius took over the monarchy from the murdered Fruela I, a certain suspicion must exist that more complicated procedures are thereby being masked. A slightly later episode is, however, revealing. In 783 Alfonso, the son of Fruela I, was chosen as king by his aunt, who was also the widow of the previous king, and all of the magnates of the palace. However, he did not obtain

[59] *Adefonsi Chronica*, 17 (both versions), pp. 136–7.

[60] C. Sánchez-Albornoz, 'La Sucesión al trono en los reinos de León y Castilla', *Boletín(de la Academia Argentina de Letras*, 14, (1945), pp. 35–124, reprinted in his *Viejos y nuevos estudios sobre las instituciones medievales españolas* (2 vols, Madrid, 1976), pp. 1107–72, especially pp. 1107–20.

[61] *Chronica Albeldensia*, 1–11, pp. 173–5.

The Asturian Succession

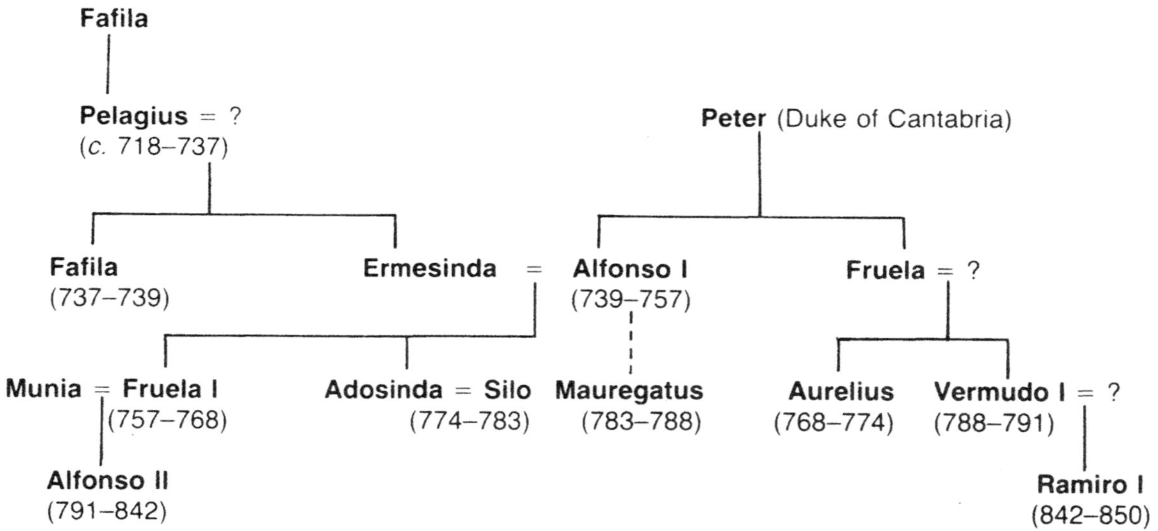

the crown because it was forcibly taken by another relative, who obviously had stronger backing.[62] This clearly did not come from the palace, and must have been regionally based. Its nature and location remain unspecified.

The succession of Aurelius, then, in 768, may also have had implications now concealed from us, and his role in the death of his cousin is not clear. Whatever the nature of its inception may have been, his short reign of six years was generally quiet. The chroniclers recorded that he was at peace with the Arabs, and fought no wars.[63] This might suggest that a formal state of peace existed, perhaps giving credence to the tenor if not the precise wording of the treaty supposed to have been made by ʻAbd ar-Raḥmān I in 759. However, it may be that Aurelius and his immediate successors were too involved in bringing the regions north of the Duero under their control to wish to essay ventures to the south of it. ʻAbd ar-Raḥmān I was equally tied down with concerns in the south and later in the Ebro valley.

The major event of Aurelius's reign looks to have been a servile revolt, eventually supressed by royal action. The wording used by all three chronicle sources to describe the event and its suppression is strikingly uniform, other than for the characterization of the rebels. In the *Chronicle of Albelda* they are just called *servi*. The 'B' or Roda text of the *Chronicle of Alfonso III* gives the same impression with its *servilis origo*. On the other hand the 'A' text offers a contradictory impression by calling them *libertini*, which is to say freedmen.[64] In all cases they are said to have risen against their own lords. It is particularly regrettable that no further details are provided in any source concerning this episode. The geographical location is unknown both as far as the start and the spread of the uprising, and its causes are equally hidden. It is possible that the revolt stemmed from a recent imposition of servitude on previously free inhabitants of those northern areas brought under Asturian control by the campaign of Alfonso I and Fruela I.

On the other hand some form of more widespread servile revolt may have resulted from particular economic difficulties of the time.

[62] *Adefonsi Chronica*, 19 (both versions), pp. 136–9.

[63] Ibid., 17 (both versions), pp. 136–7.

[64] Ibid., *Chronica Albeldensia*, 5, p. 174. On the subject of *Liberti* see C. Sánchez-Albornoz, 'Los Libertos en el reino asturleonés', *Revista Portuguesa de Historia*, 4 (1949), pp. 9–45.

That there was a class of cultivators tied to the land and obliged to work it for the landlords is clear enough from numerous documents of the next two centuries, although few survive from the eighth. They were transferred and sold with the land, though not, in later periods at least, separately from it. Their unfree status was transmitted to their descendants, who became their lords' property from birth. That they were permitted to retain a proportion of the produce of their labour would seem a reasonable assumption, in that it was the most obvious means of providing for their subsistence.[65]

The economy of the Asturian kingdom was entirely non-monetary. No coinage seems to have been minted at all. This was not to reappear in Christian Spain, other than Catalonia, before the eleventh century. Such exchanges as took place were conducted on a system of barter, although a nominal unit of value, the *solidus* features in ninth- and tenth-century charters.[66] Towns, as has been mentioned, were conspicuous by their absence, and there seems to be no evidence of any form of longer distance trading. The creation of the Duero frontier might alone inhibit much traffic with the south. Thus a closed economy existed within the frontiers of the Asturian kingdom. Landlords supported themselves on the proceeds of their own estates, and these could be adversely affected by poor weather. Certainly the peninsula suffered from severe drought, in turn leading to famine, on a number of occasions in the middle of the eighth century. Additionally, the movement of population from the northern Meseta in the time of Alfonso I into the Asturias must have intensified the pressure on limited resources. Thus if the lords were to cut down the amount of the surplus produce that their *servi* were able to retain for their own subsistence, severe hardship and increasing unrest could have ensued.[67]

The nature of Aurelius's solution to this problem remains as opaque as most of the rest of the episode. It does not look as if there was a battle, and thus resistance cannot have been organized on a large scale. Instead all of the chroniclers remark on how the

[65] For *Servi* in the Asturian kingdom see C. Sánchez-Albornoz, 'Los Siervos en el noroeste hispano hace un milenio', *Cuadernos de Historia de España*, 61/2 (1977), pp. 5–95.

[66] See C. Sánchez-Albornoz, 'Moneda de cambio y moneda de cuenta en el reino asturleonés', *Cuadernos de Historia de España*, 31/2 (1960), pp. 5–32.

[67] C. Sánchez-Albornoz, *El Regimén de la tierra en el reino asturleonés hace mil años* (Buenos Aires, 1978).

rebels were reduced to their previous state of servitude by royal *industria*. This could indicate localized or small-scale military activity, or for that matter some other means entirely for the settling of the issue. In any event, whatever the solution, it appears to have worked.

On the death from natural causes of Aurelius in 774 the throne passed to Silo, the husband of Alfonso I's daughter Adosinda.[68] Again some form of selection must have taken place. It is tempting to look for some kind of hidden principle of succession, but it would seem instead that there existed a number of throneworthy candidates, all enjoying various degrees of familial relationship to the royal line, amongst whom the nobility of the kingdom could choose. In 783 the main selectors were the nobles with office and followings at court, but then they were subsequently overpowered by what may be called the provincial nobility.[69] In that Adosinda was closely associated with the move to elect her nephew Alfonso in that year, it is a reasonable supposition that her own husband had the backing of the palatine nobility in 774, and was probably one of their number.[70]

As under Aurelius, the reign of Silo was marked by no hostilities with the Arabs. Elusively, the *Chronicle of Albelda* attributes this to Silo's mother.[71] The general tendency has been therefore to believe that she was an Arab or Berber, but the brief remark does not require such an interpretation; nor could this be held to be a sufficient explanation in its own right.[72] This passivity may seem particularly surprising in the light of the difficulties faced by 'Abd ar-Raḥmān in the Ebro valley around the years 776 to 778, which could have been exploited by the Asturians. Nor do Charlemagne and the Franks seem to have been aware of the small Christian kingdom at the time of their disastrous expedition to Zaragoza in 778. Silo was faced in the course of his reign by a revolt in Galicia, and thus, like his immediate predecessor, would have been more

[68] *Adefonsi Chronica*, 18 (both versions), pp. 136–7.

[69] Ibid., 19 (both versions), pp. 136–9. The nature and the development of the social organization of the Asturian kingdom will be considered in a subsequent volume.

[70] On which see C. Sánchez-Albornoz, 'El *palatium regis* asturleonés', *Cuadernos de Historia de España*, 59/60 (1976), pp. 5–104.

[71] *Chronica Albeldensia*, 6, p. 174.

[72] J. Pérez de Urbel, *España cristiana*, p. 38, who wishes to make her a relative of 'Abd ar-Raḥmān I as well!

concerned with events closer to home.[73] In general, except when itself threatened, the kingdom of the Asturias seems to have remained content within its own boundaries as far as the powers in the south were concerned for a considerable period, extending from perhaps 759 to 791. It is only the later perspective of *Reconquista* that may make this seem surprising. By those standards the Asturian kingdom should have been engaged in a perpetual war to extend the limits of Christian ruled territory at the expense of the Muslims. Those rulers not so engrossed in this anachronistic struggle have received little sympathy from modern historians.

The Galician revolt against Silo may again need to be seen more as a war of conquest on the part of the Asturian monarchy than a rebellion by one group of its subjects. For once an actual battle is mentioned, and it is located *in monte Cuperio*; as a result of this victory Silo is said to have 'subjugated the people of Galicia to his imperial rule'.[74] Here the word *imperium* means rule over more than a single people. This the Asturian kings had achieved by their conquest of Galicia and the subjection of various parts of Basque territory to their authority.

The death of Silo should have opened the way for the succession of Fruela I's son Alfonso. The 'B' or Roda text of the Alfonsine chronicle makes him out to have been 'governing the palace' during the reign of Silo; that is to say that he was the principal palatine noble, and by Visigothic precedent would have had a title such as *Comes Palatii*.[75] His own youth made him an improbable candidate at earlier points, and it is possible that to some extent Silo had been selected in 774 to keep the throne warm for Alfonso. If such 'legitimist' sentiments had been nourished amongst the court circle they were rudely dashed by the seizure of power in 783 by Mauregatus, a bastard son of Alfonso I.[76]

This seems to have been achieved by sheer force. Alfonso was expelled, and took refuge amongst his mother's relatives in Alava. In that obviously neither these Basques nor the Asturian court nobility supported Mauregatus's *coup d'état*, it is legitimate to

[73] *Adefonsi Chronica*, 18, (both versions), pp. 136–7.
[74] Ibid.
[75] *Adefonsi Chronica – Rotensis*, 18, p. 136. For such an office see C. Sánchez-Albornoz, 'El *palatium regis*', pp. 5–20.
[76] Ibn al-Athīr, p. 133, also records this, but states mistakenly that Alfonso was then killed by Mauregatus.

wonder where such overwhelming force came from. The answer may well be Galicia. This had been the principal area of expansion of the kingdom since the days of Alfonso I. At the same time the Galicians had shown themselves able to resist quite effectively, and had shown themselves opposed to Silo. That Mauregatus drew his support from the marcher nobility of Galicia and tapped indigenous hostility to rule from Pravía, which Silo had made his capital, is an at least plausible hypothesis.

After an apparently uneventful and unchallenged reign Mauregatus died in 788. Even this failed to provide the opening for the long expected rule of Alfonso the son of Fruela I. Yet another member of the royal house, a certain Vermudo, brother of the former king Aurelius and son of the brother of Alfonso I was elected instead.[77] If this was the act of the palatine nobility, it was a group whose composition can hardly have been unaffected by the ascendancy of Mauregatus. It is quite possible to regard Vermudo as the candidate of those who had deprived Alfonso of the kingdom in 783.

The latter was finally able to remount the throne to which he had been elected with the disappearance of Vermudo I in 791. The causes of this are by no means easily explained in the sources. The *Chronicle of Albelda*, which characterizes him as being 'merciful and pious', states that he abdicated voluntarily. The 'B' text of the Alfonsine chronicle elaborates on this by saying that he set aside his kingship because he was a deacon.[78] Even more extraordinary is the remark of the 'A' text that he abdicated because 'he remembered that he was a deacon'. This can not have been too easy to forget!

It is quite plausible that Vermudo had been in holy orders; this adds to the sense of the determination of those who had elected him to keep out Alfonso at all costs. However, if it had not been a problem for him in 788, it is not easy to understand why it became one in 791. For once the *Chronicle of Albelda* is more informative than its rival, and refers to a battle fought by Vermudo 'in Burbia'.[79] The nature of the enemy is not specified here, but it was almost certainly an Arab army. The Muslim accounts make it clear

[77] *Adefonsi Chronica*, 20 (both versions), pp. 138–9.
[78] Ibid., and *Chronica Albeldensia*, 8, p. 174.
[79] *Chronica Albeldensia*, 8, p. 174.

that under the reign of the second Umayyad Amir, Hishām I (788–96), almost regular campaigns were undertaken against the Christians in the north from 791 onwards. An account of a major defeat inflicted on the Christians in that year by the Amir's general Yūsuf ibn Bukht almost certainly should be linked to the chronicler's reference to the battle of Burbia.[80]

Thus the context of Vermudo's abdication was one of military disaster. Whether he felt himself personally inadequate to the task or was forced to step down is irrelevant in that, as in the preceding Visigothic period, the inadequacy of a king in war created a crisis of confidence leading to usurpation or deposition. In this case what is striking is that, despite earlier conflicts, family solidity prevented any threat to dynastic continuity from developing, and Alfonso II was able to take the power denied him since 783 under the cover of an abdication, real or obligatory. According to the *Chronicle of Alfonso III*, Vermudo I, later known as 'the Monk', continued to live for many years, and on the best of terms with his supplanter.[81] Quite how Alfonso II viewed those who had kept him from power for so long is not known, but one of his first acts was to move the capital away from Pravía and establish a new and permanent one in Oviedo.

This was not the only way in which the reign of Alfonso II marked a break with those of his predecessors. Under his rule the kingdom was to develop not so much territorially as ideologically, and in directions far removed from the more limited and regional aspirations of the previous kings. Furthermore, the campaign of 791, which proved so politically fortunate for Alfonso, was to initiate a period of much more intense confrontation between Muslim south and Christian north.[82] The long period of mutual neglect that characterized most of the second half of the eighth century came to an end in that year. In that major historical changes never succeed in coinciding with the pattern of chronological divisions by centuries in the neat way historians would like, it would be sensible to end the survey of the political history of the Asturian kingdom in the eighth century at this point, with the image of Vermudo I remembering that he was a deacon.

[80] Ibn al-Athīr, p. 142, who must have received his information from an ultimately Christian Asturian source. Al-Maqqarī, II, 99 merely records the battle.

[81] *Adefonsi Chronica*, 20 (both versions), pp. 138–9.

[82] See below, pp. 206–7, for the campaigns in the 790s.

7

The Maturing of a Regime

The March to the Ebro

Of all the numerous opponents that 'Abd ar-Raḥmān I had to face in the course of his reign, none were as persistent as some of the Berbers. They had provided much of the military strength of Yūsuf's regime, and had backed his attempt to regain power in 757. According to some of the Arab sources, Zanata Berbers were involved in the revolt of 774 that was centred on Seville. However, the contradictory nature of the reports of this episode make it hard to know just how much credence should be given to this particular detail. Far more significant in all respects was the sustained opposition of the Berber leader Shāqya ibn 'Abd al-Walīd.

This man was a Miknasa Berber, who in 768 proclaimed himself an *imām* of the Fāṭimid line, claiming descent through his mother from Fāṭima, the Prophet's daughter and wife of 'Alī.[1] The Shī'ite form of Islam had grown rapidly since the murder of 'Alī in 661. It had, if anything, been strengthened by the killing by the Umayyads of the grandson of Fāṭima and 'Alī in the course of an abortive rising, and its doctrines had developed apace.[2] What was, in retrospect, the last practical hope of establishing a Shī'ite Caliphate had evaporated in the immediate aftermath of the 'Abbāsid seizure of power in 750.[3] However, the doctrine of the imamate kept the

[1] Ibn al-Athīr, p. 118; Al-Maqqarī, II, p. 84. *Akhbar Machmua*, pp. 99 (Mérida cannot be correct here).

[2] S.H.M. Jafri, *The Origins and Early Development of Shī'a Islam* (London and Beirut, 1979).

[3] J. Lassner, *The Shaping of 'Abbāsid Rule* (Princeton, 1980), pp. 69–87.

potential not only for further religious revelation but also for armed insurgence very much alive.

On the other hand Shī'ism was not monolithic. Particular lines of the descendants of 'Alī were looked to for the providing of leaders of different Shī'ite communities. The Fāṭimid branch was not alone in claiming to have produced a number of *imams*, or divinely inspired leaders and teachers, from amongst its ranks, but it had one of the largest followings.

There has been a tendency amongst modern historians of Muslim Spain as much as amongst the Arab authors who provide the evidence for this episode to deride Shāqya.[4] His mother's name is said to have been Fāṭima, and this is held sufficient to have given him both a mistaken sense of his own genealogy and the idea for his self-proclamation. He was in other words just a fraud, deluded or deluding. On the other hand, his claim may have had some foundation. More important, though, than the reality or otherwise of its basis is the effect of his self-proclamation, which made him master of much of the centre of the peninsula for eight years.

Shāqya needs to be seen alongside a number of other 'messianic' figures amongst the Berbers in this same period. A Berber from Spain called Salīh ibn Ṭārif proclaimed himself as a prophet, and as such exercised power over the Bargawata tribe in western Morocco and in opposition to the 'Abbāsids, until supressed in 776/7.[5] Even more significant is Idrīs, a descendant of 'Alī, who was accepted by the Zanata Berbers in 789, and founded a dynasty that ruled much of northern Morocco until 926.[6] Again, there has been a tendency to secularize these men, and to regard the role of Shī'ism in their seizure of power as being marginal at best. However, what is clear from all three examples is that there was considerable potential amongst the Berbers for support of leaders held to be divinely inspired. In this sense Shāqya, Salīh ibn Ṭārif, and Idrīs I seem to be functionally identical to such pre-Islamic figures as the

[4] E. Lévi-Provençal, *Histoire de l'Espagne musulmane* (Paris and Leiden, 1950), vol. I, p. 112 writes of 'la foule assez crédule de ses compatriotes Berbéres d'Espagne'.

[5] Ibid., p. 113.

[6] C.E. Bosworth, *The Islamic Dynasties* (Edinburgh, 1967), p. 20. It is tempting to wonder if the general recognition of Idrīs I's Alīd descent really just derives from his success. Thus, if Shāqya had made himself master of *Al-Andalus*, would he not have come to be accepted as a legitimate Fāṭimid?

'prophets' Koseyla and the Kahīna, who led Berber resistance to the Arab conquest.[7] What is different is that the Berbers were now looking for such figures with an Islamic context, albeit a heterodox one, which concentrated upon the role of the revealed charismatic leader.

An account of the activities of Shāqya and of the campaigns directed against him by 'Abd ar-Raḥmān I is preserved in the work of Ibn al-Athīr, whose *Kamil*, written *c.* 1231, contains much of interest for the history of *Al-Andalus*. He himself was working in Baghdad, and dependent on written sources for his information relating to Spain. Unfortunately, he did not include references to these or the long lists of 'authorities' that had previously been a standard feature of Arabic historiography.[8]

According to Ibn al-Athīr, Shāqya's rising had its origins in Santaver in the modern province of Cuenca. On his self-proclamation in 768 he surprised and killed the nearest representative of Umayyad authority, the governor of the fortress of Santaver (Sontebria), and ravaged the district of Coria. He was able to avoid the punitive expedition led against him by the Amir the following year by taking refuge in the mountains, and used the same procedure to evade other armies in the course of the next two years (770 and 771) as well. In 772 he was able to take the offensive against an unwary Umayyad commander and scatter his army. By another ruse he was able to capture and kill the governor of the fortress of Medellín.[9] In 774 he himself was besieged in a stronghold, but the siege was not brought to a conclusion because of the Yemeni revolt in Seville. In 775 the Berber garrison of Coria betrayed the town to him, but it was retaken by 'Abd ar-Raḥmān I who chased the Berbers into the mountains. In the two succeeding years Shāqya was again able to resist Umayyad sieges in his principal fortresses of Santaver and 'Shebat'ran' (in the vicinity of Toledo), only to be murdered by some of his followers later in 777. They sent his head and their submission to the Umayyad Amir.[10]

[7] On whose activities in leading the resistance to the Arab conquest of North Africa see C.E. Julien, *Histoire de l'Afrique du nord* (Paris, 1931), pp. 319–27.

[8] D. Dunlop, *Arab Civilisation to A.D. 1500* (London and Beirut, 1971), pp. 128–9.

[9] This identification, suggested by Fagnan, p. 119, n. 2, would seem improbable in the light of the geographical location of Shāqya's other known activities. The name given in the text is *Mad'ain*.

[10] For these campaigns see Ibn al-Athīr, pp. 118–19, 120–1.

The whole episode is very revealing of the problem of public order faced by any of the medieval rulers who tried to impose their authority on the peninsula. This was the impossibility of maintaining permanent control over the kind of territory that supported large scale banditry and guerrilla warfare.[11] Shāqya based himself on a number of small fortresses, and apart from Coria, which was looted rather than held, did not seek to centre his rule on towns. He dominated the countryside from his hideouts and controlled communications. When threatened, he and his followers were able to take refuge in the mountains and evade pursuit by the less mobile Umayyad armies. The Berbers were, from their experiences in North Africa, adept at living and campaigning in mountainous terrain, which always seems to have posed problems for Arab forces. The same kind of pattern would be seen again in the long-lived revolt of 'Umar ibn Hafṣūn in the late ninth and early tenth centuries, or for that matter in the activities of the guerrilla leaders who resisted French domination in the Napoleonic period.[12]

Ultimately only a reversal of loyalty on the part of some of Shāqya's supporters saved 'Abd ar-Raḥmān I from yet more years of fruitless campaigning. This is similar to the Berber reactions to the self-proclaimed *Mahdis* and *Imams* who were thrown up in the period of the great revolt against Arab rule in the 740s. There too they ultimately perished at the hands of their own followers. Perhaps in both instances a crisis of credibility was provoked by the failure of the Berber leaders to achieve the kind of success their claims about themselves should have led to.[13]

The elimination of Shāqya in 777 meant that Umayyad authority was once more re-established across a wide region in the centre of

[11] It is worth noting that even in the mid-seventeenth century it was impossible for John Evelyn to travel the relatively small distance and easy countryside between Calais and Paris without having to join an armed convoy, due to the threat of bandits: *The Diary of John Evelyn*, ed. J. Bowle (Oxford, 1983), pp. 132, 136.

[12] Perhaps the best modern illustration of the kind of career and effect of a religious guerrilla leader of the kind that Shāqya appears to have been may be found in the activities of Muḥammad ibn 'Abdallāh Hāssan, the so-called 'Mad Mullah', who was able to resist regular forces and maintain a personal regime for over twenty years; see D. Jardine, *The Mad Mullah of Somaliland* (London, 1923).

[13] Cf. D. Jardine, *The Mad Mullah*, pp. 46–56, while attributing the ability of the Mullah to attract a following almost exclusively to the desire for loot, has some interesting reflections on the problems of preserving it in times of difficulty and defeat.

the peninsula. In particular it opened up the route from Córdoba to the Ebro valley. By this same period a new pattern of relationships between different regions seems to be established. For most of the Visigothic period Toledo had been the focus of attention as seat of the king and the dominant ecclesiastical power in the peninsula. This was to a certain extent an artificial creation, as the Madrid of Philip II was to be in the sixteenth century.[14] Neither in terms of communications nor economically did Visigothic Toledo make an obvious capital. Its geographical location, however, gave it a symbolic value as the centre of a peninsula monarchy. The Arab rulers, on the other hand, had preferred to base their rule in the Guadalquivir valley. This, and their apparent lack of initial interest in suppressing it, allowed a small Christian kingdom to come into being in the extreme north.

In consequence the region that had been, at least theoretically, the heart of the Spanish kingdom in the preceding Visigothic period became a frontier zone by the second half of the eighth century. For the Asturians, established behind the *cordon sanitaire* of the depopulated Duero valley, the towns of the central and southern Meseta became the natural prey for raiding expeditions. Similarly, the commanders of the Arab and Berber garrisons directed punitive expeditions northwards into Christian territory whenever the opportunity arose. These do not seem to have become a matter of interest and concern for the Ummayad Amirs themselves until the reign of 'Abd ar-Raḥmān I's son Hishām (788–96), largely because of involvements elsewhere, and an imperfect control of the frontier regions.

The removal of the supporters of Yūsuf from Toledo in 764 and the disposal of the threat presented by Shāqya and his Berber followers in the region of Santaver and Coria in 777 left 'Abd ar-Raḥmān I in a much stronger position as far as the central marcher regions of the peninsula were concerned. Even so, Toledo remained a potential centre of opposition, as seen in the support given to the rising of the last of the sons of Yūsuf there in 785, and it provided the base for the revolt of the brothers of Hishām I against the new Amir in 788–91.[15] It is, however, probably significant

[14] A. Alvar Ezquerra, *Felipe II, la corte y Madrid en 1561* (Madrid, 1985), pp. 23–59.

[15] J. Porres Martín-Cleto, *Historia de Ṭulayṭula (711–1085)* (Toledo, 1985), pp. 22–5.

that it is only after the temporary pacification of this region by 777 that we become informed of events taking place in the Ebro valley, and find 'Abd ar-Raḥmān I imposing his authority there in the course of the next few years. As previously mentioned, communications between Córdoba and the Ebro valley ran directly through the region that had been dominated by Shāqya.

During the reign of Yūsuf the newly-established 'Abbāsids had tried to regain the direct caliphal authority over *Al-Andalus* lost during the civil wars of the mid 740s, and in 754 the Caliph al-Manṣūr had secretly nominated as governor an Arab living in the peninsula, who was distinguished by being a descendant of the man who had carried the Prophet's standard in some of his most celebrated battles. He was not slow to find supporters. Disgruntled Yemeni Arab detachments in the north eastern frontier regions, particularly the Ebro valley, had collaborated with the 'Abbāsid pretender and had revolted against their commander, Yūsuf's nominee As-Ṣumayl, who was a member of the faction of Qays.[16] After some initial difficulties, the revolt was suppressed, and the 'Abbāsids' intended governor executed. This, however, coincided with the Umayyad rising, and was followed by the collapse of Yūsuf's regime. It looks as if Yūsuf had intended to entrust the governing of this marcher area to his elder son 'Abd ar-Raḥmān, but the latter fell into the hands of the Umayyads in Córdoba, and was executed soon after his father's death.[17]

There may have ensued something of a power vacuum in the March (*Tagr*) with the fall of Yūsuf and the ensuing slow period of the building up of the Umayyad regime from its centres in the Guadalquivir valley. Nothing is heard of what was going on in the Ebro valley and the coastal regions of Catalonia south of the Pyrenees between 756 and *c.*775. North of the mountains conditions had become equally unstable in the 750s. The Aquitanian duke Waiofar had been able to sack Narbonne in 751, and the following year the towns of Nîmes, Maguelonne, Agde and Béziers were betrayed to the newly created Frankish king Pippin by a Goth called Ansemund. When, however, the latter also tried to take Narbonne he was murdered by his own men.[18] There seems to

[16] Ibn al-Athīr, pp. 90–91; *Akhbar Machmua*, pp. 67–8.
[17] *Akhbar Machmua*, p. 77. For his execution, ibid., p. 94.
[18] M. Rouche, *L'Aquitaine des Wisigoths aux Arabes, 418–781* (Paris, 1979), p. 121, and p. 522, n. 63.

have ensued a seven-year struggle for influence in the region between the dukes of Aquitaine and the Franks, now under the Arnulfing or Carolingian dynasty, with the Muslims left as no more than impotent on-lookers. The issue was decided in 759 when the inhabitants of Narbonne massacred the Arab garrison and handed over the city to king Pippin.[19] Neither support nor reprisals seem to have been expected from other Muslims to the south of the mountains. With this extinguishing of Arab control in Septimania, the eastern Pyrenees became the frontier between the dominant powers in Francia and in the peninsula for the first time ever, and control of the Ebro valley gained even greater strategic importance.

The dominant figures in the Ebro and central Pyrenean area in the mid-770s may be assumed to have exercised power by virtue of their local following. There is no suggestion that any of them were appointed by 'Abd ar-Raḥmān I or any other external authority. The autonomy of these local potentates is confirmed by the next attempt of the 'Abbāsids to establish their control over *Al-Andalus*. At some point in the first half of the 770s an 'Abbāsid appointed governor called 'Abd ar-Raḥmān ibn Ḥabīb proclaimed the authority of his master the Caliph Al-Manṣūr in Tudmir.[20] In itself this is interesting, as it indicates that this region, still possibly under the direction of Athanagild the son of Theodemir when the *Chronicle of 754* was written, had lost its earlier autonomy by this time. Rather than directing his attention to the Umayyad ruler of Córdoba, then embroiled with Shāqya, the 'Abbāsid pretender demanded the support of a certain Sulaymān ibn Yaqẓān al-Arabī, then controlling Barcelona. When this was refused 'Abd ar-Raḥmān ibn Ḥabīb marched against him, but was defeated in a battle near Valencia. He was subsequently murdered by a Berber.[21]

It seems paradoxical that the 'Abbāsid challenger should have been more concerned with an opponent in distant Barcelona if the latter was no more than the appointee of the Umayyad Amir. The Yemenis of the Ebro valley had provided a powerful body of support for a previous 'Abbāsid delegate, the opponent of Yūsuf

[19] *Chronicle of Moissac*, s.a. 759, p. 294.
[20] Ibn al-Athīr, p. 125.
[21] Ibid.; *Akhbar Machmua*, p. 102.

and As-Ṣumayl in 755/6. The contest between 'Abd ar-Raḥmān ibn Ḥabīb and Sulaymān ibn Yaqẓān could be seen as a bid by the former to win over the loyalty of the latter's following. Another reason why ibn Ḥabīb was not immediately concerned with the Umayyad ruler will be considered below. In practice it looks as if sympathy for the 'Abbāsids had greatly waned in *Al-Andalus* since the period 754–63, and after 'Abd ar-Raḥmān ibn Ḥabīb's failure no further attempts were made to instigate such risings in the peninsula.

This episode, however, was to be the prologue to a more complicated series of events that, amongst other things, involved the expedition of the Frankish King Charlemagne to Zaragoza and his defeat at Roncesvalles. This is particularly interesting in that it is one of the few subjects in the history of the peninsula at this time for which it is possible to correlate the accounts of the Arabic historians with nearly contemporary Latin sources. Of the various Arab histories that provide an account of these events, that of Ibn al-Athīr (d. 1233) has generally been preferred, largely because it is sequential and comprehensible. It also has an absolute chronology within itself, which, however, is out of synchronization with that of the Latin sources. These latter consist primarily of the *Annales Regni Francorum*, a set of annals composed at the court of Charlemagne, and the section concerning these years is believed to have been written between 787 and 793.[22] To these can be added supplementary material in the 'Revised' version of the same annals, written around the year 814, and some further details to be found in a small number of other Frankish chronicles of early ninth-century date.[23]

Priority has always to be given to the datings proposed by the Frankish sources, because they were composed so close in time to the events in question, and the difficulty of someone like the first compiler of the *Annales Regni Francorum* being able to make a major chronological error in his work without the whole scheme of it being thrown out of its relationship to the time of his writing.

[22] *Annales Regni Francorum*, ed. F. Kurze, *MGH SRG*. On the dating see Wattenbach–Levison, *Deutschlands Geschichtsquellen im Mittelalter*, vol. II (Weimar, 1953), pp. 247–57, 260–5.

[23] Revised version of the *Annales Regni Francorum*, once attributed to Einhard, and thus known as *Annales q.d. Einhardi*, ed. F. Kurze, *MGH SRG*, on pages facing the original version.

Thus the Frankish intervention must have occurred in 778, and Ibn al-Athīr's placing of it in 781 is plainly erroneous.[24] However, what is striking is that all of the major Arab accounts of the interrelated series of events extending from 'Abd ar-Raḥmān ibn Ḥabīb's proclamation of the 'Abbāsids to the final submission of Zaragoza to the Umayyad 'Abd ar-Raḥmān I, are essentially mutually consistent and indeed largely parallel one another. In other words they all derived from a common source. That this was itself or was related to the version found in the *Muktabis* of Ibn Ḥayyān is a reasonable supposition, but for this early period that work too consisted of extracts from earlier authors.[25] The unusual consistency suggests that this does represent a survival from the earliest level of historiography in *Al-Andalus*, which may date to the first half of the ninth century. In this respect the core of the Islamic tradition is not much later in date than that of the Frankish Latin one.

The reason for Ibn al-Athīr's chronological errors are not hard to seek. An almost identical version of the major events may be found in the eleventh-century, anonymous *Akhbar Machmua*.[26] Here, however, the system of chronology employed is not absolute but relative, and it is likely that this was also true of the original text from which all these later ones derive. Ibn al-Athīr, who was giving his work a year by year annalistic structure, had to sort out the unstated chronology of his model, which if it was anything like the *Akhbar Machmua* also may have led him to separate out sequentially the description of distinct episodes that overlapped chronologically. Thus Ibn al-Athīr placed the series of events in which the Franks had a part to play in the years immediately following the elimination of Shāqya. On the other hand the *Akhbar Machmua's* account commences the sequence of events in the middle of the period of Shāqya's activities. The two distinct episodes have to be interleaved chronologically.

The 'Abbāsid proclamation of 'Abd ar-Raḥman ibn Ḥabīb must have occurred during the time of the Umayyad 'Abd ar-Raḥmān's conflict with Shāqya. Ibn al-Athīr places it in the year 778, which is patently wrong, whilst the *Akhbar Machmua*, without stating a

[24] Ibn al-Athīr, pp. 128–30.
[25] Ar-Rāzī is the most probable first source of this information.
[26] *Akhbar Machmua*, pp. 103–04.

precise date, locates it around the year 775.[27] This was just after the crushing of the Yemeni revolt based upon Seville, and the elimination of this likely base of support may help to explain Ibn Ḥabīb's greater interest in the Ebro than the Guadalquivir as 'Abbāsid recruiting grounds. It was in the final stages of 'Abd ar-Raḥmān I's campaign against Shāqya in 777 that the revolt of Sulaymān ibn Yaqẓān and Al-Ḥusayn ibn Yaḥyā al-Ansārī is said by the *Akhbar Machmua* to have taken place in Zaragoza.[28]

As with some of the earlier conflicts, it is legitimate to wonder to what extent this was, formally speaking, a revolt. It is by no means clear that 'Abd ar-Raḥmān I's authority had previously been accepted in Zaragoza, a former stronghold of Yūsuf. Why Sulaymān, last heard of in Barcelona, should now be located in Zaragoza, and in what capacity, it is not possible to say. An initial Umayyad expedition sent to reduce the city in the same year proved a fiasco, and the army was dispersed and its commander captured in a sortie. This was another example of the kind of warfare encountered in the campaigns of 763 and 774.

Despite this first victory the leaders of the opposition clearly expected a far more serious Umayyad onslaught the following year, and in looking about for possible allies settled upon the Franks. This part of the picture is much better filled by Frankish than Arab sources, just as the former are totally uninformative about the events in the peninsula leading up to Charlemagne's intervention. The *Annales Regni Francorum* describe how various 'Sarracens' came to Charlemagne at his assembly at Paderborn in Saxony in the winter of 777. They are named as being 'Ibin al-Arabi', and the son and son-in-law of 'Deiuzefi, who in Latin is named Joseph'.[29] Historians have been unanimous in hailing the first of these as Sulaymān ibn Yaqẓān al-Arabī.[30] However, the chronicler is quite clear that the person in question was *Ibin al-*

[27] Ibn al-Athīr, p. 125 (A.H. 161, which commenced 8th October, 777); *Ajbar Machmua*, p. 102.

[28] *Akhbar Machmua*, p. 103. Al-Ḥusayn ibn Yāḥya was said to be a descendant of Sa'd ibn 'Abāda, an early follower of Muḥammad and a competitor for power against the first caliph Abu Bakr after the Prophet's death. Sa'd's son Qays was a leading Shī'ite and supporter of 'Alī. From either of these roots the authority of Al-Ḥusayn might have stemmed.

[29] *Annales Regni Francorum*, s.a. 777, p. 48.

[30] E.g. L. Halphen, *Charlemagne et l'empire carolingien* (reissued Paris, 1967), p. 82; P. D. King, *Charlemagne* (London, 1986), p. 12.

Arabi, that is to say the *son* of Al-Arabi. Such an identification also makes sense of a subsequent apparent contradiction between the Latin and Arab sources. The latter record the murder of Al-Arabī inside Zaragoza, while the Frankish chronicler's 'Ibin al-Arabi' was later taken off as a hostage into Francia.[31] If the latter be accepted as the son of the former then the two versions of the fate of one man happily become those of two separate if related individuals.

The son and son-in-law of 'Joseph' have been recognized as the relatives of the former ruler Yūsuf.[32] In itself this is not improbable. Zaragoza had been a centre of Yūsuf's supporters in 756, and his son Abu al-'Aṣwād continued the family's unremitting hostility to the Umayyad seizure of power until his death in 786. Interestingly, the Arab sources make no mention of the role of these man, and no further reference to them can be found in the Frankish texts. It is only the 'Revised' version of the *Annales Regni Francorum* that adds to the account of this embassy that they came to Charlemagne to submit their cities to him.[33] To judge by what resulted some form of military intervention may have been sought.

If so, it was peculiarly ill-received by those who had solicited it. In 778 two Frankish forces were despatched, one to go around by each end of the Pyrenees and probably unite in the Ebro valley. Charlemagne took one army across the western end of the mountains, taking Pamplona *en route* and descending the Ebro to Zaragoza. He received hostages from Abu Tāhir the ruler of Huesca.[34] The other army, of which little is recorded, made its way by the eastern route to Barcelona. It may be that both of these cities were the objectives of the Frankish operation, as both seem to have been in the hands of those usually considered to be Charlemagne's allies, Sulaymān al-Arabī and Al-Ḥusayn ibn Yaḥyā. In neither case were the Franks admitted to the city, and it may have been this that caused the second force to proceed from Barcelona to Zaragoza. A joint withdrawal was obviously there decided on, and the Frankish army retreated by the western route

[31] E. Lévi-Provençal, *Histoire de l'Espagne musulmane*, vol. I, p. 124.
[32] Ibid., vol. I. pp. 122–3.
[33] *Annales q.d. Einhardi*, s.a. 777, p. 49.
[34] *Annales Regni Francorum*, s.a. 778, p. 50.

across the Pyrenees via the pass of Roncesvalles. There, memorably, Charlemagne's rearguard was set upon and obliterated by the Basques.[35]

At some stage in 778 Sulaymān ibn Yaqẓān al-Arabī was murdered in Zaragoza by his associate Al-Ḥusayn.[36] What relationship this had to the city's failure to co-operate with Charlemagne is not clear. It may be that the two men differed fundamentally over the Frankish alliance; it was Sulaymān's son who had gone to Paderborn in 777, and who was now carried back as a hostage into Francia.[37] On the other hand their murderous falling out could have been a local power struggle. There are no certain indications that either man had envisaged the kind of Frankish intervention that had actually taken place. Perhaps the first alternative is the preferable one, but the failure of Sulaymān's stronghold of Barcelona to co-operate was as marked as that of Zaragoza.

Although from the Western medievalist's point of view it is the Frankish intervention that has attracted the greatest degree of attention, it is necessary to realize that this was virtually an irrelevancy in terms of the struggle for domination in the Ebro valley in the 770s and 780s. It has been suggested, on the basis of a letter sent by Charlemagne to Pope Hadrian I in 778, that his action was intended as some form of pre-emptive strike against the bases from which Arab pirates were conducting increasingly threatening raids on parts of Italy.[38] Barcelona might fit the bill for such a naval base, but Zaragoza could not, and if this was the main purpose of the expedition it is surprising that the main force under Charlemagne's own control should have concentrated on the latter city rather than the former.[39] The alternative view that sees this whole operation as a piece of opportunism designed to achieve the long-term Frankish ambition of securing a march south of the Pyrenees may be preferable. In neither case was it a success, and, apart possibly from bringing about the murder of Sulaymān, does

[35] *Annales q.d. Einhardi*, s.a. 778, pp. 51–3; R. Collins, *The Basques* (Oxford, 1986), pp. 118–23.

[36] *Akhbar Machmua*, p. 104.

[37] E. Lévi-Provençal, *Histoire de l'Espagne musulmane*, vol. I, p. 124.

[38] P.D. King, *Charlemagne: Translated Sources* (Kendal, 1987), p. 48.

[39] J.M. Salrach, *El procés de formació nacional de Catalunya (segles VIII–IX)* (2nd edn, Barcelona, 1981), p. 8, suggests that contingents of troops from Barcelona actually joined the Frankish forces in the march to Zaragoza.

not seem to have affected the balance of power between the other competitors.

'Abd ar-Raḥmān I arrived with his forces outside Zaragoza but was unable to take the city, and so made a treaty with Al-Ḥusayn, now its sole master.[40] The making of such an agreement, even though it involved the surrender of the latter's son as a hostage, suggests the relationship between sovereign powers rather than between lord and dissident subject. 'Abd ar-Raḥmān followed the trail of the departed Franks up the Ebro and sacked the now defenceless Pamplona, whose walls had been raised by Charlemagne. He seems to have destroyed the fortresses of some local Basque potentates, and to have secured the co-operation of another of them, called in the *Akhbar Machmua* 'Ibn Belascut'.[41]

Even though it cost the life of his hostage son, Al-Ḥusayn broke the agreement with 'Abd ar-Raḥman the following year.[42] How he did so is not specified, but it may have been in the matter of tribute. This led to a renewed siege of the city by the Umayyad Amir, this time equipped with 36 mangonels, an unusual piece of detailed information supplied by all of the Arab accounts.[43] With their aid he was able to take Zaragoza. Al-Ḥusayn was put to death slowly, and the citizens temporarily expelled from their city. Thus by the end of 779 Umayyad authority had become a reality for the first time in the Ebro valley. This may have been the point at which 'Abd ar-Raḥmān I dreamed of sending an expedition to Syria to regain his ancestral rights.

Thus in gradual stages the Umayyad regime had extended itself from its first foothold in the extreme south into the Guadalquivir valley, then on to Toledo, Mérida and the marcher lands in the centre of the peninsula, and finally into the Ebro and the foothills of the Pyrenees. There has been a tendency in the past to regard the creation of the Umayyad Amirate as the product of a single year, that of 756, and to imagine it thenceforth existing as if already fully grown to its greatest extent. On the contrary, it is far more logical

[40] Ibn al-Athīr, p. 128; *Akhbar Machmua*, p. 104.

[41] *Akhbar Machmua*, p. 105. Ibn al-Athīr, p. 129 records that from Zaragoza 'Abd ar-Raḥmān I advanced up the Ebro to Calahorra, and into the Basque region, where he took the fortress of 'Mothmin', and besieged a certain 'Maldutun ibn Atlal'; neither of these can be identified.

[42] Ibn al-Athīr, p. 130; *Akhbar Machmua*, p. 105.

[43] Ibid.

to envisage it growing gradually, and against the opposition of numerous local groups and potentates. Like the Visigothic king Leovigild in the later sixth century, ʻAbd ar-Raḥmān I had to reconstitute a fragmented unity.

The governors had taken over a powerful and centralized unitary state, but had only been able to maintain parts of it, whilst conceding a large measure of autonomy to the rest. The treaties made in the years of conquest broke the strongly centralized pattern of Visigothic government in the interests of expediency. The civil wars of the 740s and 750s, of which the Umayyad seizure of power in Córdoba was but a stage, further dissolved the fragile bonds that had once linked the disparate parts of the peninsula together in a political and cultural whole. This period saw the emergence of rival local powers, not just in the form of the Christian kingdom in the Asturias, but amongst the Arabs and Berbers too. It took ʻAbd ar-Raḥmān I a quarter of a century to emerge on the top of this pile of rivals and competitors, and in the meantime the Christian rulers of the Asturias had had time to consolidate their hold in the north, crushing their own regional opponents.

It would be too simple to say that by the 780s the situation in the peninsula as a whole had clarified itself. To a certain extent, though, this is true. The two principal protagonists of centuries of future conflict had emerged in the form of a dwarf Christian state in the north and a giant Muslim one in the rest of the peninsula. However, many of the earlier divisions that marked their formative phases continued to exist and to produce internal conflicts as severe as any external ones. Other participants in the peninsula's complex future, such as the Basque kingdom of Pamplona and the Catalan counties of the Frankish March, had yet to make their appearance, although their embryo forms are visible with hindsight.

Despite the complexities of the history of the peninsula in the ninth and tenth centuries, a certain clarity does seem to descend upon the delineation of political and cultural conflicts by the end of the eighth century. In part this may be a reflection of the improved quality of the available evidence. Although the date of writing of the earliest extant Arab texts dealing with the history of the peninsula is still some centuries off, they are at least in part themselves using sources of nearly contemporary date. Likewise with the Latin materials, ninth-century Asturian and Frankish chronicles have more that is comprehensible to say about times closer to their own than they did about the dimmer realities of the eighth century. On the other hand, there also takes place a genuine tidying up of the participants. Some of the losers in the game of the eighth century disappear. Messianic Berbers, Arab factions deriving from ever more distant rivalries in the vanished Syria of the Umayyad Caliphate, the partisans of Yūsuf al-Fihrī, and secret 'Abbāsid governors all vanish or cease to loom large in the record of events. The reader may regret their passing, but their contemporaries probably did not.

The 'Arab Leovigild'

Like Leovigild before him, at the end of a period of almost continuous warfare 'Abd ar-Raḥmān I was able to turn instead in the last phase of his reign to a programme of urban planning, building and artistic patronage. This is not to say that his final years were entirely peaceful. The house of Yūsuf launched its final bid to regain its lost power in the years 785/6.[44] Within the Umayyad dynasty itself strife broke out, possibly as the question of the succession became more acute, and three close relatives of the Amir were executed for their parts in conspiracies against him in the 780s. Nor, on the other hand, were all of 'Abd ar-Raḥmān's more peaceful endeavours delayed until these final years. Some of the work attributed to him in the building of public amenities and utilities in the city of Córdoba may belong to earlier periods of the reign. But his greatest monument, the first stage of the Mezquita of Córdoba, may only have begun to be constructed in 785.[45]

The history of the development of the city of Córdoba under Arab rule looks, superficially, to be easy to chronicle. Although archaeological confirmation is almost impossible to obtain, because the continuous occupation of the site makes the possibilities for excavation both limited and rarely occurring, the literary evi-

[44] Ibn al-Athīr, pp. 131–32. Even after the death of Abu al-'Aṣwad Ibn Yūsuf, another brother by the name of Qāsim emerged to give short-lived leadership to the revolt.

[45] On this building see O. Grabar, *The Formation of Islamic Art* (New Haven and London, 1973), pp. 111–23, 130–4. For the date see Ibn 'Idārī, II, p. 378.

dence would seem to be substantial both in the quantity and the variety of information it appears to provide.[46] However, the reality proves to be quite otherwise.

The elaborate and detailed accounts of the city to be found in a number of late sources, above all the seventeenth-century work of Al-Maqqarī, are unreliable and dangerously misleading. Particularly alluring are the precise statistics given for such quantities as the number of houses or of shops to be found in the city, or for the present enquiry in particular, for the number of mosques that existed in it during the reign of 'Abd ar-Raḥmān I. In a number of cases Al-Maqqarī is citing, as was his custom, extracts from other earlier works, though sometimes without specifying the names of their authors. In certain instances such citations take the form of personal assurances on the part of the writers that their information was validated on the grounds that they themselves had actually compiled their statistics from first-hand observation.[47]

Such precision, however, is invariably spurious. The figures given are, in all cases, patently absurd. In general, numbers appearing in Arab historical texts, be they the quantity of a certain type of building or the revenues of the 'Abbāsid Caliphs given to the nearest dinar, should be treated with profound caution and suspicion.[48] This is not just a problem affecting the study of Muslim Spain, but is a flaw at the very heart of the Arab historical tradition. In terms of the study of towns, it is as true of Baghdad as of Córdoba.

Both cities, moreover, acquired particular significance in retrospect, becoming in themselves symbols of what later generations looked back to as lost golden ages. Just as the Baghdad of Ḥarūn ar-Rashīd and the 'One Thousand and One Nights' took on a spurious glamour in the period of 'Abbāsid decline, so Umayyad Córdoba could become a symbol of a lost grandeur for writers working either after the fall of the Spanish Caliphate or indeed after the expulsion of the Arabs from the peninsula in 1492. From fear of both this retrospective romanticism and of the Arab his-

[46] Many of the principal texts are conveniently collected in A. Artajona Castro, *Anales de Córdoba musulmana* (Córdoba, 1982), see p. 263 for index of relevant documents.

[47] Al-Maqqarī, I, pp. 200–31.

[48] 331,929,008 dirhems a year in the reign of Al-Mamun! P. Hitti, *A History of the Arabs* (8th edn, London, 1964), pp. 320–1, quoting from Ibn Khaldūn.

torian's insatiable love of spurious statistics it is necessary to be very wary about making too many firm statements about the appearance and organization of Córdoba in the eighth century.

Despite the force of such necessary reservations, it is possible to make some kind of assessment of the way the city developed in the early Islamic period. Its importance stemmed only in part from its Roman and Visigothic past. What little is known of it in the seventh century merely reinforces the sense of the greater importance of Seville at that time. However, its selection as the administrative centre for the first governors and subsequently for the Umayyad Amirs transformed its role and gave it a pre-eminence matched by no other city in the peninsula before the eleventh century. By the end of the period of Umayyad rule, Córdoba was not only the governmental but also the cultural heart of their regime, and the city benefited from the dynasty's patronage to an unparalleled degree. Indeed Umayyad interest in the other cities and towns of *Al-Andalus* seems to have been remarkably slight, and the collapse of their caliphate opened the way for a remarkable cultural florescence in a series of provincial urban centres previously overshadowed by the dominance of the capital.[49]

How far the process of building up, both literally and metaphorically, the artistic and cultural splendours of Córdoba had reached by the end of the reign of 'Abd ar-Raḥmān I is hard to say. A number of the most important buildings in the city are said in later sources to have been his work. In particular, one of the principal palaces, known as the Risafāh, together with its gardens and an aqueduct are claimed to date from his reign.[50] In itself this is not improbable. The enhanced status as well as the descent of the new ruler of *Al-Andalus* doubtless required a suitable setting for his family and entourage, and that Córdoba was used to recreate something of the palace culture of the Umayyad caliphs of Syria is a reasonable assumption.[51] As no material remains of these or other major public buildings in Córdoba itself have come to light it is

[49] D. Wasserstein, *The Rise and Fall of the Party Kings: Politics and Society in Islamic Spain, 1002–1086* (Princeton, 1985), pp. 163–246.

[50] Al-Maqqarī, II, p. 86. Cf. *Ajbar Machmua*, p. 105 for mention of it.

[51] For some impression of this see the account of the excavations of the palace complex of Qusayr 'Amra: M. Almagro, L. Caballero, J. Zozaya, and A. Almagro, *Qusayr 'Amra: residencia y baños omeyas en el desierto de Jordania* (Madrid, 1975).

both impossible and unnecessary to worry about the architectural character and composition of the first Umayyad palaces in *Al-Andalus*. That they bore a resemblance to those still extant in Jordan and Israel that were erected by members of the same dynasty earlier in the eighth century is, though, a reasonable supposition.

Some maintenance work on public buildings had taken place earlier, during the period of the governors. As-Sāmh is reported to have restored the Roman bridge over the Guadalquivir at Córdoba around the year 719.[52] This is sometimes held to prove that the previous Visigothic regime had been incapable of maintaining such vital works of Roman engineering.[53] In that the same sources used to justify this claim have the Arabs crossing the bridge in 712, the damage to it must have been either very limited or more recent in date. Furthermore, the absurdity of such a line of argument can be seen if applied instead to the restoration of the bridge over the Guadiana at Mérida carried out under Visigothic auspices.[54] Is this supposed to prove that the late Romans were therefore previously incapable of keeping their bridges in order?

Interestingly, no record exists of this type of work being undertaken by 'Abd ar-Raḥmān I. Most of the buildings attributed to him were of a more private character. On the other hand the kinds of public building, such as theatres, hippodromes and circuses that had once been the staple ways of displaying the munificence of the individual patron or of the imperial regime in the time of the Roman Empire had ceased to play their primary functions in urban life. Even in Constantinople in this same period the limited imperial building programmes were confined to the erection or restoration of palaces and churches.[55]

Within the Islamic community the mosque was indeed the public building *par excellence*, in that it was still the place in which the whole male Muslim population of any given settlement gathered once a week for the Friday prayers. Thus as well as its

[52] *Akhbar Machmua*, p. 35.

[53] T.F. Glick, *Islamic and Christian Spain in the Early Middle Ages* (Princeton, 1979), p. 31.

[54] *Inscripciones cristianas de la España romana y visigoda*, ed. J. Vives, (Barcelona, 1969), no. 363, pp. 126–7.

[55] C. Mango, *Le Développement urbain de Constantinople (IVe–VIIe siècles)* (Paris, 1985), pp. 51–62.

purely religious importance, it served as the regular meeting place and political pulse of the local Muslim community. This was the place in which a Muslim ruler would wish to make his presence felt. The prohibition on the mention of the name of the 'Abbāsid caliph in the Friday prayers from 757 was only the first step as far as the Umayyad regime in *Al-Andalus* was concerned. For various reasons previously discussed, 'Abd ar-Raḥmān I was in no position to have his own name substituted for that of the Caliph, but by the end of his reign he was able to link his own dynasty's achievements to those of Islam in a very material way by undertaking the construction of a new mosque for the Muslim community of Córdoba, in itself probably the largest in *Al-Andalus*.

The first mosque in the city was, according to later Arab accounts, half of the Church of St Vincent, one of the three principal Christian patron saints of Córdoba. This claim requires to be treated with considerable caution in that it parallels a story relating to the founding of the great Umayyad mosque in Damascus.[56] Whether or not a church had previously existed on the site, the location of the new mosque, adjacent to what is thought to have been the former Roman and then Visigothic governor's palace, and also close to the bridge across the Guadalquivir was carefully chosen, and may also testify to an initial defensiveness on the part of the Muslims. There may also have been a symbolic significance in the deliberate re-use in the mosque of capitals and columns from earlier Roman and Visigothic buildings.[57] Many early mosques incorporate pieces of stonework, principally columns and capitals taken from earlier buildings, in a number of cases from churches. It is usually assumed that this was done for reasons of speed or convenience. On the other hand a strong case has been made for seeing the motif of crowns in the mosaic decoration of the Dome of the Rock in Jerusalem as symbolizing the conquests of various non-Muslim states by the

[56] Al-Maqqarī, I, pp. 217–18, Artajona Castro, *Anales*, doc. 16, pp. 24–5. This paralleling has rightly led to considerable suspicion being thrown on the truth of the Cordoban case. See K.A.C. Cresswell, *A Short Account of Early Muslim Architecture* (Harmondsworth, 1958), p. 213.

[57] See, for example, N. Harrazi, *Chapiteaux de la grande Mosquée de Kairouan* (2 vols, Tunis, 1982), which studies the Roman and early Byzantine capitals reused in the prayer hall of the Great Mosque of Kairouan (*c*.860).

forces of Islam.[58] The re-use of architectural spoils taken from non-Islamic places of worship may have similar significance. In the case of the mosque in Córdoba this may have been reinforced by the later Arab traditions that located the building on the site of a former Christian church. In an even more elaborate form of the story the Church of St Vincent itself was made out to have been built on the site of an earlier synagogue erected by King Solomon. Thus in itself the Muslim building symbolized the stages of the progressive revelation of true religion.[59] This in its developed form was probably a later mystical rationalization, but the possible selection of a major Christian church for the location of the first mosque, can be paralleled in a number of North African cities, and may have some factual basis.[60]

For his new mosque 'Abd ar-Raḥmān I is said to have had the rest of the Church of St Vincent taken from the Christians, who were compensated by being allowed to build another church in the suburbs of the city, and then demolished to make way for an entirely new structure, architecturally related to the type of mosque being erected elsewhere in the Islamic world in the same period.[61] This can still be seen as a section of the vastly expanded late tenth-century mosque later transformed into the cathedral of Córdoba after the Christian conquest of the city. In itself the physical structure of the mosque of 'Abd ar-Raḥmān I can give some impression of the size of the male Muslim community of Córdoba in the 780s. Although clearly increased from that of the first mosque erected in the time of the governors, it still appears to have been relatively small. The dimensions of the prayer hall were no more than 35 by 75 metres. Even allowing only one square metre per man, an absurdly small amount of room for the perform-

[58] O. Grabar, *Formation of Islamic Art*, pp. 66–7.

[59] In view of the suspicious relationship of this story to the one relating to the Umayyad mosque in Damascus, it would be unwise to put too much weight on its reality. There exist a number of unique or unparalleled features in the Cordoban mosque; see K.A.C. Cresswell, *Short Account*, pp. 225–8. For the Damascus mosque see L. Golvin, *Essai sur l'architecture religieuse musulmane*, vol. 2 (Paris, 1971), pp. 125–86, esp. 129–30 for its relationship with a previous church of St John.

[60] This was very probably the case in Sousse, the former Hadrumetum.

[61] Al-Maqqarī, I, pp. 218. Cresswell stresses Syrian parallels, largely based on an estimate of the earlier forms of the late Umayyad mosque of Al-Aqsā in Jerusalem.

ance of the necessary prostrations, such a structure could not have held more than 2,000 people.[62] The reality must be something nearer half that number. Some allowance might be made for the additional use of the courtyard intended for ritual ablutions that provided the entry into the prayer hall, but even so, in that the mosque begun by 'Abd ar-Raḥmān I in 785 was new and purpose-built, the community it was intended to serve was clearly small. It may have numbered less than 4,000 members of both sexes. Such a calculation, rather than the preposterous statement to be found in al-Maqqarī to the effect that there were 490 mosques in Córdoba in the time of 'Abd ar-Raḥmān I gives more of a sense of the Arab achievement in eighth-century Spain.[63]

Administration and Control

One crucial area of enquiry that so far has been given little attention here is that of the administration and governmental structures of Muslim ruled Spain in the eighth century. This has been both deliberate and necessary in that the evidence on which an assessment of them could be made is depressingly thin, and it is not possible to use it in a chronologically specific way as far as this period is concerned. There has been a tendency in the historiography of Muslim Spain to take source material relating to governmental practices of the ninth and tenth centuries and treat it as if, *a priori*, it must also be true of the situation in the eighth. However, if anything is clear it is that this latter period saw extraordinary variations in the political and economic ordering of the peninsula. It would be legitimate enough to expect that something very like the mature administrative structure of Umayyad *Al-Andalus* had emerged by the end of the eighth century, and that this was structurally related to earlier forms of organization. But to assume

[62] For the making of this kind of calculation, using a North African example, see A. Lézine, *Deux villes d'Ifriqiya* (Paris, 1971), pp. 17–23, who thereby estimates that the Muslim population of Sousse around the year 780 was approximately 700.

[63] Al-Maqqarī, I, p. 215. There may have existed some sectional mosques in the city by this time (see O. Grabar, *Formation of Islamic Art*, p. 112), but the whole male Muslim population would still have had to gather in the main mosque once a week.

that it had already reached this state by 756 or that the exigencies of the period of the 740s to 760s did not impose a large measure of change and improvisation would be too optimistic.

In the earliest period of the conquest two administrative systems had co-existed. By the terms of such treaties as that made with Theodemir it is clear that various towns and districts retained their previous forms of local government, which were those of the Visigothic period. In the seventh century responsibility for the local administration of a town had been shared between the *Comes Civitatis* and the *Iudex*, the one effectively a military official and the other a civilian judge.[64] Both were appointed by and were answerable to the king. In origin this may have related to the division between Roman and German inhabitants, with the count having responsibility for the Goths and the judge for the rest. In legal matters in particular this has been taken as reflecting the essential cultural divide between the two sectors of the population, and the need to be able not only to operate two separate and racially oriented systems of law but also to provide mechanisms to resolve disputes in which Roman and Germanic traditions conflicted.

However, the supposedly distinctive Germanic elements in the earlier Visigothic royal law codes tend to evaporate on close inspection, and the whole question of when territorial codes as opposed to racially specific ones were first issued by the Visigothic kings remains at least debatable.[65] It is indeed far more likely that the Roman/German divide should rather be seen as a civilian/military one. The roots of the separate systems of law and administration should thus be sought in the practices of the Late Roman Empire, rather than in any sense be seen as a response to the presence of a racially distinct element in the population. In any case the distinction was not one with much or perhaps any meaning in the last decades of the Visigothic period. To such a degree had assimilation and the reformation of a new common ethnic identity advanced that it is impossible to detect ethnically distinct Romans in Spain by the end of the seventh century.[66] Similarly, the

[64] E.A. Thompson, *The Goths in Spain* (Oxford, 1969), pp. 139–42.

[65] R. Collins, *Early Medieval Spain: Unity in Diversity, 400–1000* (London, 1983), pp. 24–30.

[66] On the re-formation of ethnic identities see A. Smith, *The Ethnic Origin of Nations* (Oxford, 1986).

older arrangements by which a separate Visigothic element in any given town might be expected to have been military in character were probably obsolete. There seems little reason to believe in the continued survival of such garrisons of Germanic soldiery as may have existed in the fifth century. Thus it is by no means easy to say whether or not the kind of administrative structure that can be worked out from the normative regulations of the *Forum Iudicum*, some of which were two centuries old, still existed in practice in the late Visigothic kingdom. Even less likely is it that the organization envisaged in the *Breviarium* of Alaric of 506 still had any contemporary manifestations.

Argument also exists as to the degree to which, if at all, urban councils still existed in Visigothic Spain.[67] The local aristocratic families that provided the *curiales* or councillors are generally seen as being in a state of economic crisis and decline from at least the fourth century onwards, but some of them were still using senatorial titles in the seventh. The survival of the organs of urban government which they had previously dominated is another matter, though, and such councils may well have ceased to play any significant local function long before 711. If the civilian oligarchy had lost power or perhaps interest in the towns and their government, their loss had been the episcopate's gain.[68] From the time of the emperor Constantine onwards bishops had come to play a more and more prominent role in urban administration, initially in respect of the dispensing of justice, but increasingly in a wider social and economic context. In the Visigothic kingdom this was recognized and manipulated in the way in which the national councils of the Church in the peninsula came to take responsibility for the promotion of secular law and governmental measures, as well as for the elaboration of the ideology of the monarchy.

The impact of the Arab conquest was inevitably to weaken the role of the episcopate and, initially at least, strengthen or leave intact that of the indigenous counts in those parts of the peninsula

[67] C. Sánchez-Albornoz, 'El Gobierno de las ciudades de España del siglo V al siglo X', *Settimane di studio del Centro italiano di studi sull'alto medioevo*, 6 (Spoleto, 1959), pp. 359–91.

[68] This is well illustrated in part of the hagiographic text, the *Vitas Patrum Emeretensium*; on this see R. Collins, 'Mérida and Toledo, 550–589', in *Visigothic Spain: New Approaches*, ed. E. James (Oxford, 1980), pp. 189–219, especially pp. 192–8.

not taken directly under the rule of the conquerors. A number of local aristocrats, such as Theodemir and perhaps the Count Cassius said to be the eponymous ancestor of the Banu Qasī, probably benefited in the short term from the removal of the centralized authority of the kings and the Visigothic Church.[69]

How long such arrangements as those envisaged in the treaty made by 'Abd al-Azīz ibn Mūsā with Theodemir lasted in practice is by no means easy to say. The only case for which any clear evidence survives is indeed that of the region of 'Tudmir'. The peculiar nature and location in the *Chronicle of 754* of the material relating to Theodemir, and the subsequent and very much later claims to descent from him on the part of various local potentates in the area make a degree of caution necessary. But there is nothing in the three extant versions of the text of the treaty to make it necessary to suspect its essential reliability. That the quasi-autonomous region still survived under the direction of Theodemir's son Athanagild around the year 745 has also generally been held to be established by the words of the chronicler.[70] In fact this latter asumption is less secure than has been appreciated. All that the *Chronicle of 754* confirms is that Athanagild was very rich, and was obliged to pay a fine of 27,000 *solidi* by the governor Abu al-Ḳattar. This he did within three days and was restored to favour.[71] The context suggested by the chronicle might well be the time of the civil war, when Abu al-Ḳattar had been expelled from Córdoba, and such financial assistance as that provided, albeit involuntarily, by Athanagild was peculiarly welcome. The episode testifies to the wealth but not explicitly to the status of the son of Theodemir in the mid 740s. It is thus possible that the arrangements made by the treaty of 713 had already ceased to exist.

They certainly cannot have still been in the course of implementation by the late 770s, when the 'Abbāsid nominee tried to win the support of the Arabs in the region. The only other locality known with certainty to have made a treaty of capitulation is Pamplona, and there too by 798 at the latest an alien governor was in control.[72]

[69] On the Banu Qasī see A. Cañada Juste, 'Los Banu Qasī (714–924)', *Príncipe de Viana*, 158/9 (1980), pp. 5–96.

[70] J.B. Vilar, *Orihuela musulmana* (Murcia, 1976), pp. 47–52.

[71] *Chronicle of 754*, 87, p. 114.

[72] Muṭārrif ibn Mūsā of the Banu Qasī; see E. Lévi-Provençal, *Histoire de l'Espagne musulmane*, vol. I, p. 176.

Thus, in the second half of the eighth century, if not before, the distinction between areas retaining their local forms of self-government and those under direct Arab rule seems to have disappeared and something of a more uniform pattern may be held to have emerged. The nature of this depends upon the estimate to be made of the character of Arab rule over those towns and regions the conquerors had kept for themselves from the start.

It is probably necessary to say that conditions in Córdoba should not be taken as being typical of or applicable to all other parts of *Al-Andalus*. The only period in which the city could be expected to have been little different to the other major urban centres of the peninsula was the time of the first two governors, under whom Seville had been the preferred place of residence. The creation of a fixed capital and centralized royal administration by the Umayyad rulers obviously made Córdoba increasingly distinct. It would thus be unwise to extrapolate too confidently from the evidence relating specifically to this city. However, starting in the period of the governors, it is possible to work out some of the basic features of the Arab administration, and in consequence to form some impression of what it will have required in terms of organization and personnel.

As has been seen, at this time the Arab and Berber elements of population were proportionally very small, as had been that of the Visigoths in the fifth century.[73] Their principal functions look to have been twofold: warfare and perhaps enforcing the collection of tax.[74] The making of treaties and the granting of local self-government in return for tribute greatly facilitated both of these tasks, in that from the areas thus covered revenue could be collected without the need to maintain garrisons and the apparatus of central administration. In the regions and towns under direct control it is clear that a number of key fortresses had to be manned for reasons of internal security, the keeping open of routes of communication, or as bases for aggressive campaigns against areas

[73] This is to minimize or discount the notion of a large settlement of a Visigothic 'peasantry' on the Meseta.

[74] All too little is known about the details of tax assessment and collection, but the *Chronicle of 754*, 91, p. 122, records Yūsuf ordering the making of a new tax census, and requiring the *scrinarii* to check the old records in the *codex publicus*. See W. Goffart, *'Caput' and Colonate: towards a History of Late Roman Taxation* (Toronto, 1974), pp. 7–16 for parallels.

outside of Arab control. The information relating to later eighth-century events makes the identity of a number of such centres clear, and they include amongst others Elvira-Granada, Jaén, Mérida, Talavera, Toledo, Zaragoza, Tarragona and Barcelona. Although early confirmation exists for no more than two of these, Córdoba and Narbonne, it would seem likely that some form of permanent garrisoning was maintained in all of these towns.

It is very likely that from this the latter structure of the *quras* developed.[75] These were the provincial sub-divisions of *Al-Andalus*, each of which was centred on a town or major fortress from which the region was administered and controlled. The full pattern of *quras* had emerged by the middle of the tenth century, but it is unclear, due to the lack of evidence, just how far back it can be traced. They certainly bore little relationship to the previous Visigothic and Roman provincial structure.[76] On the other hand, that the major urban centres just mentioned should be found at the centre of administrative units is hardly surprising, and with the exceptions of Talavera and Jaén they also all featured as episcopal sees in the Visigothic period. However, several of the later *qura* centres do not look to have been places of significance either in the civil or the ecclesiastical administration of the Visigothic kingdom, and it is unlikely that the fully extended pattern of these regional units could have been constructed in the eighth century.[77]

Some very interesting work has been done by Spanish scholars on the administrative divisions of *Al-Andalus*, and a recent trend in emphasizing elements of continuity between the pre- and post-conquest phases has proved both revealing and also a useful counterweight to the tendency to believe that the Arab invasion

[75] On these see J. Vallvé, *La División territorial de la España musulmana* (Madrid, 1986), pp. 225–340 for the full range of *quras* that had developed by the end of the tenth century. Also A. Arjona Castro, *Andalucía musulmana: estructura político-administrativa* (2nd edn, Córdoba, 1982), pp. 31–61, which is concerned only with the area of Andalucia.

[76] Which consisted of only six large units; J. Orlandis *La España visigótica* (Madrid, 1977), pp. 216–20, and map on p. 143. No equivalent to the Visigothic *dux* seems to have existed in *Al-Andalus*. J. Vallvé, *La División territorial*, pp. 181–223, argues for a grouping of *quras* within the context of the previous provincial structure. This, perhaps, does not make enough allowance for the antiquarianism of his sources.

[77] The only references to such units in the eighth century relate to a number of southern districts, such as Rayyā (Malaga), Mouron (Morón), and Siduna (Medina-Sidonia): Ibn al-Athīr, p. 99.

marks a totally new beginning in virtually all aspects of society in the peninsula.[78] However, it is necessary to admit that in evidential terms a mighty gulf exists across most of the eighth century, and that offices and structures that can be shown to have existed in later periods of Umayyad rule may not have been found in this earliest age. Similarly, where incontrovertible evidence does exist, as in the case of the coinage, the Arab rulers can be seen as introducing into the peninsula forms and practices with which they were familiar in the eastern Mediterranean or which they had developed in North Africa. Thus the earliest Islamic coins in Spain derive from African prototypes and not from the designs and weight standards of the Visigothic kingdom.

To a certain extent such arguments need not be taken too far, in that late Roman prototypes will be found behind virtually all of the variants of administration practised in Spain and Africa both before and after the Arab conquest. However, it is clear that caution is necessary, and the pattern of events in the peninsula throughout the eighth century would seem to indicate a process of the gradual dissolution of previous structures of government and society until at least the later part of the reign of 'Abd ar-Raḥmān I, rather than one of smooth continuity from the Visigothic period. Mere changes in nomenclature of office are not the issue here, and modern research may be right to stress that similarity of function can lurk behind the linguistically very different appearance of Latin and Arabic titles.[79]

The introduction of a regular system of urban governorships probably took place during the rule of Al-Ḥurr (715–718). Even so, whilst a functional identity between the Visigothic *Comes Civitatis* and the Arab *Sahīb al-Madīna* might be admissable in certain respects, a number of major changes in Spanish society in the early eighth century clearly make such an equation very approximate at best. For one thing the Visigothic state was not organized for war to anything like the extent of the one that existed in the peninsula in the time of the governors. An almost endemic

[78] J. Vallvé, 'España en el siglo VIII: ejército y sociedad', *Al-Andalus*, 43 (1978), pp. 51–112, makes a number of important suggestions as to continuities. The idea that references to Berbers in the Arab sources may indicate Visigoths ('Barbarians') in Arab service may arouse less enthusiasm!

[79] J. Vallvé, 'España en el siglo VIII' on functional similarities between the *Sahīb al-Medīna* and the *Comes Civitatis*.

state of war, initially totally aggressive, was maintained in the north-east of the peninsula and across the Pyrenees throughout the 720s and 730s. Nothing like this seems to have existed in the Visigothic period since the late sixth century. Similarly, internally the requirements of garrisoning and local control may be reminiscent of the earlier phases of the Visigothic occupation of the peninsula and the regulations needed to govern this, but the conditions existing in the seventh century had been very different.

The racial exclusivity of the Arabs, and the ethnic and linguistic divisions between themselves and the Berbers and between both of them and the indigenous population again meant that the governors of the cities were no longer operating against a background of consensus and cultural uniformity. The ideological framework of Visigothic government was one of the first casualties of the invasion. This itself had been fragile enough in the light of the difficulties of imposing effective centralized rule on the peninsula as a whole, but the addition of new and alien elements in the form of the Muslim Arabs and their Berber allies destroyed the previous Latin Christian basis of social integration without at first having anything to put in its place. The Muslims made no attempt to proselytize, and apart from allowing initial local autonomy in various parts of the peninsula the conquerors showed no inclination to assimilate themselves with the conquered in the way that the Visigoths had.[80] This process, when it got under way, proved to be oriented in quite the opposite direction with the gradual Arabization of various sectors of indigenous Spanish society.

The earliest stages of the conquest resemble nothing more than an armed occupation, and the introduction of the new elements of population only added to the cultural fragmentation of the peninsula, with regional variations being reinforced by the differences in the patterns of settlement. The Berbers were particularly dominant in the frontier zones, especially around Toledo and Talavera, in Mérida and, at least initially, in the eastern Pyrenees and Catalonia.[81] The question of Arab groupings and their location has been discussed previously. The establishing of the Syrian forces who accompanied Balj ibn Bishr into the peninsula is particularly

[80] R.W. Bulliett, *Conversion to Islam in the Medieval Period* (Cambridge, Mass., 1979), pp. 114–27.

[81] P. Guichard, *Al-Andalus* (Barcelona, 1973), pp. 403–9.

interesting, in that they look to have been concentrated in the south-east, and this may have included the formerly quasi-autonomous area of 'Tudmir'.[82]

There are important questions that need to be asked in respect of the organization of the Arab and Berber occupation, and also how it came to be transformed into a more permanent form of settlement. Those who are particularly anxious to stress a continuity of indigenous procedures in the administration and social organization of Islamic Spain have pointed to the Late Roman system of *hospitalitas*, particularly in the form in which it was practised in the Iberian provinces as providing the model on which the establishment of the Arabs and Berbers was carried out.[83] By such a view the conquerors received, as the Visigoths had before them, two-thirds of the land and movable property of the principal local landowners in the regions which they occupied directly.[84] This would have been supplemented by the distribution of a fixed percentage of the tribute obtained annually from the areas that had capitulated by treaty.

In that the character of *hospitalitas* itself remains controversial, it would be unwise to be too dogmatic about the precise procedures implied by this argument.[85] However, in that the practical application of the system in the Spanish context was by this time as much as three centuries old it is unlikely to have been this precedent that was being consciously employed in the organization of the Arab and Berber settlement. As with other issues it is very likely that the conquerors imported practices that were already familiar to them and were being applied elsewhere in the Arab world at the time. Once again, though, a common grounding of so many of these areas in the traditions of Late Roman government and administrative thinking must have made such procedures comprehensible and relatively acceptable to the indigenous population.

[82] Ibn 'Idārī, II, p. 33.

[83] J. Vallvé, 'España en el siglo VIII', and *La División territorial*, pp. 181–223.

[84] On the application of this system in Visigothic Spain see E. A. Thompson, *The Goths in Spain*, pp. 132–4, and P. D. King, *Law and Society in the Visigothic Kingdom* (Cambridge, 1972), pp. 204–08.

[85] See the very controversial but ultimately convincing arguments of W. Goffart, *Barbarians and Romans, A.D. 418–584: the Techniques of Assimilation* (Princeton, 1980).

It is probably sensible to assume that the first decade or so of the existence of *Al-Andalus* was marked by the conquerors maintaining a purely military presence, supported by the distribution, perhaps largely in kind, as this is what the treaty with Theodemir seems to suggest, of fixed proportions of tribute and loot. A personal allocation of land, as opposed to fiscal revenues, took place in the governorship of As-Sāmh (718–21), approximately ten years after the initial conquest.[86] The numbers of Arabs taking part in the conquest were relatively small, and such a distribution to the heads of households rather than to all individuals, including clients, would not have involved too complicated a process or too great a fragmentation of existing estates. As has been mentioned rectification of unjust seizures of land from the Christians was carried out very soon after the conquest itself. In the case of the Berbers the nature of their social structure could enable land to be given to them as whole tribal units for common ownership rather than being subdivided by household.

In such circumstances it is not surprising that the existing forms of social and political power amongst the units employed in the particular garrisons were maintained. Thus in the case of the Berber commander Munnuza his status would have come from his role in his own tribal society and not because of his designation by an Arab governor. In the creation of authority amongst the Arabs, as instanced by Yūsuf al-Fihrī, a range of social factors such as Qurayshi descent and relationship to the line of 'Uqba ibn Nāfi' could come into play. It may in the early stages of the conquest and again by the end of the century, when the Amirate of Córdoba looks to have been more securely established, have been possible for status to have been conferred just by designation by the Umayyad ruler.

Amongst the Christians and, from the second half of the century, amongst those indigenous inhabitants of the peninsula who embraced Islam there may have existed forms of status that antedated the conquest. However, in the Visigothic period office was held at royal pleasure and in a very large measure standing and fortune depended on the continuance of the king's favour.[87] There was no independent Gothic aristocracy with its roots lost in a

[86] *Chronicle of 754*, 69, p. 84.
[87] R. Collins, *Early Medieval Spain*, pp. 114–15.

hoary antiquity. Thus, as in the case of Theodemir's son, contemporary wealth probably conferred more power than heroic ancestry. In due course, by the end of the tenth century at least, distinguished lineage had once again become a determinant of status, and fictitious genealogizing became a necessary pastime in the way it had been in the Later Roman Empire. Thus it is more reasonable to assume that in the eighth century it was entrepreneurial skill and ruthlessness that threw up the leaders of society. Inherited wealth could only survive the conditions that prevailed in much of the peninsula in the middle of the century if backed by the strength needed to protect it.

While a general level of internal peace existed throughout the Arab world and the power of the Umayyad Caliphs commanded respect, control could be exercised, even in so remote a limb of it as *Al-Andalus*, by the ruler's designated deputy the governor or *Wali* on the basis of delegated authority. However, with the breakdown of order in North Africa and the disintegration of the Umayyad regime new forms of more localized authority that were still province-wide had to be developed to replace the older system. This was all the more difficult when the entrenched regional power of the Arab and Berber tribal and garrison commanders be considered. Both 'Abd ar-Raḥmān I and Yūsuf al-Fihrī were able to call upon some support that derived from the nature of their particular ancestry and family connections, but this had to be extended by diplomacy, bargaining and the use of force when necessary. Thus, as been suggested above, 'Abd ar-Raḥmān I had to create his own kingdom rather than find it ready and waiting for him just on the strength of his having seized control of Córdoba.

Apart from the designated commanders of garrisons and armies, much of whose power may have derived from their own followings and their personal reputations, the other principal figures upon whom the governors and later the Amirs had to rely for the maintenance of loyalty and support amongst the Arab and Berber population were the *qāḍīs*.[88] These were the men who were appointed to judge Muslims according to the regulations contained in the Koran, and the interpretations that had developed in the Islamic community since the time of the Prophet. Although this became their definitive function, in the early stages of the forma-

[88] N.J. Coulson, *A History of Islamic Law* (Edinburgh, 1964), pp. 28–35, 121–7.

tion of Islamic society they may also have exercised wider administrative and governmental powers. They were thus required to be not only educated in the law, but also, because of its fundamental rooting in the religious message of Islam, men of peculiar uprightness and probity. These qualities were highlighted in the anecdotes, many of which were probably apocryphal, that were recounted of them in the later biographical collections recording their deeds and sayings.[89] To be effective their reputation had to be high in their own community.

It is not too superficial a parallel to liken the role of the early Muslim *qāḍīs* to that of revolutionary commissars. They could serve as the touchstone of Islamic orthodoxy. Not only did every urban Muslim community have its own *qāḍī*, but one was also appointed to accompany every major military expedition.[90] Their roles extended beyond the settlement of legal disputes to the exercise of what might be called political functions. They took the oaths of loyalty from the leaders of the community whenever a change of ruler took place, and their pre-eminence in a society in which the secular and the religious were not easily divided gave enormous weight to their support or otherwise for the existing regime.[91] Thus the appointment of the *qāḍīs*, particularly in Córdoba, was amongst the most important and sensitive functions that the Umayyad Amirs had to perform.

The rules of Islamic law obviously did not extend to the majority Christian population, for whom the rules of the Visigothic *Forum Iudicum* continued in force. This is also the implication of the governor 'Uqba's decree that each community should be judged by its own law. Previously under Visigothic rule all disputes would have come under the jurisdiction of the urban counts and judges, or even in some instances the court of the king, but with the Arab conquest all of the major administrative posts in the towns ruled directly by the conquerors were held by Muslims, and

[89] *Historia de los jueces de Córdoba de Aljoxami*, ed. and tr. J. Ribera (Madrid, 1914); similar traditions exist relating to early Islamic judges in Egypt, and are treated with due reserve in J. Schacht, *The Origins of Muhammadan Jurisprudence* (Oxford, 1950), pp. 100–3.

[90] R. Castejón Calderón, *Los Juristas hispano-musulmanes* (Madrid, 1948), p. 21; N.J. Coulson, *A History of Islamic Law*, p. 29 for the gradual consolidation of the functions of the office.

[91] *Crónica anónyma de Abderrahmán III*, ed. and tr. E. Lévi-Provençal and E. García Gómez (Granada, 1950), pp. 91–5.

thus an alternative judicial organization had to be developed for the settlement of disputes between Christians. In the ninth and tenth centuries there existed a class of men known as 'Judges of the Christians', who were probably to be found in all of the major settlements, and this is very likely true of the eighth century as well.[92] They may have been mainly or exclusively clerics. A rule of law, for members of both religious communities, was not always easy to maintain, especially in periods when the authority of the ruler was weak, as in the time of the succession crises that rocked Umayyad rule in the last two decades of the eighth century.

[92] For one of these in the region of Lérida see R. Collins, 'Visigothic law and regional custom in disputes in early medieval Spain', *The Settlement of Disputes in Early Medieval Europe*, eds W. Davies and P. Fouracre (Cambridge, 1986), pp. 96–7.

8

Some Winners and Some Losers

The Struggle for the Succession

Like his Umayyad predecessors in Syria, 'Abd ar-Raḥmān I established a system of succession based upon designation by the existing ruler.[1] Thus he passed over his eldest son Sulaymān in the interests of a younger one called Hishām. The reasons for this are hidden, and later traditions that make of Sulaymān a *bon viveur* and Hishām an assiduous attender of the counsels of the wise can be no more than rationalizations.[2] One source, here of dubious worth, even suggests that the decision was left to chance.[3] Whether his motives were personal or political, 'Abd ar-Raḥmān's arrangements created a political crisis on the accession of his designated successor in 788. However, the relative ease with which it was resolved, and the limited damage it inflicted on the stability of the Umayyad regime testify to the strength of 'Abd ar-Raḥmān's achievement in the central and southern parts of *Al-Andalus*.

Hishām had been his father's governor in Mérida, the principal fortress city of the western section of the frontier area and also a major Berber stronghold. His elder brother Sulaymān was simi-

[1] In practice there were various hidden constraints on such a choice, and an 'entailed' designation could inhibit the freedom of a ruler to make a free selection. Thus traditionally Walīd II succeeded Hishām in 743 not so much thanks to the latter's choice as by a prior designation by his own father Yazīd II in 724. See M.A. Shaban, *Islamic History, A.D. 600–750: a New Interpretation* (Cambridge, 1971), p. 153.

[2] Al-Maqqarī, II, pp. 95–6.

[3] Ibn 'Idhārī, II, p. 98.

larly placed in Toledo, at least from after the suppression of the revolt of Abu al-'Aṣwad ibn Yūsuf in 785.[4] Thus the two brothers had their own natural followings from their frontier commands. A third brother, 'Abdallāh, who may even have been the eldest of the three, supported Sulaymān against their father's designated heir. On 'Abd ar-Raḥmān I's death in Córdoba on 18 September 788, Sulaymān and 'Abdallāh rebelled in Toledo. Judging by later attested procedures this involved the refusing of an oath of allegiance to the new ruler, which should have been taken in the principal mosque of all major settlements by the leaders of the community.

In many ways this revolt follows a pattern to be seen in the previous Visigothic period, in which the credibility of a new ruler could be tested by a localized revolt.[5] Failure to meet such a challenge successfully would expose the monarch's weakness and lead to a more widespread reaction against him. In this case Sulaymān was quickly besieged by his brother Hishām I in Toledo, again testifying to the almost total reliance on siege warfare as opposed to open battle in this period. This was what might be regarded as standard procedure. As with 'Abd ar-Raḥmān I's campaigns in the Ebro valley, the besiegers lacked the necessary numbers or technology to bring the investment of the city to a military conclusion. The psychology of the waiting game and developments in other regions at the same time were the real determinants of the outcome of this type of warfare. For, leaving his confederate 'Abdallāh to hold Toledo, Sulaymān left the city with a following to try and win over support elsewhere whilst the new Amir was tied down by the siege.[6] His very escape is itself proof that the investment of Toledo was far from total.

Sulaymān's first move was towards Mérida but here he was rebuffed and his forces defeated by the new governor, who remained loyal to Hishām. He then tried to make a descent on Córdoba, but was similarly repulsed, and instead had to be content with taking control of the region of Tudmir in the south-east. Although Hishām was unable to press the siege to a conclusion, the failure of Sulaymān to win wider backing or control of any of

[4] Al-Maqqarī, II, 95; Ibn 'Idhārī, II, p. 98.

[5] R. Collins, *Early Medieval Spain: Unity in Diversity, 400–1000* (London, 1983), pp. 114–15.

[6] Ibn al-Athīr, pp. 137–40 for the revolt and its failure.

the other principal cities led ʻAbdallāh to submit to his brother the following year, thus giving the Amir control of Toledo.[7] Thus freed, Hishām was able to send his son with an army to expel Sulaymān from Tudmir. The latter took refuge with the Berber garrison of Valencia, but his bid had clearly failed, and in 790 he came to terms with Hishām, agreeing to go into exile in North Africa, together with all of his immediate family.

This episode, which was to be re-run on the premature death of Hishām in 796, when Sulaymān made another unsuccessful bid for power, illustrates something of the structure of Andalusi society in the late eighth century. Practical power rested in the control of a number of key points, the fortress towns of the south and centre of the peninsula, with their important garrisons of Berber or Arab warriors. Control as such depended ultimately on the acquiescence of the leaders of the local community, whose own authority largely rested on tribal status, allied to the display of particular virtues as soldier and patron. The loyalty of these garrison communities to particular families is marked. The kind of ideological ties between the central royal administration and the provinces, largely articulated through the Church and the Councils, that had existed in the Visigothic kingdom lacked a counterpart in the early Umayyad period.

The unified state of the seventh century, compromised and finally undermined by the treaties made by the governors and the civil wars of the 740s and 750s, had given way once more to the regionalism that is so often a feature of the history of the peninsula. On the other hand, for a variety of reasons, most of those with significant local power in the crucial centres were in 788–90 prepared to back and thus accept the authority of the ruler of Córdoba. Only in areas or amongst groups with a history of previous dissidence or opposition to ʻAbd ar-Raḥmān I was Sulaymān able to find support, and it clearly was not powerful enough.

Equally patent is the fact that, whilst the decisions made in the major fortress towns of the centre and south could determine the future of the regime, events in the Ebro valley could not. Unsurprisingly, this area only so recently subjected by ʻAbd ar-Raḥmān I reverted to its previous traditions of local autonomy on his death,

[7] Ibn ʻIdhārī, II, p. 98; J. Porres Martín-Cleto, *Historia de Ṭulayṭula (711–1085)* (Toledo, 1985), pp. 23–4.

while his successor was tied down with the revolt of his brother. Nor is it unexpected that the local leaders who re-emerged at this time should turn out to be the relatives of those who had been eliminated by the first Umayyad Amir. As with the family of Yūsuf, such local power was clearly dynastic in character.

The first to declare his hand was Sa'īd ibn Al-Ḥusayn, who had escaped to Sagunto when his father was betrayed to 'Abd ar-Raḥmān I in 779.[8] His revolt may have broken out just prior to the Amir's death. He seems to have appealed to those who had backed his father, and made himself master of Tortosa at the mouth of the Ebro, the first stage on his return to Zaragoza. However, there he was soon defeated and killed by a certain Mūsā ibn Fortūn, who himself was able to seize power in the city in consequence. This proved short-lived, as he was soon afterwards murdered by a freedman of the family of Al-Ḥusayn, a typical act of vengeance in the blood feud created by the killing of Sa'īd.[9]

This Mūsā ibn Fortūn appears in the pages of the *Kamil* of Ibn al-Athīr as if from nowhere. For Ibn 'Idhārī, he was the leader of the local Muḍari or Qays faction, but this may be a typical example of the later chroniclers imposing factionalism as the motivation for developments they did not understand. It is clear enough from the subsequent history of his family, the Banu Qasī, that he was a *mawali*, an indigenous convert to Islam.[10] His line took their name from their claim to descent from a Visigothic count called Cassius.[11] Whether this was more than the spurious antiquarianism that became fashionable in the later Umayyad period is now impossible to say. This Mūsā ibn Fortūn is the first of the family to appear in a clear historical context. From his father's name, an Arab form of the Latin Fortunius, it would seem that he was born a Christian, and that it was he who converted to Islam, perhaps around the middle of the century. The power of Mūsā ibn Fortūn in 788 and the subsequent continuing influence of his family suggest that they had acquired considerable local standing. It is conceivable that they were an Ebro valley equivalent to Theodemir and his son Athanagild in the region called Tudmir. If so the roots

[8] Ibn al-Athīr, p. 141.
[9] Ibid.; Ibn 'Idhārī, II, p. 98.
[10] Ibn 'Idhārī, II, p. 98.
[11] A. Cañada Juste, 'Los Banu Qasī (714–924)', *Príncipe de Viana*, 158/9 (1980), pp. 5–96 for the history of this family.

of their local power might lie in the late Visigothic period, but unlike the family of Theodemir they were able to retain and enhance it until it was finally extinguished in the early tenth century.

The failure of both Sa'īd ibn Al-Ḥusayn and of Mūsā ibn Fortūn to retain control of Zaragoza opened the way to another challenger, Matrūh, one of the sons of Sulaymān ibn Yaqẓān al-Arabī, the confederate of Al-Ḥusayn in 777/8. Like his father before him, his first support came from Barcelona. Again, like Sulaymān, he was able to extend this, in the power vacuum following the death of Mūsā ibn Fortūn, to bring both Zaragoza and Huesca under his control. While Hishām I was kept busy in the south he was thus able to make himself master of most of the Ebro valley. The end of Sulaymān ibn 'Abd ar-Raḥmān's resistance in Valencia led to the re-establishment of Umayyad authority in the Ebro valley. An expedition was sent against Matrūh in Zaragoza, and although, as usual, the city could not be taken by storm, Hishām's general established himself higher up the valley at Tarazona. Within a short time, in 791, Matrūh was murdered by some of his closest associates, who sent his head to Hishām and submitted Zaragoza to his rule.[12]

The developments in the Ebro valley in the years 788–91 showed that if the central authority of the Amirs was weak, then this region would revert to its own traditions of local independence. On the other hand, it is equally clear that it was not able to stand against the resources of an Umayyad Amir in full control of the south and centre of the peninsula. Claimants to local power continued to exist, and as late as 826/7 other descendants of Sulaymān al-Arabī were still causing problems in the area of Barcelona, though by then for the Franks rather than the Umayyads.[13] Others, though, and these included the heirs of Mūsā ibn Fortūn, were used by the Umayyads to maintain their authority in this turbulent area. This they could do on the basis of their existing local standing, but proved as willing as ever to go their own ways when central power seemed weak. Throughout the next two centuries the Umayyad

[12] Ibn al-Athīr, pp. 141–3.

[13] The Aizo recorded by the *Annales Regni Francorum* as having escaped from the Frankish court, and raising a rebellion in the March could be identified with the Ayso reported as a son of Suleymān ibn Yaqẓān in 778. J. M. Salrach, *El Procés de formació nacional de Catalunya (segles VIII–IX)* (2nd edn, Barcelona, 1981), pp. 81–7.

hold over the region depended on the effective playing off of local rivals or occasionally on building up the power of one of the contestants at the expense of others.

In general the inadequacy, from the point of view of the Amir in Córdoba, of the kind of rule by consensus needed to keep the loyalty of the dominant elements in the major urban centres of *Al-Andalus* must have been made very apparent by the events of the years 788 to 791. It is thus perhaps no coincidence that the ending of the campaigns required to secure acceptance of Hishām I's rule saw the instigation of a series of annual expeditions directed against the Christian kingdom in the north.[14] The emergence of the Asturian monarchy had gone unchallenged by Córdoba. Where there had been conflicts they had been conducted from the Muslim side by the governor of Toledo, as for example in a raid in force into the kingdom in the time of Mauregatus (783–88).[15] Larger-scale operations directed by the Amir had not previously been envisaged, but from late in 791 onwards such expeditions, often involving two independent field forces penetrating different Christian regions, became a standard occurrence until the end of the reign.

Although on occasion these could result in pitched battles, as in the defeats suffered by Vermudo I in 791 and by Alfonso II in 794, at no point do these expeditions seem to have been intended actually to subjugate and destroy the Christian kingdom.[16] It is possible that this might have been achieved in the 790s, but it almost looks as if the conducting of such operations had become an end in itself. This is credible, in that the despatch of armies from Córdoba under appointees or relatives of the Amir, which picked up reinforcements from the frontier regions as they advanced, could become instruments of political control over the Muslim-ruled territory in the centre of the peninsula. They made manifest the power of the ruler of Córdoba, and also removed elements of the temperamental garrison forces from their local contexts. Furthermore, the direction of such operations against the Christians and the loot that could be and was acquired helped to distract attention from potentially divisive conflicts inside Andalusi society. For the first time since the 730s the Muslim war ethic could be revived and

[14] Ibn al-Athīr, pp. 144–52.
[15] Ibn al-Athīr, p. 133.
[16] R. Collins, *Early Medieval Spain*, pp. 196–200 for this argument.

jihad be directed against non-Muslim neighbours with a great measure of success.[17]

This pattern was interrupted by the unexpected death of Hishām I in April 796, and the resulting attempts of his brothers to overturn the succession of his son Al-Ḥakam I (796–822).[18] This, and renewed problems in the Ebro valley, kept the new ruler busy for several years, and when he had emerged at the end of that period he did not return entirely to the expedients of his father. In part this may have been because he was able to rely on a new source of military power, the first appearance of which, though, may be found in the reign of his grandfather.[19]

Like the Visigoths before them, the Arabs were numerically a very small minority of the population of the peninsula, and yet dominated it without any real threat being posed to their rule by the indigenous inhabitants. The same is equally true for much of North Africa, though there the apparently rapid conversion of various Berber tribes to Islam is a complicating factor. In Spain too the presence of the Berbers, who seem to have been kept well away from the major urban centres of the south, has also to be taken account of. Yet what they contributed in terms of manpower and military strength was often vitiated by the racial and cultural conflicts between the Berbers and their Arab masters.

The Arabs themselves had become increasingly disunited as a result of internal conflicts in the middle of the century, many of which owed their origins to events in the Near East, and the consequences of these continued to effect the politics of the peninsula for several decades thereafter. In the circumstances it is not surprising that, like the 'Abbāsids, the Umayyad rulers tried to make themselves increasingly independent of the old tribal armies.[20] Although this process is said only to have reached maturity in the time of his grandson Al-Ḥakam I (796–822), the use of slave soldiers linked directly to the ruler is reported to have been introduced in the reign of 'Abd ar-Raḥmān I.[21] If this is the case such a development is probably only to be looked for in the last years of the reign. For one thing this depended upon the existence

[17] See article 'DJIHAD' in *Shorter Encyclopedia of Islam*, p. 89.
[18] See below pp. 208–10.
[19] Al-Maqqarī, II, p. 106.
[20] J. Lassner, *The Shaping of 'Abbāsid Rule* (Princeton, 1980), pp. 102–36.
[21] Al-Maqqarī, II, p. 85.

of an accessible supply of suitable slaves. From the early ninth century the 'Abbāsids were drawing these from the Turkish tribes of Central Asia, on the fringes of their empire. The Umayyads in Spain were in this respect less fortunately placed, until the rise of the Vikings and the stability of the Pyrenean frontier made possible the growth of both sea-borne and land-based slave trading from the Baltic and the areas of Slav settlement.[22] Both of these were essentially early ninth-century developments, and it is probably not until then that the Umayyad slave armies should be looked for.

The pattern of events that had followed on from the succession of Hishām I to his father 'Abd ar-Raḥmān was paralleled almost exactly by what happened at the beginning of the reign of his designated heir and eldest son Al-Ḥakam. All of the regions in which Umayyad control was weak or where local contenders for power were still entrenched proved troublesome, and the repercussions of the succession dispute of 788 reasserted themselves. The disappointed brothers of Hishām I, who had been forced into exile in 790, had been forging new links with the Berbers in North Africa, especially with the Karijite ruler of Tahert, and were quick to seize the opportunities offered by the succession of their nephew.[23] The new Amir's uncle, 'Abdallāh ibn 'Abd ar-Raḥmān returned from North Africa at once, and seems to have made for the Ebro valley, but with initially limited effect. 'Abdallāh's more formidable brother Sulaymān did not mount his challenge until 798. Elvira, Ecija and Jaén are recorded as being his centres of operation in the course of the fighting that followed over the next two years. Sulaymān's principal supporters seem to have been Berbers established in these regions. Despite a number of minor defeats in 798 and 799, the issue was only finally decided in 800 when Sulaymān was decisively beaten and forced to flee to Mérida, another Berber stronghold. However, he was captured before he reached safety and was taken to Córdoba for execution.[24]

As in the period 788–90 the consequences of the change of ruler

[22] See C. Verlinden, *L'Esclavage dans l'Europe mediévale*, vol. I, *Péninsule ibérique – France* (Bruges, 1955), pp. 181–247.

[23] For these and ensuing events see E. Lévi-Provençal, *Histoire de l'Espagne musulmane* (Paris and Leiden, 1950), vol. I, pp. 150–7, who here used a still unpublished fragment of the *Muqtabis* of Ibn Ḥyyān.

[24] Ibn al-Athīr, pp. 153–4, 160–2; Ibn 'Idhārī, II, pp. 110–11.

and the ensuing fighting between the rival Umayyads in the south included the loss of control over more distant regions. Toledo broke free again in 797, and a certain Balūl ibn Marẓuq set himself up as an independent ruler in Zaragoza in the same year.[25] In these circumstances the Asturians under Alfonso II, who had suffered a major defeat in 794, were able to raid their southern neighbours with impunity, and in 798 an expedition from the north reached as far down as Lisbon, which was captured and sacked.[26]

Al-Ḥakam I was able to take more rapid and more immediately effective action against some of these threats than had been possible for his father. This may testify to the greater stability achieved by the Umayyad regime in the course of the intervening eight years, though, as will be seen, the Ebro valley and Pyrenean regions proved especially resistant. Although Al-Ḥakam himself had been governor of Toledo from 792 until his accession, the city had followed its previous tendency to throw up local potentates and to oppose rule from the south.[27] The Arab accounts are mutually contradictory as to the identity of the leader of the Toledan revolt. Three alternative names are given, and one source suggests that two of the men ruled consecutively. This may be no more than a rationalization of the confusion over naming. What is perhaps more interesting than this particular insoluble question, as in none of the three cases is anything else known of the men in question, is the role played in the revolt of a local poet called Girbīb ibn 'Abdallāh. His verses are said to have played a major role in instigating the opposition to Umayyad rule.[28]

Al-Ḥakam was able to dispose of the threat from Toledo with relative ease, largely through the efforts of one of his newly appointed commanders, 'Amrus ibn Yūsuf. This man had been one of the leading supporters of the house of Sulaymān al-Arabī, who had opposed Umayyad attempts to obtain control of the Ebro valley. However, 'Amrus had changed sides in the course of the

[25] Ibn 'Idhārī, p. 110; Ibn al-Athīr, p. 156.

[26] On the Battle of Lutos in 794 see C. Sánchez-Albornoz, *Los Orígenes de la nación española: el Reino de Asturias*, vol. II (Oviedo, 1974), pp. 491–508. For the campaign of 798 see ibid. pp. 531–40, and see below.

[27] Ibn al-Athīr, pp. 143–4.

[28] J. Porres Martín-Cleto, *Historia de Ṭulayṭula*, pp. 25–6; for poetry in Arab society see E. Wagner, *Grundzüge der klassischen arabischen Dichtung*, vol. I (Darmstadt, 1987).

previous conflict, and is said to have been one of those who murdered Matrūh ibn Sulaymān at Zaragoza in 791.[29] Although such a background might not have inspired confidence, in 797 Al-Ḥakam put him in charge of the Berber garrison in Talavera. From there he was able to suborn the loyalty of some of the rebels in Toledo, and persuade them to murder their leader. They themselves were in turn put to death by his troops. According to one account this merely led to the substitution of another rebel leader in Toledo and the whole process had to be repeated. However, as has been suggested, such a duplication of events renders this rather suspicious. In any event, with the problem of Toledo for once rapidly dealt with, 'Amrus seems to have governed the city until despatched in 802 to restore the Amir's authority in the Ebro valley.[30]

The Return of the Franks

In the Ebro valley in the later 790s the pattern of events is somewhat more confusing, but both contemporary Frankish and later Arab sources have things to say about it. For the year 797 the *Royal Frankish Annals*, which were probably at this point being composed annually, records that a certain 'Zatun' returned Barcelona to Frankish control.[31] The phraseology is a little strange in that no evidence exists of any earlier period of Frankish rule over Barçelona. The chronicler's view of the city having previously revolted against Charlemagne and now having been returned to him probably derives from a legalistic interpretation of some of the events of 777/8. As previously mentioned, in the former year one of the sons of Sulaymān al-Arabī, then ruling Barcelona, had come to Charlemagne's assembly at Paderborn, and in the campaign of 778 the second Frankish army had entered the Ebro valley by way of the eastern Pyrenees, which is to say in the vicinity of Barcelona. On either occasion some form of expedient capitulation could have

[29] On 'Amrus see F. de la Granja, tr., 'La Marca Superior en la obra de Al-'Udri', *Estudios de Edad Media de la Corona de Aragón*, vol. VIII (Zaragoza, 1967), pp. 447–545, sections 21–6, pp. 465–8, and genealogical table III. See also the comments of J. Salrach *El Procés de formació*, pp. 81–8.

[30] E. Lévi-Provençal, *Histoire de l'Espagne musulmane*, vol. I, p. 156.

[31] *Annales Regni Francorum*, ed. F. Kurze, *MGH SRG*, s.a. 797, p. 100.

been made, on the strength of which the Frankish ruler could have claimed a lordship over the city, which was denied him in practice.[32]

At a subsequent point in 797, when Charlemagne was at Aachen, he received 'Abdallāh, the son of 'Abd ar-Raḥmān I, who made some form of agreement with him, which was interpreted by the Frankish chronicler as an act of homage.[33] In November he sent off 'Abdallāh in company with his third son Louis, the King of Aquitaine. The anonymous compiler of the *Royal Frankish Annals* does not record any further developments, but in a revised version of the Annals, written *c.* 814, an addition has been made reporting that in this year Charlemagne sent Louis with an army to besiege the Pyrenean town of Huesca.[34] In the Revised Annals this precedes the arrival of 'Abdallāh in Aachen, and thus it may be the revived Frankish activity in the eastern Pyrenean area, sparked off by the action of the governor of Barcelona, which led this rebellious uncle of Al-Ḥakam to seek Frankish aid. Conversely, though, it is possible that the expedition to Huesca resulted from the agreement made between Charlemagne and 'Abdallāh. 'Abdallāh's ally Balūl also came to meet Louis at Toulouse.[35]

The Arab accounts record some of these Frankish involvements, and provide additional details that augment the complexity of the events. According to the annalistic account of Ibn al-Athīr, 'Abdallāh was the ally of the rebel ruler of Zaragoza, Balūl ibn Marẓuk, and the approach to the Franks was made by them jointly.[36] The Latin chroniclers do not record the developments in the Ebro valley after 797 and before the Frankish capture of Barcelona in 801. However, it seems as if a number of contenders for local power emerged. A certain Abu Imrān is found in opposition to Balūl of Zaragoza in 799, and in 800 this Abu Imrān appears as the new ally of 'Abdallāh and the two of them made themselves masters of Huesca. In the same year Umayyad generals dislodged Balūl ibn Marẓuk from Zaragoza. The alliance between 'Abdallāh and Balūl had clearly ended, as the latter besieged his former

[32] The revised form of the *Annales Regni Francorum* states that the Arabs who visited Charlemagne at Paderborn in 777 submitted their cities to him. This would include Barcelona. *Annales q.d. Einhardi*, s.a. 777, p. 49.

[33] *Annales Regni Francorum*, s.a. 797, p. 100.

[34] *Annales q.d. Einhardi*, s.a. 797, p. 101.

[35] E. Lévi-Provençal, *Histoire de l'Espagne musulmane*, vol. I, p. 179.

[36] Ibn al-Athīr, pp. 160–2.

associate in Huesca later in that year and took it. In consequence, in 801, 'Abdallāh withdrew to Valencia, where the following year he finally came to terms with his nephew the Amir Al-Ḥakam. He was permitted to retain his quasi-independent rule over Valencia and its immediate hinterland.[37]

Other pieces of the same puzzle, though usually taken as independent items, might be the Asturian sack of Lisbon and the revolt in Pamplona, both of which occurred in 798. The Asturian campaign, which may have led to a short-lived occupation of the town, was preceded by the dispatch of an envoy, called Froia, from Alfonso II to Charlemagne at the beginning of the year. After the success of the operation a second embassy was sent bringing some of the spoils to the Frankish court.[38] Flanked as it was by this diplomatic activity both before and after, it is hard to believe that the campaign against Lisbon had not been planned with at least the foreknowledge and moral support of the Carolingian ruler. Similarly, it is not easy to believe that the fact that the revolt of the Christian inhabitants of Pamplona against their *muwallad* governor occurred in 798 was just a coincidence.

Clearly a great deal of Frankish fishing in the troubled waters of the affairs of the peninsula, and above all the Ebro valley, was taking place in 797/8. Why, though, did nothing very substantial come of it, and why was there no major royal intervention at this time? The answer here probably has to do with events in the eastern Frankish regions. Charlemagne's wars with the Avars had come to a successful conclusion in 796, thus potentially freeing his hands for more effective meddling in the Iberian peninsula, but 797 and 798 saw the renewal of difficulties with the Saxons.[39] It was not until 801, after the imperial coronation, that Charlemagne, through his son Louis the King of Aquitaine, was able to direct the major Frankish strike south of the Pyrenees in the form of the campaign that took Barcelona.[40] Although successful in itself, it proved to be the limit of the undertaking, and in this sense was probably ill-timed. Had it been launched four years earlier in the year 798 more spectacular results might have ensued. As it was it is notable

[37] Ibn 'Idhārī, II, pp. 110–13.
[38] *Annales Regni Francorum*, s.a. 798, pp. 102, 104.
[39] *Annales Regni Francorum*, s.a. 797–9, p. 102–6.
[40] On this expedition see J. Salrach, *El Procés de formació*, pp. 14–26.

that Charlemagne's erstwhile ally the governor of Barcelona had by this time changed sides, and the Asturians are not recorded as having renewed any of the contacts that had existed in 798. 'Abdallāh had also been dislodged from Huesca and Zaragoza was back in Umayyad hands.

The events of the late 790s and of 801 in the eastern Pyrenees may be seen as having established the stake of another significant player in the struggles for regional ascendancy over various parts of the Iberian peninsula in the ninth century. In terms of central royal involvement, Frankish participation was to be short-lived, but the cultural effects of Carolingian rule on the 'Gothic' and 'Spanish' Marches, and the re-establishment of an administrative structure (perhaps mirroring the Visigothic one) were to prove longer lasting.[41] In general this was an area always torn between the political and cultural imperialisms of the dominant societies of the Iberian peninsula and of France. After a long period, extending back into the early sixth century, in which political ties to the south had pre-dominated, most of the region was now transferred into the sphere of influence of the northern power. However, in the heady days of the later 790s, this was not the only area of the peninsula in which an expansionary Frankish empire was showing an interest. The roots of these involvements go back to the time of the fall of the Visigothic kingdom and before.

The Arab conquest of the peninsula, and perhaps even more the savage fighting, massacres and destruction that seem particularly to have affected the Ebro valley and the area of the former Visigothic Septimania in the 720s, produced a flight of refugees into Francia. Some may also have sought refuge in the northern mountains of the peninsula itself, but it is probably Provence and southern Aquitaine that received the majority of those who went into voluntary exile from their homeland. Some continued on as far as Italy. Thus Sindered, metropolitan of Toledo in 711, took refuge in Rome.[42] Some unknown person or persons brought a book of prayers from Tarragona to North Italy and ultimately Verona.[43] A

[41] See R. d'Abadal i de Vinyals, 'La Catalunya carolingia', in his *Dels Vinigots als Catalans* (2 vols, Barcelona, 1969), vol. I, pp. 135–494.

[42] *Chronicle of 754*, 53, p. 70.

[43] *Oracional visigótico*, ed. J. Vives (Barcelona, 1946), pp. xxxii–xxxv of the 'estudio paleográfico' by J. Claveras.

Spanish priest is known to have been at Monte Cassino in the 730s.[44]

As well as personnel, manuscripts and doubtless other portable objects transferred themselves across the Pyrenees. Amongst the best known of these are the *Liber Orationum*, or Prayer Book, that seems to have originated in Tarragona around the year 700 and which migrated to Italy in the eighth century, and is now preserved at Verona. Less well travelled are two manuscripts of patristic texts that seem to have belonged to Bishop Nambaudus of Urgel in the Pyrenees, probably the man killed by the Berber leader Munnuza in the 720s, which made their way to Autun, and were there possibly annotated by Claudius, later to be bishop of Turin, himself a refugee from Spain.[45] As well as manuscripts such as these, produced in the late Visigothic kingdom, especially in Septimania and the north of the province of Tarraconensis, in other words the future Catalonia, the exodus of texts and scholars from the peninsula can be detected in other less direct forms. Certain Italian manuscripts of the eighth century show such strong traces of Hispanic influence in their script and decoration that there has often been uncertainty as to which of the two peninsulas they should be attributed.[46] Similarly, it is arresting to find the contents of a later Italian law book, probably produced in Monte Cassino, being composed of a mixture of Roman elements and unattributed extracts from the Visigothic *Forum Iudicum*.[47]

The full extent and character of the Spanish impact on the politics and the cultural revival of Francia under the Carolingian dynasty have never been fully assessed, but the careers of a number of well-known individuals have received considerable scholarly attention. It would be unwise to make too much of the possible influence of such men on the growing Frankish interest in the Iberian peninsula from the mid-eighth century onwards. The earliest generations of these Spanish refugees seem to have made

[44] Huneberc of Heidenheim, *The Hodoeporicon of St. Willibald*, *MGH SS*, XV, pp. 80–117.

[45] On these see the exhaustive study of R.P. Robinson, *Manuscripts 27 (S.29) and 107 (S.129) of the Municipal Library of Autun* (Rome, 1939).

[46] MS Corpus Christi College, Cambridge, 304, written in eighth-century uncial, see E.A. Lowe, *Codices Latini Antiquiores*, no. *127, vol. II, p. 4; see the commentary for palaeographic parallels in other manuscripts.

[47] London, British Library MS Add. 47676, formerly Holkham MS 210. This is 'R3' in Zeumer's edition of the *Lex Visigothorum*.

little personal impact, and their greatest period of influence seems to have been the first half of the ninth century. Even Theodulf bishop of Orléans, a self-proclaimed Goth, and the most significant figure of Hispanic origin in the court of Charlemagne, is unlikely to have arrived there before 778. As has been suggested, Charlemagne's initial venture across the Pyrenees in 778 had an impromptu and improvisatory character to it. This was in contrast to the more cautious and firmly based approach adopted by the Franks in the first decade of the ninth century.

It may have been the expedition of 778 that persuaded Charlemagne to take a more informed interest in the affairs of the Iberian peninsula, and led in due course to the rise of such influential Spaniards at his court as Theodulf. Although there is no contemporary evidence that the ill-fated venture into the Ebro valley was seen in this way at the time, by the 830s it was being presented as an intervention on the part of the Frankish ruler to bring succour to the distressed Christian communities of the region.[48] Although such an ideological interpretation was consistent with the general image of Charlemagne that was being developed in the later period, it is likely that it owes its particular character to the influence of Spanish refugees in Francia and the contacts that had grown up with the Christian kingdom in the Asturias.[49]

Information on these latter is both limited but unequivocal. Einhard in his *Life of Charlemagne* records the sending of Asturian envoys and letters to Charlemagne on the part of Alfonso II.[50] No record of such contacts can be found in the very limited Asturian sources, but there is no reason to doubt their existence. Although they must have had something to do with the military

[48] 'Astronomer', *Vita Hludowici Imperatoris*, 2, ed. R. Rau, *Quellen zur karolingischen Reichsgeschichte*, vol. I (Darmstadt, 1968), p. 260.

[49] A Frankish presence became established across the Pyrenees when in 785 the inhabitants of Gerona seem to have put themselves under Charlemagne's protection. This was extended to Vic in 786. Such a development looks very similar to the urban revolts in Septimania in the 750s which led to Narbonne and the other major towns of the region putting themselves under Frankish protection. Although localized evidence is lacking, these moves may represent reactions to the bad relations between the urban communities and their garrisons. In 794 the Berber garrison of Tarragona massacred much of the civilian population of the city, which was then abandoned for about a decade. Ibn 'Idārī, II, p. 102. See in general J. Fontaine, 'Mozarabie hispanique et monde carolingien', *Anuario de Estudios Medievales*, 13 (1983), pp. 17–46.

[50] Einhard, *Vita Caroli Magni*, 16, ed. L. Halphen (Paris, 1938), pp. 44–6.

aspirations of both parties, the roots of this relationship were both older and more pacific. A letter of Charlemagne's advisor Alcuin makes it clear that Spanish pilgrims from the Asturian kingdom were coming to Tours to visit the shrine of St Martin.[51] Such connections between the north-west of the peninsula and the Loire valley were at least as old as the mid-sixth century, when relics of St Martin were sent from Tours to the Suevic kingdom. Martin of Braga may also have travelled directly from one to the other at the same period.[52] Such communications, probably sea-borne around the coasts of the Bay of Biscay, may indeed have been much older, as the despatch of such significant relics from Tours can hardly have been accidental, and they may relate to a pattern of trade of considerable antiquity. The commercial and cultural contacts between northern Spain and Francia assumed greater significance as the older Visigothic order in the peninsula disintegrated under the increasing strains placed upon it in the course of the eighth century.

From the unitary, and by Early Medieval standards highly centralized, state of the late Visigothic period the eighth century saw an extraordinary transition. The Arab and Berber conquest, with its introduction of new elements of material and above all intellectual culture, was in itself fatal as far as the Romano-Gothic ideology and practice of peninsular unity on the basis of a common religious and political allegiance was concerned. The period of the governors had to some extent seen the beginning of the processes that led to the rapid dissolution of the measure of the administrative uniformity and cultural cohesion achieved by the upper classes of Roman and Gothic society in the seventh century. The slighting of Toledo in favour of the towns of the Guadalquivir valley, and the making of the various regional treaties that allowed a large measure of local autonomy, dissolved the structures around which the previous order had developed.

[51] Letter of Alcuin to Beatus of Liébana, ed. W. Levison in his *England and the Continent in the Eighth Century* (Oxford, 1946), Appendix XI, p. 318.

[52] E. James, 'Ireland and western Gaul in the Merovingian period', eds D. Whitelock, R. McKitterick and D. Dumville, *Ireland in Early Medieval Europe*, (Cambridge, 1982), p. 374.

Adoptionism and the Decline of Toledo

Although the Christians retained a numerical predominance in *Al-Andalus*, certainly until the eleventh century if not longer, and were able to preserve many features of their previous culture and social organization, it is clear that from the middle of the eighth century onwards several of these were under threat.[53] The elimination of the concessions made to those towns which had submitted under treaty introduced Muslim rulers and their followers into virtually all of the major settlements. The impact of Arab dominance was thus brought into regions perhaps initially sheltered from the effects of the conquest. As with the civil administration, many aspects of the institutional organization of the Christian Church in southern and central Spain were slowly forced to adapt to the new social realities engendered by Muslim rule and the breakdown of order in the middle of the century.

The Church of Toledo was able to retain an intellectual pre-eminence well on into the eighth century, but the turbulent politics of the city and its region in the period 756 to 797, together with the enhanced importance of Córdoba and Seville under Arab rule, threatened its standing as the primatial see. It is notable that, although the holding of episcopal councils continued on an occasional basis throughout the Umayyad period, they were located in Seville and Córdoba, and no longer in Toledo.[54] However, although derived from tradition rather than contemporary realities, the prestige of the holder of the see of Toledo remained unequalled throughout the eighth and early ninth centuries. It is notable, though, that when the metropolitan bishops of Toledo are encountered in the scanty evidence relating to the Church at this time, they are rarely to be found in their titular city.

In terms of episcopal continuity the Arab conquest was disruptive but far from catastrophic. The nature of the evidence means that little is heard of individual bishops and their sees in the eighth century, but information from the better documented period that followed shows a number of bishoprics still functioning, especially

[53] For the large Christian rural population in the mid-tenth century see Ibn Hawkal, *Configuración del mundo*, tr. M.J. Romani Suay (Valencia, 1971), p. 63.

[54] These will be discussed in subsequent volumes.

in the south, and there is no reason to assume any significant hiatus in episcopal succession in these cases. On the other hand, the creation of an internal frontier in the peninsula with the emergence of the Asturian kingdom and the depopulation of the Duero valley seems to have led to the disappearance of a number of bishoprics in the Meseta and the Ebro valley. The metropolitan see of Galicia at Braga may have been extinguished when the town was abandoned, and a similar fate will have befallen the bishopric of Tarragona in 794 if not before.[55] There may also have been a break in the episcopal succession in Narbonne before the city fell into Frankish hands. Whatever short-term problems may have occurred, Mérida and Seville both continued to function. Thus of the six metropolitan sees of the old Visigothic kingdom only three survived with certainty the first hundred years of Muslim rule.

It would be unwise to exaggerate the difficulties of communication to be faced in any given instance, but the general impression suggested by the pattern of events in the peninsula from the 740s to the end of the 770s would be that travel and exchange across the centre of Spain became increasingly difficult. More generally the orientation of the Church in the peninsula became increasingly southwards facing, as the new Umayyad Amirate developed its base in the Guadalquivir valley. Inevitably, contact with Christian communities across the Pyrenees became more difficult. Periods of conflict between the Arabs and the Franks, and Arab sea-borne raids on the coasts of Italy can only have exacerbated the problems.[56] The supposed isolation of the Church in Spain in the seventh century has been seen to be largely mythical. Conditions in the decades following the Arab conquest, however, were such that sustained contacts with the wider Christian world must have become harder to maintain. On the other hand, the quarter century following the first establishment of Umayyad power in the Ebro valley around the year 780 saw, in terms of the available evidence, the period of the most active exchanges ever recorded between Christians in Spain and the Church in Rome and in the Frankish kingdom.

[55] For Tarragona see Ibn 'Idhārī, II, p. 102.

[56] The Balearic Islands, whose nominal allegiance had remained with the Byzantine emperors, were plundered by a sea-borne Arab raid in 798, and transferred themselves to Frankish rule in 799; see *Annales Regni Francorum*, s.a. 798, 799, pp. 104, 108.

Thus it would be unwise to become too committed to the image of the post-conquest Church as becoming increasingly fossilized and out of touch with the developments in Christianity elsewhere. In addition, the eventual disappearance, though not before the eleventh century at the earliest, of Christianity in North Africa has deprived us of an enormous body of valuable evidence. The very close relations between southern Spain and North Africa, not only in the period of the governors but at many subsequent points, could be expected to have affected the Christian communities in both areas, but this remains only a subject for speculation. Liturgical and palaeographical traces in some manuscripts from the monastery of Saint Catherine on Mount Sinai remain the only real clues to possible Hispano-African ties at this time.[57]

From a western perspective, though, the Christian Church in Spain may have looked dangerously isolated by the time regular contact was re-established in the 780s. This consideration may have lain behind the initiative of Archbishop Wilcharius of Sens in deciding to consecrate as bishop a Goth called Egila, and send him into the peninsula around the year 780 with a commission to preach.[58] This was an unusual move in that an itinerant bishop without an at least titular see, as Egila appears to have been, was an anomaly in the ecclesiastical organization of the Early Middle Ages. The information relating to Egila is, however, so limited that certainty is not possible. In the 830s a reference to a former bishop 'Agila of Ementia' may relate to the same person, and the name 'Ementia' could be a scribal error for *Emerita* or Mérida.[59] Even so, the fact of his consecration having taken place in Francia is itself a matter for some surprise.

His consecrator, Archbishop Wilcharius, is also an odd figure. He has been identified with an Italian holder of the suburbicarian bishopric of Nomentum, that is to say a suffragan see of the Roman Papacy, who had served as diplomatic envoy to the Frankish monarchs in the times of Popes Stephen II (752–57) and Paul I (757–67). If the identification be correct the same man then became

[57] E.A. Lowe, 'An Unknown Latin psalter on Mount Sinai', *Scriptorium*, 9 (1955), pp. 177–99.

[58] For the history of the events relating to the Migetian and then the Adoptionist controversy the best narrative is still that of E. Amann, in *Histoire de l'Eglise*, ed. A. Fliche and V. Martin, vol. VI (Paris, 1947), pp. 129–52.

[59] In the *acta* of the Council of Córdoba of 839, *CSM*, I, p. 139.

Archbishop of Sens by 769.[60] He must have died around the year 786. In his signature to the acts of the Lateran Council of 769 and in references to him in the later correspondence between Charlemagne and Pope Hadrian I, he is credited with the unique title of *Archiepiscopus Galliarum*. The implication would seem to be that he had been invested with the approval of both Papacy and Carolingian monarchy with some form of primatial authority over the Frankish Church.[61] If this be the case nothing practical seems to have come of it; and such an appointment was not repeated. However, one step that he took would seem to have been the consecration of Egila, which despite the difficulties this would eventually lead to, was never regarded by the Papacy as uncanonical, although it clearly was. The implication must be that the ordination and sending of Egila had at least tacit papal support if not original sanction and inspiration. This could be paralleled by the popes' involvement in the creation of bishoprics in the mission areas amongst the Frisians and Saxons.

However unusual the Frankish consecration of Egila may be, there are no known instances in Late Antiquity and the Early Middle Ages of a bishop being appointed to minister to other than an existing Christian community.[62] The implication must be that in this case too the intention was that he should be carrying out episcopal functions amongst a Christian population otherwise deprived of the services of a bishop. This in turn must suggest that it was in response to contact from such a body of Christians that the Frankish bishop, and behind him perhaps the Papacy, were acting. As has just been mentioned, though, the indications are that a large measure of episcopal continuity was preserved in the sees of most areas of the peninsula. Furthermore, had a sizeable enough Christian population survived in such areas as the Duero valley or the lower Ebro whose bishoprics seem to have ceased functioning, it is improbable that they would have felt that sending to Sens for a bishop was the most practiceable thing to do, when other Christian

[60] L. Duchesne, *Les Fastes épiscopeaux de l'ancienne Gaule* vol. II (2nd edn, Paris, 1910), Sens no. 33, pp. 418–19, who makes the identification with the Italian bishop.

[61] For correspondence in which this title is used see P. Jaffe, *Regesta Pontificum Romanorum* (Leipzig, 1885), nos. 2413, 2429, 2445, 2479.

[62] E. A. Thompson, *The Visigoths in the Time of Ulfila* (Oxford, 1966), p. xvii.

metropolitanates were still operating in the peninsula. The suggestion might be made, therefore, that the Christian communities to whom Egila was sent were ones who had broken off communion with other indigenous congregations. In other words there existed some form of schism in the Spanish Church.

Such a conclusion is supported by what little is known of the subsequent activity of Egila and those associated with him in the peninsula. In 785 Bishop Elipandus of Toledo wrote a letter condemning the teaching of a certain Migetius.[63] This was in response to a short treatise or *libellus* that the latter had sent to him. The doctrine he opposed, and for which his letter is the only evidence, is not easy to understand. According to Elipandus, Migetius was teaching that the Trinity had manifested itself as three corporal persons in the forms of David, Christ and Paul. As expressed in the letter this is a quite extraordinary notion, and modern commentators have tended to be dismissive of Migetius on the strength of it. Although Elipandus was clearly being deliberately polemical and indeed abusive in the letter, the fact that it was a reply to an extant text must imply that he could not distort Migetius's arguments beyond a certain rhetorically acceptable limit. He probably intended, though, not just to controvert a particularly odd piece of theology, but also to discredit a whole movement in his Church.

It is from other sources that other aspects of Migetius's ideas and following come to light. In a letter sent by Elipandus and the Spanish bishops to the Pope they complained that Egila, whom they clearly regarded as a papal representative, had become a follower of Migetius, and it is reasonable to suspect that Migetian notions could be found in his correspondence with Rome. In 782 Pope Hadrian I had sent two letters to Egila in reply to some lost communications of his own.[64] In them Hadrian had explicitly condemned, probably at Egila's insistence, any form of marriage between Christians and either Muslims or Jews. In general it would seem that Migetius and Egila found the Church in the south and centre of Spain dangerously open to the influence of Islamic and Jewish ideas and practices. The earlier letters of Evantius and Peter to Christian communities in Zaragoza and Córdoba show

[63] *Elipandi Epistula in Migetium*, ed. J. Gil, *CSM*, I, pp. 68–78.
[64] P. Jaffe, *Regesta*, nos. 2445, 2446.

the degree to which such influences could make themselves felt.[65] It was not a question of the possibilities of direct conversion so much as a convergence, which threatened to compromise distinctively Christian ideas and practices. Migetius and Egila looked to Rome as the source of orthodoxy, and also as the only authority that could be employed to correct what they regarded as the shortcomings of the rest of the Spanish Church of their day. It may well be, then, that it had been the representations of this group that had led to the sanctioning of Egila's mission and his consecration at the hands of a papal envoy and Frankish archbishop. Their refusal to accept the authority of the Spanish episcopate would follow on from the nature of their complaints, though the nature of Migetius's trinitarian ideas was clearly kept concealed.

Thus it looks as if Migetius and his followers were representing themselves as purists, trying to keep themselves and their fellow religionists clear of such contamination. This is a phenomenon that can be paralleled in early periods of Christian history, when rigorist movements such as those of Donatism and Novatianism came into being in response to what was held to be compromise on the part of majority opinion in a regional Church. In the case of Migetius, however, this became allied to some forms of doctrinal unorthodoxy, as implied by Elipandus's letter to him, and the Spanish bishops were thus able to secure papal condemnation of him and of Egila. Their movement, thus isolated from its source of authority, did survive into the ninth century, but is not heard of after 839.[66]

Migetianism as a heretical movement is generally considered of importance not for itself but because of the way it gave rise almost accidentally to the Adoptionist controversy.[67] In his condemnation of Migetius Elipandus first used the terminology of Christ's adoptive humanity, which caused the dispute. However, as has been suggested, limited as the evidence for it may be and peculiar as are some of the theological notions related to it, Migetius and his followers represent a movement in Spanish Christianity in the later eighth century that is not without interest in its own right. They

[65] See above pp. 67–71, and *CSM*, I, pp. 2–5, 55–7.

[66] *Acta* of the Council of Córdoba, *CSM*, I, pp. 135–41, following Amann's identification of the *Acebaleos nomine Casianorum* with the earlier Migetians.

[67] J.F. Rivera Recio, *El Adopcionismo en España (S. VIII)* (Toledo, 1980), pp. 33–7.

testify to the possible intellectual ferment in southern peninsula Christianity, no longer obliged to be rigidly orthodox, and exposed to powerful currents of influence not just from long present Judaism but also from the new and politically dominant Islam. Bishop Cixila's Sabellian heretic returns to mind here.[68] At the same time the new conditions in the peninsula and the channels of communication opened up by the assimilation of much of Spain into the wider Arab world may also have led to the introduction of heterodox Christian ideas from the East.

This at least is the argument of one powerful school of the interpreters of the theology of Adoptionism, who see the roots of Elipandus's teaching as having to be found in the influence on him of Nestorian ideas.[69] There are certain theological justifications for such a view, and, just as significantly, there is evidence that Nestorian Christian texts were circulating and being translated into Latin in Spain or North Africa at this time.[70] At the same time, though, there are features of Elipandus's arguments that indicate that he was actually being influenced by the use of phrases implying that Christ's humanity was adopted in some of the works of the leading writers of the Visigothic period. Such a view is supported by the nature of the defence that Elipandus and his supporters put up to their critics.[71] In reality it seems that earlier Spanish adoptive phraseology was impeccably orthodox, and that Elipandus had either misunderstood its precise intent or deliberately distorted it to serve his own polemical purposes.

In itself the Adoptionist controversy is a rather disappointing affair. Attention has always concentrated on the reactions of the Franks, especially Charlemagne, on those of his Anglo-Saxon adviser Alcuin, and on those of the Pope. However, although all of these created a great deal of sound and fury, the significant developments were always those taking place in Spain, and on which

[68] See above pp. 73–4.

[69] J.F. Rivera Recio, 'La Irrupción de los Sirios en Hispania', in *I Congresso internacional 'Encuentro de las Tres Culturas'* (Toledo, 1983), pp. 179–83, who sees the Syrian Arab immigration as the most likely route for the arrival of Nestorian ideas in the peninsula. For the fullest theological discussion of Adoptionism see J.F. Rivera Recio, *Adopcionismo*, pp. 85–154.

[70] G. Levi della Vida, 'I Mozarabi tra Occidente e Islam', in *Settimane di studi dell Centro italiano sull'alto medioevo*, vol. XII (1965), pp. 667–95, especially pp. 677–8.

[71] See the citations in the *Epistula Episcoporum Hispaniae*, *CSM*, I, pp. 82–93.

we are extremely ill-informed. Despite an usually full pageant of councils and theological debates, Charlemagne only ever had one Adoptionist in the whole of his domains, the unfortunate Bishop Felix of Urgel, whom he was able to harry for over twenty years, and there was never any real possibility of this teaching establishing itself in Frankish territory or in Rome.[72] To a considerable extent there must exist a suspicion that this was just something of an exercise to enable the newly revitalized Frankish Church to flex its intellectual muscles, and for the Carolingian monarchy to display its unimpeachable orthodoxy at a time when the purity of Byzantine official theology was in question.

The sequence of events is simple enough. The letter of Elipandus against Migetius was obviously intended for wide circulation amongst the Christian communities in the peninsula, and at least one copy of it reached the Asturian kingdom, where it came to the attention of a certain Beatus, who felt compelled to complain about the unorthodox nature of the bishop's view of the Incarnation. Although he never held high office in the ecclesiastical hierarchy, Beatus was by no means an insignificant figure, and requires some attention here. The literary and intellectual culture of the Christian north in the eighth century might almost be summed up in this one name. He is best known, though, for what later generations did to his major work by way of illustrating it rather than for the content of the work itself. The *Commentary on the Apocalypse* attributed to Beatus has survived in approximately two dozen manuscripts ranging in date from the tenth to the twelfth century, many of which contain a highly elaborate scheme of decoration.[73] The illuminated Beatus manuscripts constitute the best examples of the so-called Mozarabic art, and have deservedly attracted much scholarly attention.[74] The author of the commentary itself, however, has remained a shadowy and rather enigmatic figure.

[72] *Liber Alcuini contra haeresim Felicis*, ed. G.B. Blumenshine (Vatican City, 1980), pp. 14–24, who (p. 14) takes the supposed threat of Adoptionism in Francia more seriously. For Alcuin's, as opposed to Charlemagne's, concern see D. Bullough, 'Alcuin and the Kingdom of Heaven', in *Carolingian Essays: Andrew W. Mellon Lectures in Early Christian Studies*, ed. U.-R. Blumenthal (Washington, 1983), especially pp. 39–40, 49–59.

[73] For a listing of the MSS see T. Marín Martínez, 'La escritura de los Beatos', in the introductory volume to the facsimile of the *Codex Gerundensis* (Madrid, 1975), pp. 179–80. In general see H. Stierlin, *Die Visionen der Apokalypsen* (Zurich and Freiburg, 1978).

[74] E.g. M. Mentré, *La Peinture mozarabe* (Paris, 1984).

What little is known of him comes primarily from his own work, principally the polemical treatise written in 785 jointly by himself and Eterius bishop of Osma denouncing the Adoptionist Christology of Elipandus of Toledo.[75] This can be augmented by information to be gleaned from a letter sent to him by Alcuin around the year 797/8, and some highly abusive references in various letters of Elipandus.[76] In itself this material is hardly substantial, and historians have often been tempted to supplement it by recourse to a *Life of Beatus*. This latter, however, is in all probability a late forgery, and lacks any independent authority.[77]

From these various texts it can be deduced that he was both a priest and an abbot, and that his *floruit* should be placed in the period *c.* 785–800. That the monastery under his charge was that of Santo Torribio de Liébana is possible but no means definite. He attended the monastic profession of the former queen Adosinda, daughter of Alfonso I and widow of Silo in 785, but this in itself is insufficient to make her into his particular patron, as has often been believed.[78] Of the small number of works with the authorship of which he is attributed, only the polemical letter against Elipandus can be assigned to him with absolute security. A hymn in honour of St. James, with an acrostic reference to king Mauregatus, is almost certainly not his work.[79]

That the substantial commentary on the Apocalypse is the work of Beatus has long been an almost dogmatic certainty amongst scholars. However, in none of the various extant medieval manuscripts of the work is his authorship explicitly attested. It was not until the sixteenth century that the name of Beatus was linked to the commentary. This was the suggestion of the antiquary and *cronista real* Ambrosio de Morales (1513–91). He based his con-

[75] *Beati et Eterii Adversus Elipandum*, ed. B. Löfstedt, Corpus Christianorum, continuatio medievalis, vol. LIX (1984).

[76] Letter of Alcuin to Beatus of Liébana, ed. W. Levison, *England and the Continent*, Appendix XI, pp. 318–20.

[77] *Acta Sanctorum, Februarii*, vol. III, pp. 147–8; see L. Vázquez de Parga, 'Beato y el ambiente cultural de su época', in *Actas del simposio para el estudio de los códices del 'Comentario al Apocalipsis' de Beato de Liébana* (Madrid, 1978), vol. I, p. 37 on the uselessness of this text.

[78] C. Sánchez-Albornoz, 'El *Asturium Regnum* en los días de Beato de Liébana', ibid., vol. I, p. 28.

[79] M.C. Díaz y Díaz, 'Los himnos en honor de Santiago de la liturgía hispánica', *Compostellanum*, 11 (1966), pp. 457–502, reprinted in his *De Isidoro al siglo XI* (Barcelona, 1976), pp. 237–88, especially pp. 251–61 for the argument about authorship.

jecture upon the dated references in the work, which are all to the years 776 to 786. This, from the letter to Elipandus, is the beginning of the period in which Beatus was known to be working. As few other named Christian authors were known to have been writing in the peninsula at this time, Morales made the tempting association. A possible corroboration might come from a later letter of Elipandus, in which he refers in slighting terms to some millenarian doctrine he accused Beatus of disseminating, and which might be thought appropriate for someone with an interest in apocalyptic exegesis.[80]

To say that the grounds for the assumption are decidedly thin is to state the obvious. However, no other contenders for the honour exist, and there are certain features of the argument that might give it some support in the absence of other challenges. But, it is important to recognize the provisional nature of the trust to be placed in the identification. Were it to be undermined or the evidence provided in support of it held to be of insufficient quality, then the whole question of the authorship would remain open and the main testimony to the intellectual culture of the Asturian kingdom somewhat weakened.

In itself the *Commentary on the Apocalypse* may not seem a work of great originality. Like most exegesis of the Carolingian period, it consisted of sections taken from earlier works devoted to the study of the book of the Bible in question reassembled in scissors and paste fashion to provide a continuous commentary on the text. Thus it is more of a witness to the books available to Beatus, if his authorship be assumed, than to the quality of his own composition. In this sense, however, it is striking. Amongst the works of authors cited by Beatus either explicitly or without being named may be found treatises and commentaries by Ambrose, Jerome, Augustine, Fulgentius, Gregory, Isidore, and the Donatist Tyconius.[81] For the reconstruction of the text of the latter's commentary on the Apocalypse this work of Beatus's is invaluable. He

[80] The question of authorship was reopened by Prof. Díaz y Díaz in the discussion following L. Vázquez de Parga's lecture to the Beatus conference: *Actas del simposio*, vol. I, p. 47.

[81] *Beati Liebanensis, Commentarius in Apocalipsim, praef.*, 5, ed. H.A. Saunders (Rome, 1930), pp. 1–2; see S. Alvarez Campos, 'Fuentes literarios de Beato de Liébana', in *Actas del simposio*, vol. I, pp. 119–62.

also knew the *Tractatus* on the Apocalypse of the shadowy mid-sixth-century Spanish bishop Apringius of Beja.[82]

Thus, in taking on the learning and authority of the primate of the Spanish Church, Beatus was by no means ill-equipped. His co-author, Eterius, is less easy to delineate. That he was bishop of *Oxoma* or Burgo de Osma is attested in the manuscript tradition of their joint epistle. The problem lies in the location of this see, which is on a confluent of the Duero, and in the very heart of an area that traditional historiography requires us to believe had been depopulated in the middle of the eighth century. This difficulty has been got round by seeing him, following more recent precedents, as a bishop *in partibus infidelium*, in other words holding a titular office with no direct relationship to its actual location.[83] This is ingenious, but totally unacceptable in an Early Medieval context, in which such a concept and the procedures involved in realizing it would be quite anachronistic. The fact that there was a bishop of Osma in the 780s can only imply the existence of some form of Christian community in the town at this time.

The extant treatise or letter of Beatus and Eterius denouncing Elipandus's adoptionist theology was itself written in response to a letter the latter had sent to an Abbot Fidelis of the monastery of San Torribio in the Asturias de Liébana in October of 785 in reply to their initial criticisms.[84] The ensuing controversy soon made itself felt in Rome, and Pope Hadrian's letter to the Spanish bishops, written sometime between 785 and 791, warning them against the teaching of Migetius also contained a condemnation of Elipandus's adoptionist terminology. How Rome came to be informed of the issue would be interesting to know. It only became an active question in Francia after 791, with Felix of Urgel, Elipandus's Pyrenean supporter being summoned to Ratisbon to defend his views before Charlemagne.

The only other named supporter of the Adoptionist Christology is a bishop Ascaric, who was also condemned in Hadrian's letter.[85] Some have thought he was the metropolitan bishop of Braga, and,

[82] On whom see Isidore, *De Viris Illustribus*, XVII, ed. C. Codoñer Merino (Salamanca, 1964), p. 143.

[83] Alternatively, he can be presented as a refugee: J.F. Rivera Recio, *Adopcionismo*, p. 40, but if so then his see must have been in existence until *c.*780.

[84] *Elipandi Epistula ad Fidelem*, ed. J. Gil, *CSM*, I, pp. 80–1.

[85] P. Jaffe, *Regesta*, no. 2479.

although there is no proof to back so specific a claim, a reference in a letter he wrote on corporeal resurrection would at least seem to locate his see in the Asturian kingdom.[86] A ninth-century mention of the dispute seems to suggest that the bishop of Seville at this time, Theudila, was opposed to Elipandus's teaching.[87] Thus, what is immediately striking is the degree to which the whole Spanish Church became involved in the debate, with clerics as far removed as the Asturias, Urgel and Seville all taking a direct part in it. It was clearly in Spain a far livelier and more divisive issue than it ever was or could have been in Francia. Without the support of a Christian secular power there was also no way in which uniformity could be imposed or dissent quelled.

Although the metropolitan of Seville may have been fishing in troubled waters, and perhaps hoping to see his titular superior in Toledo humiliated, the majority opinion amongst the Spanish bishops would seem to have favoured Elipandus's views.[88] In part this may have been due to the traditional prestige of the holders of the see, who in the later seventh century acted as theological mentors and spokesmen for the whole of the Church in the Visigothic kingdom. Elipandus and the Spanish bishops in letters sent to Charlemagne after the Frankish condemnation of Adoptionism at the Synod of Frankfurt in 794 placed much stress on the apparent justification of the teaching in the works of earlier Spanish fathers and of those such as Fulgentius of Ruspe who had been particularly venerated in the peninsula.

In this sense the whole question ended in impasse. Charlemagne and Pope Leo III were able to harry the recalcitrant Felix of Urgel whenever they could get their hands on him, and common opposition to Elipandus led Alcuin to write to Beatus in 797 or 798, at a time when Frankish and Asturian political liaison was at its height. However, there was no formal renunciation of the doctrine of Christ's adoption of his humanity either by Elipandus or by the

[86] *Ascarici Epistula ad Tuseredum*, ed. J. Gil, *CSM*, I, pp. 114–16.

[87] *Albari Epistula IV*, 27, ed. J. Gil, *CSM*, I, p. 181. Another, but anonymous, Spanish opponent of Adoptionism *c*.800 was the writer of the marginalia in Visigothic script added to MSS 4 and 19 of the library of Monte Cassino; see D. de Bruyne, 'Un document de la controverse adoptioniste en Espagne vers l'an 800', *Revue d'histoire ecclésiastique*, 27 (1931), pp. 307–12. De Bruyne would, however, like to present him as an Adoptionist.

[88] See the corporate letter of the Spanish episcopate to the Gallic bishops: *Epistula Episcoporum Hispaniae*, *CSM*, I, pp. 82–93.

Spanish bishops that supported him. Yet within thirty years or so of Elipandus's death, probably *c.*804, the whole issue was a dead one within the Spanish Church, with if anything a recognition that Adoptionism had been wrong.

Arguments that make of the question an assertion of independence on the part of the Christian community in the nascent kingdom of the Asturias against the traditional authority of Muslim dominated Toledo are probably anachronistic.[89] No Asturian metropolitanate emerged from the struggle, and an ideological goal was achieved when the Christian kingdom was able to capture Toledo in 1085. On the other hand, the blending of the issues of Migetianism and Adoptionism in the 780s, and the contacts and alliances that were created by the dispute in the 790s seem to have broken finally the residual unity of the Spanish Church, which had survived the destruction of the Visigothic kingdom by over three quarters of a century.

Elipandus may not have been the greatest representative of an intellectual tradition that stretched back to the first quarter of the seventh century in the see of Toledo, but he was far from being out of step with his illustrious predecessors. Indeed his very sense of the great tradition that he had inherited, and whose integrity he clearly felt was being threatened by the attacks made on his theological pronouncements, probably accentuated the sharpness of tone of the controversy. In itself, though, what may seem to the modern reader to be little more than sheer vulgar abuse in his epistolary exchanges with his adversaries had a distinguished past not only in the Toledan school, with such model compositions as Julian's *Insultatio in Tyrannidem Galliae*, but in the wider Late Antique rhetorical tradition, which that school preserved. Where Elipandus did diverge from his predecessors was in getting his theology wrong. He had the doctrinaire self-assurance of Julian and Ildefonsus, but lacked their grasp of the content of the arguments, whilst sharing their forensic skills in expressing them.

It would be too much to claim that the Adoptionist controversy alone broke the hold of Toledo over the Spanish Church, but the three centuries that passed between the death of Elipandus (*c.*804) and the pontificate of Bernard of Cluny (1086–1124) are the

[89] R. d'Abadal i de Vinyals, *La Batalla del Adopcionismo en la desintegración de la iglesia visigoda* (Barcelona, 1949).

darkest in the history of the primatial see. To what extent it could exercise even a theoretical primacy between the mid-ninth century and 1085 is very much open to question. The securing of the Umayyad regime, with its inflexible base in the Guadalquivir valley, by the end of the eighth century ensured that the link between what was effectively the political heart of the peninsula and its foremost Christian centre, that had been so vital in the Visigothic period, was not to be renewed. Thus, another feature of the previous order withered away.

As a whole the eighth century may, like the fifth, seem to have been a peculiarly violent and unstable time in the history of the peninsula. Certain continuities can be detected, but against a background of change. This latter was not so much the immediate product of the Arab conquest, which initially preserved more of the status quo, particularly at a local level, than it has often been given credit for, as it was the result of the breakdown of order in the middle decades of the century. At the same time, though, it was this peculiarly troubled period that opened up the opportunities that led the dominant features of a new political and cultural order to emerge. Here lay the chances for various competitors for power on the local and the wider stages to make their bids for power. In the end most of them failed, but those who succeeded, above all the Umayyads, did so spectacularly. Even so, for various reasons, the latter were unable or insufficiently interested to revive the peninsula-wide rule of the Visigothic kings, and this allowed peripheral regions, such as the Asturias, Galicia, the Ebro valley and Catalonia, to continue to develop their own independent sources of authority. From such beginnings the more complex economies and the more sophisticated states of the ninth century would emerge.

Bibliographical Essay

Relatively little has been written exclusively about the history of Spain in the eighth century, and this book is the first to treat both the Arab ruled parts and the Christian ones in the compass of a single work. Those books that deal with the history of Islamic or of Christian Spain more broadly tend to devote very limited space to the eighth century. Thus, a number of items mentioned here will be found to extend well beyond the confines of this period, and it is also necessary to divide up the existing literature according to whether it relates to *Al-Andalus* or to the kingdoms of the Asturias and of Pamplona and their satellite territories. A more comprehensive bibliography will be offered in the next volume in this series. This will also take account of the substantial amount of archaeological work that has been published in recent years concerned with the early Islamic period in the peninsula. Little of this, however, relates to sites that can be dated to the eighth century. For the one very significant exception, the Visigothic village of El Bovalar that appears to have been hurriedly abandoned in the course of the Arab conquest of the Ebro valley, see P. de Palol i Salellas, *El Bovalar (Seròs; Segrià)* (Lérida, 1989).

For an introduction to the history of the rise of Islam and the Arab conquests prior to the invasion of Spain see W. M. Watt, *Muhammad at Mecca* (Oxford, 1953), and *Muhammad at Medina* (Oxford, 1956) for the classic account of the life of the Prophet. A more zestful version will be found in M. Rodinson, *Mohammed* (Eng. tr. London, 1971), and M. Cook, *Muhammad* (Oxford, 1983) provides an introduction to a modern revisionist school of interpretation. On the conquests, F. M. Donner, *The Early Islamic Conquests* (Princeton, 1981), A. J. Butler, *The Arab Conquest of Egypt* (revised edn by P. M. Fraser, Oxford, 1978), and W. E. Kaegi, *Byzantium and the early Islamic conquests* (Cambridge, 1992) all offer substantial accounts, with a variety of interpretations. See also M. A. Shaban, *Islamic History A.D. 600–750: a New Interpretation* (Cambridge, 1971), P. Crone, *Slaves on Horses: the evolution of the Islamic polity* (Cambridge, 1980) provides a challenging new perspective. For North Africa there is an excellent treatment of the period up to the late ninth century in M. Brett, 'The Arab conquest and the rise of Islam in North Africa' in J. D. Fage (ed.), *The Cambridge History of Africa* (Cambridge, 1978), pp. 490–555.

The standard general history of early Islamic Spain remains that of E. Lévi-Provençal, *Histoire de l'Espagne musulmane* (3 vols, Paris and Leiden 1950/1), of which only the first two chapters concern themselves with the period considered here. The older work of Reinhart Dozy, *Histoire des Musulmans d'Espagne* of 1861, was translated into English by F. G. Stokes as *Spanish Islam* (London, 1913), and retains value as a narrative account, deriving uncritically from the Arab sources. R. Arié, *España musulmana siglos VIII–XV)* (Barcelona, 1982) offers a short narrative of the whole history of Islam in Spain, followed by a series of analytical chapters on the social, cultural and economic life of *Al-Andalus*. For a more recent synthesis of the same kind see M. Cruz Hernández, *El Islam de Al-Andalus* (Madrid, 1992). For the architectural remains of this period see M. Barrucand and A. Bednorz, *Moorish Architecture in Andalusia* (Cologne, 1992), pp. 38–45, and J. D. Dodds, 'The Great Mosque of Córdoba' in J. D. Dodds (ed.), *Al-Andalus: the Art of Islamic Spain* (New York, 1992), especially pp. 11–15.

The most accessible translations of the main Arab sources are listed at the front of this book. Very useful English translations of both the *Chronicle of 754* and of the Roda version of the *Chronicle of Alfonso III* have become available in K. B. Wolf, *Conquerors and Chroniclers of Early Medieval Spain* (Translated Texts for Historians, vol. 9: Liverpool, 1990). The best edition of the *Chronicle of 754* is that of J. E. López Pereira, *Crónica mozarabe de 754* (Zaragoza, 1980), and it is accompanied by its editor's *Estudio crítico sobre la crónica mozarabe de 754* (Zaragoza, 1980). On the *Chronicle of 741*, the only study remains that of C. E. Dubler, 'Sobre la crónica arábigo-bizantina de 741', *Al-Andalus* vol. 11 (1946), pp. 298–332; some of his conclusions are over-optimistic. Other eighth-century Latin texts from the south will be found in J. Gil (ed.), *Corpus Scriptorum Muzarabicorum* vol. 1 (Madrid, 1973). There are now several competing editions of the two versions of the *Chronicle of Alfonso III* and of the *Chronicle of Albelda*. The best of these, textually, is J. Gil Fernández, J. L. Moralejo and J. I. Ruiz de la Peña, *Crónicas asturianas* (Oveido, 1985). The edition of Y. Bonnaz, *Chroniques asturiennes* (Paris, 1987) tends to over-classicize the texts, but has a useful long introduction. On the *Chronicle of 754* and the *Chronicle of Alfonso III* see M. C. Díaz y Díaz, 'La historiografia hispana desde la invasión arabe hasta el año 1000', in his *De Isidoro al siglo XI* (Barcelona, 1976), pp. 203–29. The works of Beatus of Liébana can be found in E. Romero-Pose (ed.), *Sancti Beati a Liebana Commentarius in Apocalypsin* (2 vols, Rome, 1985), and B. Löftstedt (ed.), *Beati Liebanensis et Eterii Oxomensis Adversus Elipandum Libri Duo* (Turnholt, 1984).

On the Arab conquest and the ensuing settlement see J. Vallvé Bermejo, *Nuevas ideas sobre la conquista árabe de España* (Real Academia de la Historia, Madrid, 1989), and the same author's 'España en el siglo VIII: ejército y sociedad', '*Al-Andalus*, vol. 43 (1978), pp. 51–112. More relevant to the succeeding centuries, but with some treatment of the eighth is another book by Joaquin Vallvé: *La división territorial de la España musulmana* (Madrid, 1986); see in particular the third section comprising pages 179 to 223. On Arab and Berber social structure and settlement there is P. Guichard, *Tribus arabes et berberes en Al-Andalus* (Paris, 1973). Apart from a controversy over the location of the supposed 'battle of Guadalete', there has been little written on the immediate events of the conquest outside of the general histories. For those who wish to inspect that debate see C. Sánchez-Albornoz, 'Guadalete' in his *Orígenes de la nación española*, vol. I (Oviedo, 1972), pp. 271–317. For some of the arguments about the internal conflicts in the peninsula at the time of the Arab invasion see M. Coll i Alentorn, *Els successors de Vititza en la zona nord-est del domini visigòtic* (Reial Acadèmia de Bones Lletres de Barcelona, 1971). On the Umayyad seizure of power in *Al-Andalus*, as well as to the general histories referred to above, recourse should be made to P. Chalmeta, 'El nacimiento del estado neo-omeya andalusí' in *Homenaje a Manuel Ocaña Jiménez* (Córdoba, 1990), pp. 95–106.

Although there has been an increasing amount of work done on Islamic towns and town life, the limitations of the evidence, both literary and archaeological, has meant that little of this is concerned directly with this period. See, however, E. A. Llobregat, 'De la ciudad visigótica a la ciudad islámica en el este peninsular' in M. de Epalsa, *Simposio internacional sobre la ciudad islámica* (Zaragoza, 1991), pp. 159–88. And also J. L. Corral Lafuente, 'Las ciudades de la Marca Superior de Al-Andalus' in *ibid.* pp. 253–87. See too the latter's 'El sistema urbano en la Marca Superior de Al-Andalus', *Turiaso*, vol. VII (1987), pp. 25–64. Some of the articles in P. Senac (ed.), *La Marche Supérieure d'Al-Andalus et l'occident chrétien* (Madrid, 1991) also take their starting point in the eighth century; see in particular C. Esco and P. Senac, 'Le peuplement musulman dans le district de Huesca (VIIIe-XIIe siècles)', and J. Giralt i Balagueró, 'Fortifications andalusines à la Marca Superior d'Al-Andalus'.

Amongst other regional and local studies of note are M. J. Viguera, *Aragón musulmán: la presencia del Islam en el valle del Ebro* (2nd ed., Zaragoza, 1988); the first sections of J. Bosch Vilá, *La Sevilla islámica, 712–1248* (Seville, 1984); J. B. Vilar, *Orihuela musulmana* (Murcia, 1976); C. Delgado Valero, *Toledo islámico: ciudad, arte e historia* (Toledo, 1986); J. Porres Martín-Cleto, *Historia de Tulaytula (711–1085)* (Toledo, 1985); R. G. Peinado Santaella and J. E. López de Coca Castañer, *Historia de Granada II: la época medieval. siglos VIII–XV* (Granada, 1987); and F. J. Aguirre Sádaba and M. Jiménez Mata, *Introducción al Jaén islámico* (Jaén, 1979).

Turning to Christian Spain, for the kingdom of the Asturias in the eighth century the most substantial treatment will be found in the various studies collected together into a chronological narrative in C. Sánchez-Albornoz, *Orígenes de la nación española*, vol. II (Oviedo, 1974), pp. 7–396. For a shorter, and more systematic treatment see the first eight chapters of P. García Toraño, *Historia de el Reino de Asturias* (Oviedo, 1986), pp. 1–198. Other articles of D. Claudio Sánchez-Albornoz relating to Asturian history can be found most conveniently in the three volumes of his collected studies: *Viejos y nuevos estudios sobre las instituciones medievales españolas* (Madrid, 1976–9). The small number of eighth-century Asturian charters are edited in A. C. Floriano (ed.), *Diplomática española del periodo astur*, vol. I (Oviedo, 1949). There are a number of useful studies in the collection *Estudios sobre la monarquía asturiana* (Oviedo, 1949; reprinted 1971), including J. M. Lacarra, 'Las relaciones entre el Reino de Asturias y el Reino de Pamplona'. On Beatus of Liébana and his context the first volume of *Actas del Simposio para el estudio de los códices del'Comentario al Apocalipsis' de Beato de Liébana* (3 vols, Madrid, 1978) contains L. Vázquez de Parga, 'Beato y el ambiente cultural de su época', pp. 33–47, with a useful discussion appended. For the history of Galicia in this period see the relevant parts of C. Baliñas Pérez, *Defensores e traditores: un modeleo de relación entre poder monárquico e oligarquía na Galicia altomedieval (718–1037)* (Santiago de Compostela, 1988) and his *Do mito à realidade: a definición social e territorial de Galicia na alta idade media (séculos VIII e IX)* (Santiago, 1992). On the Frankish invasion of 778 see J. M. Lacarra, *La expedición de Carlomagno a Zaragoza y la batalla de Roncesvalles* (Pamplona, 1981). This is reprinted, together with his 'Navarra entre la Vasconia pirenaica y el Ebro en los siglos VIII y IX' in *idem*, *Investigaciones de Historia Navarra* (Pamplona, 1983), pp. 17–92 and 93–114. For Aragón see the first sections of A. Durán Gudiol, *Los condados de Aragón y Sobrarbe* (Zaragoza, 1988), and of A. Ubieto Arteta, *Orígenes de Aragón* (Zaragoza, 1989). On Adoptionism see R. d'Abadal i de Vinyals, *La batalla del Adopcionismo en la desintegración de la iglesia visigoda* (Barcelona, 1949); J. F. Rivera Recio, *El Adopcionismo en España (siglo VIII)* (Toledo, 1980); and J. C. Cavadini, *The Last Christology of the West: Adoptionism in Spain and Gaul 785–820* (Philadelphia, 1993). For the area of the future Catalunya see J. M. Salrach, *El procés de formació nacional de Catalunya* (2 vols, Barcelona, 1978), vol. 1 chapters 1 and 2; also R. d'Abadal i de Vinyals, 'El paso de Septimania del dominio godo al franco a través de la invasión sarracena (720–68)', *Cuadernos de Historia de España*, vol. 19 (1953), pp. 5–54 for the region north of the Pyrenees.

Index

9 780631 194057

Printed in Great Britain
by Amazon

68090199R00149